Food Security and Political Stability in Tajikistan

Maps, Figures and Tables

Contents

Published by

Vij Books India Pvt Ltd
(Publishers, Distributors & Importers)
2/19, Ansari Road
Delhi – 110 002
Phones: 91-11-43596460, 91-11-47340674
e-mail: vijbooks@rediffmail.com
web : www.vijbooks.com

First Published in 2018

Copyright © 2018, Author

ISBN: 978-81-937591-3-4 (Hardback)

ISBN: 978-81-937591-5-8 (ebook)

Food Security and Political Stability in Tajikistan

by

Raj Kumar Sharma

Vij Books India Pvt Ltd
New Delhi (India)

Foreword

The issue of food security is gradually moving to the centre stage of international politics. With rising population world over, nations are grappling with food problems and drawing up strategies to meet the challenges. In this respect, Tajikistan is no exception. Ever since it gained independence in 1991, the issue of food security has been a priority in Tajikistan's strategic thinking. One of the objectives of the Tajik opposition in the civil war which began in 1992 was to control land resources. Being a mountainous country with only seven percent of arable land, Tajikistan has always depended on food imports. Historically, Tajikistan was part of the integrated Fergana market that was a source for procuring its food requirements. Later, food imports came from the Soviet Union as Tajikistan became a part of it. The breakup of Soviet Union left Tajikistan with twisted borders and a disrupted infrastructure that cut it off from its traditional market sources. In turn, the issue of food imports got aggravated and became one of the key concerns for the government. Tajikistan's landlocked status further compounded the problem.

However, the Tajik state is taking steps to mitigate the difficulties faced by its population. For instance, land reforms were initiated and measures to improve infrastructure particularly with neighbouring countries have been taken up as well. The UN agencies and international financial institutions are forthcoming in their assistance to Tajikistan in its efforts to achieve economic development especially on connectivity issues. The government is taking steps to move away from dependence on cotton cultivation towards growing more food crops.

This is a well researched study on 'Food Security and Political Stability in Tajikistan' which has analysed all the relevant dimensions of food security in Tajikistan and its possible impact on the nation's political stability. The study will, undoubtedly, stimulate further research into other related aspects. I wish Dr Raj Kumar Sharma all the very best in his career.

Nirmala Joshi

Prof Nirmala Joshi
Former Professor
School of International Studies
Jawaharlal Nehru University,
New Delhi

Preface

Food security has become an important aspect in international relations after the world food crisis of 2007-08. Food riots were witnessed in a number of countries contributing to political instability. Tajikistan, a Central Asian country adjoining Afghanistan faces a number of food related problems. A country with poor economic indicators, Tajikistan imports almost 50 percent of its food which exposes it to food price fluctuations in the international market. Tajikistan's struggle to ensure food security can be traced to the days of Tsarist Russia when Bukhara (comprising most of the territory of present day Tajikistan) was annexed by Moscow. The Tsarist regime introduced cotton monoculture in Bukhara while its population received grains from Moscow. This made Tajikistan dependent on food supplies from Moscow till 1991. After gaining independence in 1991, Tajikistan suffered a civil war which led to severe food problems. Things have improved in recent times but ensuring food security of its people is still a big challenge for the Tajik government.

There was little academic research on Tajikistan till it became independent in 1991. However, the academic interest in the country has increased after 2001 US intervention in Afghanistan. Tajikistan shares more than 1,000 km border with the war torn country and has security linkages with Afghanistan. This work is an attempt to fill the academic void on Tajikistan, especially pertaining to its problem of food insecurity. This book traces the history of agriculture and food production in Tajikistan from mid-19th century when it came under Russian rule. From its inception, Tajikistan has been facing the 'geographic handicap' as it is a mountainous country and only 7 percent of the total land is arable. Soviet policies made Tajikistan dependent on Moscow for food supplies and once Soviet Union disintegrated, the independent state of Tajikistan lacked economic capacity to ensure food security of its citizens. Political instability has led to food problems in Tajikistan, be it the testing times of Russian revolution or the Tajik civil war (1992-97). This book is a detailed study of how Soviet economic geography introduced intensive cotton cultivation in Tajikistan at the expense of food crops. Soviet economic planners felt that a region with hot climate and large water resources should not attempt to grow grains but cotton. The book also tries to analyze whether food insecurity can lead to political instability in Tajikistan.

I am thankful to Vij Books for publishing my work which I conducted as part of my PhD thesis at the Centre for Russian and Central Asian Studies, School of International Studies, Jawaharlal Nehru University, New Delhi. I convey my thanks to my supervisor, Dr Nalin Mohapatra who helped me through thick and thin in completing my dissertation. Other faculty members at the Centre were also of immense help and encouragement. My special thanks to Prof Nirmala Joshi and Prof D Gopal who have helped in shaping my career and intellect. I am equally thankful to people at the United Service Institution (USI), Lt Gen P K Singh, Maj Gen B K Sharma, Gp Capt Sharad Tiwari, Dr Roshan and Dr Nivedita Das Kundu and faculty members at Indira Gandhi National Open University (IGNOU), Prof Anurag Joshi, Prof Jagpal Singh and Prof S V Reddy. Last but not the least; I also thank my wife, Geetanjali who has been a pillar of strength in my life despite handling motherhood and her own PhD thesis at the same time. I dedicate this work to my one year old son, Samarth whose boundless energy motivates me to work harder. Needless to say, all errors remain mine own.

LIST OF ABBREVIATIONS

AAH	Action Against Hunger
ADB	Asian Development Bank
AKDN	Aga Khan Development Network
AKF	Aga Khan Foundation
BPSR	Bukhara People's Soviet Republic
BTI	Bertelsmann Stiftung
CAREC	Central Asia Regional Economic Cooperation
CASA	Central Asia South Asia
CIA	Central Intelligence Agency
CIS	Commonwealth of Independent States
CPB	Communist Party of Bukhara
CPT	Communist Party of Tajikistan
CPSU	Communist Party of Soviet Union
DAC	Development Assistance Committee
DCC	Development Coordination Council
DDT	Dichloro Diphenyl Trichloroethane
DFID	Department for International Development
DPT	Democratic Party of Tajikistan
DRRI	Disaster Risk Reduction Initiative
EAEC	Eurasian Economic Community

EBRD	European Bank for Reconstruction and Development
FAO	Food and Agriculture Organisation
FFHC	Freedom From Hunger Campaign
FSC	Food Security Council
FSWG	Food Security Working Group
GAA	German Agro Action
GBAO	Gorno-Badakhshan Autonomous Oblast
GDP	Gross Domestic Product
GGT	Governor-Generalship of Turkestan
HYV	High Yielding Variety
ICG	International Crisis Group
ICESR	International Covenant on Economic, Social & Cultural Rights
ICRC	International Committee of the Red Cross
IsDB	Islamic Development Bank
IFAD	International Fund for Agricultural Development
IFEC	International Federation of Red Cross & Red Crescent Societies
ILC	International Land Code
ILO	International Labour Organisation
IMF	International Monetary Fund
IMO	International Organization for Migration
INGO	International Non-Governmental Organisation

IPCC	Intergovernmental Panel on Climate Change
IRPT	Islamic Renaissance Party of Tajikistan
LIFDC	Low Income Food Deficit Country
LRRD	Linking Relief Rehabilitation and Development
MBAV	Mountainous Badakhshon Autonomous Veloyat
MDG	Millennium Development Goals
NATO	North Atlantic Treaty Organization
NDS	National Development Strategy
NEP	New Economic Policy
NGO	Non-Governmental Organisation
ODA	Official Development Assistance
OPEC	Organization of the Petroleum Exporting Countries
PfP	Partnership for Peace
PRRP	Protracted Relief Recovery Operation
RRS	Region of Republican Subordination
RSFSR	Russian Soviet Federative Socialist Republic
SCISPM	State Committee on Investment & State Property Management
SCO	Shanghai Cooperation Organisation
SIPRI	Stockholm International Peace Research Institute
STTPC	South Tajikistan Territorial Production Complex
TASSR	Tajikistan Autonomous Soviet Socialist

	Republic
TSSR	Tajikistan Soviet Socialist Republic
UDHR	Universal Declaration of Human Rights
UNDP	United Nations Development Program
UNDAF	United Nations Development Assistance Framework
UNFPA	United Nations Population Fund
UNHCR	United Nations High Commissioner for Refugees
UNICEF	United Nations Children's Fund
UNIDO	United Nations Industrial Development Organization
UNO	United Nations Organisation
UNODC	United Nations Office on Drugs and Crime
UNOCHA	United Nations Office for Coordination of Humanitarian Affairs
USAID	United States Agency for International Development
UTO	United Tajik Opposition
WBCPS	World Bank Country Partnership Strategy
WFC	World Food Council
WFP	World Food Program

CHAPTER 1

INTRODUCTION

FOOD SECURITY – BACKGROUND AND FUTURE CHALLENGES

After the end of Cold War, the concept of international security has undergone a change. Earlier, states used to focus on military threats emanating outside their territorial boundaries. In the post 1991 security concept, factors other than military are also being seen as threats to national security. Food, water, energy scarcity and climate change too pose threats for nations across the world. These threats are interlinked, have a transnational character due to globalisation and nations need to work out strategies together to deal with them. However, since every nation is trying to protect its own population against such threats, this also leads to resource competition where the poor nations are marginalised while the powerful and wealthy have an advantage. Due to global food crisis which took place in 2007-08, food security has emerged as a foremost challenge that nations face amid increasing resource competition and population. The world population is expected to reach 9 billion by 2050 and to feed these people, food production should increase by 50 percent. However, climate change is likely to play spoilsport and could decrease crop yields by 25 percent (World Bank 2015). Achieving this challenge is going to be very tough if we have a look at the history. At the World Food Summit in 1996, the signatory nations had resolved that they would halve the number of hungry people by 2015 from the 1990-92 level.

Hence, the goal was to reduce the number of hungry people to 497 million by 2015 (the number stood at 994 million in 1990).

Figure 1.1. Total Number of Hungry People in the World (2001-2009).

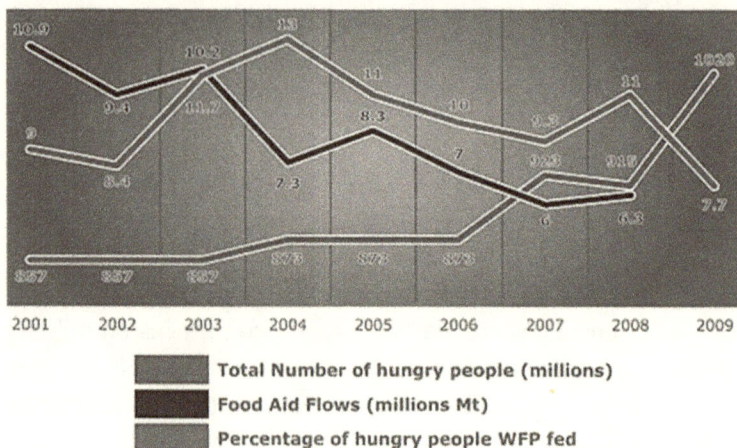

2001	2002	2003	2004	2005	2006	2007	2008	2009

■ Total Number of hungry people (millions)

■ Food Aid Flows (millions Mt)

■ Percentage of hungry people WFP fed

Source: World Food Program 2009, available at https://www.wfp. org/photos/gallery/hunger-graphs.

However, this target was not be met as 805 million people were undernourished in 2014 (World Hunger and Poverty Facts and Statistics 2015) while in 2016, the number rose to 815 million. In 2009, following the global food and economic crisis, the number of undernourished people had crossed one billion for the first time in human history, as shown in the figure 1.1. As the figure shows, while the number of undernourished people has increased in past, there has been considerable decrease in flow of food aid and number of hungry people fed by organisations like World Food Program. This shows the struggle between increasing population and food resources. The poor are most vulnerable sections in case food prices rise. Figure 1.2 shows the impact of 10 percent increase in food prices on the rural and urban households. In almost all the cases, the poorest 20 percent are the worst hit by a food price rise.

Figure 1.2. Impact of 10 Percent Food Price Increase on Rural & Urban Households.

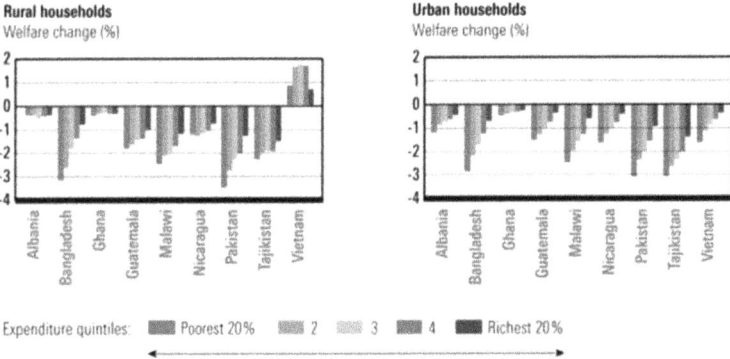

Source: Golay 2010: 6.

Former Executive Director of UN World Food Programme, Josette Sheeran in 2008 had referred to hunger as a 'silent tsunami'. She said that there are 250,000 deaths due to hunger in every ten days and it is equivalent to death toll caused by Asian tsunami in 2004 (World Food Program 2008). The Food and Agriculture Organisation (FAO) has said that there is need to increase food production else there will be social unrest and conflict in future. The predictions for increase in food demand in future have come at a time when the investment in agriculture research is decreasing in the world (Russia Today, March 10 2014). According to Fred Davies of US Agency for International Development (USAID), food related conflict could start by 2050 as the technical advancements that would increase food production are unlikely to reach the poor and small farmers, who need them the most (Wall 2014).

Tajikistan is a Central Asian country that faces problems to its food security. It is landlocked and shares borders with Afghanistan in south, China in east, Kyrgyzstan in north and Uzbekistan in north-west (CIA World Factbook Website), as shown in map 1.1.

Map 1.1. Map of Tajikistan.

Source: Nationsonline.org Website, available at http://www.nation-sonline.org/oneworld/map/tajikistan-political-map.htm.

Tajikistan faces a number of challenges in its pursuit for ensuring food security of its citizens. Mountains dominate Tajikistan's geography and form 93 percent of its terrain, stretching from west to east (Baransky 1956). Only 7 percent of the total available land is arable in Tajikistan, which limits its agrarian potential and food production. Mountainous terrain makes Tajikistan one of the least accessible countries in the world, facing problems in communication, transport, industry and agriculture (World Bank Country Partnership Strategy 2010-2013). In 2016, 30 percent of Tajikistan's population was suffering from poverty which hinders their access to food. Present day territory of Tajikistan came under the Tsarist Russian rule during second half of the 19th century. Tsarist Russia replaced grain cultivation by cotton cultivation in Tajikistan and foodstuffs were supplied to Tajikistan from Moscow. These policies were continued by Soviet authorities and Tajikistan never attained food self-sufficiency under Soviet Union. After it gained independence, Tajikistan suffered a civil war which decreased food production in the country. Hunger and starvation prevailed and the international community sent food aid to Tajikistan in order to avert a major humanitarian crisis. Tajikistan still lacks food self-sufficiency and imports around 50 percent of its food, which exposes it to fluctuations in international grain market. Factors like climate change and population growth could worsen Tajikistan's food problems in future if they are not sustainably handled.

Food security is one of the main challenges faced by Tajikistan and the government under President Emomali Rahmon has declared it as one of the three strategic goals Tajikistan would try to achieve in future. The other two goals are energy security and breaking the communication deadlock faced by Tajikistan. The food security in Tajikistan has been mainly dealt with 'economic' focus in studies conducted till now while the political factors have received less attention. There is lack of a comprehensive study that puts the food security problem of Tajikistan in historical perspective and also deals with the relationship between nature of state and food crisis in Tajikistan. This book deals with issue of food security in Tajikistan keeping its focus on the role of state in ensuring food for its citizens. Eradicating hunger has been accepted as the primary function of a state. The role of state is more prominent in ensuring availability and access to food and state can intervene directly as well as indirectly to achieve food security (Vyas 2000). Investing in agricultural research and development, land reforms and infrastructure development have indirect but significant impact on food security in a state. So, this book aims to study the role and response of state to food problems in Tajikistan. The cotton-monoculture has been widely cited as one of the reasons for food problems in Tajikistan. This work will look into the political and social factors that are behind the continuation of this trend in Tajikistan. In the post-Arab Spring world, the concept of food security has again acquired significance, especially for 'weak' states like Tajikistan. Food problem in Tajikistan is not a stand-alone challenge and this book will also focus on the food-water-energy nexus that gets severe during winter. It also aims to study institutional framework available in Tajikistan for ensuring food security. Another highlight of the book is it also explores links between food security and political stability in Tajikistan. There have been examples when political instability led to food shortages in Tajikistan but there has been no study which explores possibility of political instability in Tajikistan triggered by food insecurity. This study deals with this aspect and brings out the potential outcome of food insecurity for political stability in Tajikistan. It also analyses role of international community in alleviating Tajikistan's food security and how different donors and international non-government organisations are providing Tajikistan financial and technical resources to deal with future challenges to food security.

The book has been divided into six chapters. Chapter 1 introduces the theme.

Chapter 2 is titled 'Food Security: A Theoretical Framework'. This chapter situates food security in international security studies. It also deals with history and meaning of food security as a concept. The chapter also explores linkages between food security and political stability.

Chapter 3 is titled 'Agriculture and Food Security Situation in Soviet Tajikistan'. The chapter starts with the reasons behind the conquest of Central Asia by Tsarist Russia in second half of the 19th century. It also highlights political, economic and social aspects of emirate of Bukhara as most of the present day Tajikistan's territory was part of the emirate. The impact of First World War and Russian revolution on Bukhara and its agriculture has also been brought out. The struggle between Basmachis and the Soviet Union has been analysed and their efforts to use food as a strategic weapon are also highlighted. Other themes that are discussed in this chapter include - the social, economic and political impact of Stalin's collectivisation drive on Tajikistan, agriculture situation in Soviet Union during the Second World War, nature of uneven economic development in Soviet Union and its impact on Tajikistan, the relationship between demographic changes and agriculture in Tajikistan and impact of Gorbachev's political and economic reforms on Tajikistan's economy, society and food security.

Chapter 4 is titled 'State Response to Food Security Problem in Post-Soviet Period'. This chapter starts with the socio-economic and political milieu in Tajikistan after the breakup of Soviet Union. It briefly analyses reasons for civil war in the country and also describes impact of the war on Tajik economy and food production. State response to food insecurity has been analyzed by assessing land reforms in Tajikistan. The institutional and legal framework in Tajikistan available for food security is also included in this section. Impacts of food insecurity on society in terms of migration, health and gender issues and demographic changes are also detailed. Other important issues discussed in this chapter include – impact of 'transitional nature' of state on food security in Tajikistan and various challenges to Tajikistan' food security like natural disasters, environmental degradation, climate change, transport problems and cotton-grain dilemma faced by Tajik farmers have been analysed. Lastly, this chapter explores the linkages between food security and political stability in Tajikistan.

Chapter 5 is titled 'International Response to Food Security in Tajikistan'. It deals with the role of international financial institutions like World Bank and Asian Development Bank. Next, role of different UN agencies like United Nations Development

Program in alleviating Tajikistan's food security is discussed. Role of international non-government organisations like Mercy Corps and Welthungerhilfe or German Agro Action has been discussed as well in this chapter. The foreign aid to Tajikistan from different countries and mechanisms to ensure aid coordination and their drawbacks have been analysed as well.

Chapter 6 concludes major findings brought out in the book.

CHAPTER 2

FOOD SECURITY: A THEORETICAL FRAMEWORK

INTRODUCTION

State has played a central role in providing food security to its citizens, as control and usage of land has always been a political phenomenon. There has always been a struggle in human societies to ensure that all people have enough food for living a healthy life. Food security as a concept started developing only during 1970s; however, the issue has been finding importance in international politics since the beginning of 20th century. There has been revival of interest and research on food security after 2007-08, when increasing food prices led to food riots in many countries. Food prices were also one of the grievances that led to the Arab Spring that started in 2010 with revolution in Tunisia. In some cases, there were serious political consequences. The government in Madagascar was overthrown by a coup in 2009 as it was negotiating to lease big amount of arable land to a South Korean firm (Brinkman and Hendrix 2010). Food security forms an integral part of human security in international security studies. Before delving into the concept of food security, let us see how it fits in international security studies.

'WIDENING' SECURITY PARADIGM AND HUMAN SECURITY IN INTERNATIONAL RELATIONS

The security paradigm in international relations during the Cold war mainly relied on traditional notion of security, meaning safeguarding the territory and sovereignty of a country by military means. Security was conceptualised mainly in military terms due to the nuclear arms race that characterised Cold War international politics (Buzan 1997). Since the world was divided in to two blocs led by Soviet Union and the US, traditional security dominated international affairs and there was very less space for widening this paradigm to include other types of security. It was only in 1981 that the scholars around the world started thinking about 'widening' the security agenda to include non-traditional security threats like climate change, food security, drug-trafficking and terrorism. One of the main advocates for widening the security paradigm, Barry Buzan has further stated that in 1980s, there was increased "securitisation" of two issues, namely environment and international economy. Earlier, these issues were treated as part of 'low politics' and were not given due consideration. This started the trend where importance given to military and political security issues, seen as high politics, started declining. It was due to the issues such as pollution, biodiversity and global warming that the environment was being securitised in international politics. There was relative decline of American economy and the process of liberalisation was increasing and along with economic rise of Europe and Japan, there was simultaneous securitisation of economy in international relations (Ibid). Apart from these concerns, there was growing focus on security of an individual as a unit opposed to the earlier approach which treated the state as a unit. Middle powers such as Japan and Canada emerged after the end of Cold War and propounded the concept of 'human security' in international relations. The Olof Palme Commission report had put forward the concept of common security way back in 1982.

"Security is a process as much as a condition and one in which the participants are individuals and groups – popular and political opinion" wrote Olof Palme in his introduction to the report. One year later in 1983, Richard Ullman wrote about extended or redefined security. Historian E H Carr in 1945 had earlier argued for the individual to be main focus of security (Rothschild 2007).

Those who want to widen the international security paradigm argue that threats to the survival of a state may not be necessarily military in nature and could emanate from environment, social and economic aspects. These threats have been constantly highlighted by scholars in their attempts to redefine security arguing that these threats pose a threat to human well-being across nations. Since these threats are transnational in charter, the need is being expressed to widen the security paradigm to include them as threats to human survival (Tadjbakhsh and Chenoy 2007). Those who argue for widening the security paradigm include Ullman (1983), Ole Weaver (1993) and Barry Buzan (1983, 1991) among others. Attempts are being made to widen the international security paradigm dominated by realists and neo-realists to also include a number of potential threats which could be economic, environmental or even relate to cyber security. The neo-realist theoretical tenets that are being targeted by the 'wideners' are the ways in which security is conceptualised (state centric), how threats are understood to be mainly military in nature and the understanding of anarchy leading to security dilemma (Walt 1991). It is perhaps; little known that one of the prominent faces of classical realism, Hans J Morganthau had called food production as an aspect of national power in his book, *Politics Among Nations*. He said that states try to ensure better food production levels in order to survive under anarchy in international politics. He further added that a country which is food sufficient does not have to divert its resources for food imports and can keep their masses away from hunger during any war. He referred to regular food deficiency in a country as a sign of weakness in international relations which compel a state to behave as a weak state, since it has to import food from other countries (Morganthau quoted in Stedman 2014).

Human security represents an "ethical and methodological rupture" in the traditional security paradigm. The state assumes less importance than the individuals in human security. Since the main aim of the state is to protect its individuals, it should recognise threats to them beyond violence and military threats. It focuses on well-being and dignity of individuals. Human security does not explain threats but recognises new ones together with their inter-dependence. These threats include both, unstructured violence like the violence emanating from environmental scarcity or migration as well as violence inflicted by natural disasters, in addition to threats by states themselves (Tadjbakhsh and Chenoy 2007). In 1994, the concept of human security was underlined probably for the first time at international level by the United Nations Development Programme. It advocated safety of individuals from chronic threats as hunger and poverty. The 1994 UNDP Human Development Report recognizes threats to human security in seven areas: economic, food, health, environmental, personal, community and political. The report recognises food security as a part of human security and threats to food security like hunger, famine and poverty as direct threats to human security. It also adds that for too long, security has been shaped by disputes and conflicts among nations while states have been buying weapons to secure themselves. For most of the people around the world, insecurity arises from concerns for job, health, income and food which are emerging as human security concerns (United Nations Development Program 1994). Since human security is a multi-dimensional concept, it requires adoption of a pragmatic approach on part of state to protect its citizens (King and Murray quoted in Alkire 2003: 15).

There is complementary relationship between food security and human security. Food insecurity is a threat to human security, as it leads to malnutrition, thereby decreasing an individual's productivity. Low productivity leads to low income which lowers access to food. Hence, this becomes a vicious circle. Increasing food insecurity can also lead to conflict which has direct impact on human security. Hunger impedes political, economic and social progress of an individual which in turn threatens his human security. The various threats to human security are interlinked and their impact multiplies when two or more threats like water and food insecurity exits at the same time. The debate on broadening the concept of security takes place in the context that various human insecurities are interrelated and there is need to link human rights and development with security. There exists a connection between human rights and the human security. One of the motivational forces behind the human security is the basic foundation of human rights (Alkire 2003). Hampson (2001) argues that while it is difficult to fully and perfectly merge the notion of human rights onto that of human security but both of them are founded on the similar foundations of universality, dignity, interdependence and focus on the individual. Kaldor and Beebe (2010) say that there is need to look at security from a different perspective. There are some commonalities between human security theorists and radical, critical and feminist theorists. For all the three, individual is the prime referent of security and his security is rated above that of the state. They are committed to social and economic justice and base their postulates on rights, development and equity (Tadjbakhsh and Chenoy 2007). The works of economist Mahbub Ul Haq and Nobel laureate Amartya Sen have been instrumental in development of human security. They argue for providing suitable conditions to individuals to allow their overall development. Their approach is also reflected in Sustainable Development Goals (MDGs), which aim to tackle inter-related problems like hunger, poverty, gender inequality, health, education and environment. In the same way, human security argues that the state should increase security of the people. Human security approach links individual security to global and any threat to security of an individual is regarded as an international security threat (Ibid). There are two major constituents of human security, according to 1994 Human Security Report and depicted in the figure 2.1. First one focuses on 'freedom from want' which focuses on human needs in economic, food, health, social and environmental terms. Food security is a part of 'freedom from want' approach. The second school focuses on 'freedom from fear' and seeks to remove use or threat of force from people's daily lives (UNDP 1994).

Figure 2.1. Types of Human Security

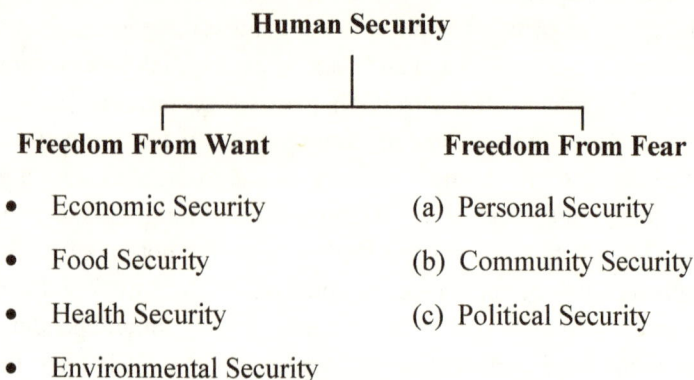

Human Security

Freedom From Want

- Economic Security
- Food Security
- Health Security
- Environmental Security

Freedom From Fear

(a) Personal Security

(b) Community Security

(c) Political Security

Source: UNDP 1994.

However, the Commission on Human Security (2003) report also includes access to healthcare, education, fair trade and basic freedoms in ambit of 'freedom from want'. The report also adds that food insecurity undermines dignity and well-being of an individual. The question is not how state governments maintain required level of food supplies but how do they put these supplies at the disposal of those who need them the most (Commission on Human Security 2003: 14). The report echoes John Rawls concept of 'distributive justice' where he advocates 'the greatest benefit of the least advantaged sections of the society' through his 'difference principle' (Rawls 2001). It means that the state should make sure that the marginal sections like the poor, women, children and elderly should have access to adequate food. It is also related to the concept of food justice which says that everybody should have access to food as it is a human right. Food justice implies that economic and social inequalities should not be allowed to keep people hungry and starved (Patricia and Melcarek 2011). Distributive justice bears significance for food security at various levels. At the international level, it has two ramifications. First, it reflects the widely held belief that the least developed countries (LDCs) have been left out of the international trading mechanism and agriculture policies. There is need to reorient trade and agriculture negotiations at the international level to reflect needs of the LDCs in order to help them achieve their food security. Second, the income levels in the LDCs should be raised by increasing their capacity to attract private investment and development aid. Distributive justice also has food security implications at national level. It means that people should not be allowed to starve by the governments and the marginalised sections should be protected against hunger by the state. Lastly, distributive justice is also relevant at the family level with respect to food security of women and children. Women and children could face hurdles to their food security and hence, should have access to nutritious food (Runge et. al. 2003).

It is clear that food security comes under human security in international security studies. Let us now examine what is the concept of food security and also trace its history in order to better understand role of international community in ensuring food security.

FOOD SECURITY: CONCEPT AND HISTORY

Towards the end of 20th century, some aspects related to food security were mentioned in the book 'Wealth of Households' written by British journalist J T Danson in 1886. He had recognised that society depended on agriculture and there was need to store food in form of reserves as a shield against starvation (Gibson 2012). Food problems surfaced around the world during the First World War. Agriculture production and food distribution was hampered by the war while food trade reduced due to naval blockades. Scarcity of food led governments to resort to price control and rationing. Russia witnessed food riots in its cities while food problems were also seen in Turkey, Austria-Hungary, Britain and Germany (Cornish 2014). The British government had even prohibited the citizens from throwing rice at wedding ceremonies and also banned feeding grains to pigeons (Williams 2014). Herbert Hoover, who later became the US President in 1929, was head of the US Food Administration and started the 'Food Will Win the War' campaign for food conservation and preservation in order to supply wheat to the Allies (Trenholm 2012). Owing to these food problems, the efforts to assess extent of hunger and under-nutrition in the world gained steam with formation of League of Nations after the First World War in 1919. This was the start of the present day food security concept in the international relations. Issues related to food security were mainly seen in local and national terms till first quarter of the 20th century. The economic and social impact of the First World War and the Great Depression during 1930s were drawing attention of experts towards food and nutritional needs of people. Health professionals were speaking against malnutrition while many European governments started taking measures to improve malnutrition by making provisions for subsidised milk and free school meals (Gibson 2012).

In this background, the Health Organisation of the League started directing its efforts to study food security related issues at global level. A number of studies were undertaken by the organisation in 1920s and 1930s in this regard. Two important conferences were held in 1932 organised by League of Nations. The Rome conference in September 1932 pondered over the issue of dietary standards and norms while the Berlin conference in December 1932 considered methods to detect malnutrition. Later, upon the proposal given by a Yugoslav delegation, the League asked its Health Organisation to come out with a report on guidelines to be followed for manufacture and sale of food products (League of Nations 1935). The report 'Nutrition and Public Health' also known as Burnet-Aykroyd report came out in 1936, authored by E Burnet and W R Aykroyd. They studied relationship between health and the institutions responsible for nutrition policies in countries like the US, France, Denmark and the Soviet Union. The report had highlighted the differential incomes between various social categories and its links with nutrition levels (Barona 2010). The report concludes with the following statement:

"Production, distribution and consumption have hitherto been considered mainly as economic problems without sufficient regard to their effect on public health, but the effect of the economic depression has directed attention to the gap which almost everywhere exists between dietary needs as determined by physiology and the means of satisfying them under existing conditions. The general problem of nutrition as it presents itself today is that of harmonising economic and public health development" (League of Nations 1935). This study was probably the earliest document which hinted about role of economic access in food security of an individual by equating 'dietary needs' and 'means of satisfying these needs'. Economist Amartya Sen later elaborated this concept in 1981.

Another important work done by the League was its 1937 study on relationship between nutrition, health, agriculture and economic factors. It was an extensive work which studied role of agriculture, social and economic aspects in relation to nutrition. The report had a slant towards the developed countries, however, it mentioned about the developing countries too. It concluded that malnutrition was prevalent in most of the countries in the world but the channels and methods to deal with it were already available. However, before anything could emerge from the League's efforts, World War II broke out which dealt a blow to its efforts related to food security (Gibson 2012). Food shortages were reported from almost all parts of the world during this war. A large portion of the Soviet Union was occupied by Germany on its western front which also included majority of the wheat producing areas. This created food shortages in the Soviet Union and it had to start food rationing from 1941 (Medvedev 1987). Food shortages and rationing were also reported from the US, United Kingdom,

Germany, Australia, Japan, France and other countries. There were 20 million deaths by starvation and related issues which exceeded 19.5 million deaths by military conflict during the World War II (Collingham 2011). Former US President Herbert Hoover again played an important role in directing American efforts towards food rationing and preservation during the Second World War. He called fats and meats as much ammunition in war as tanks and planes. The government even encouraged American citizens to change their eating habits, asking them to start eating animal organs like heart and liver despite knowing the fact that eating animal organs was considered a characteristic of low social status in the US (Romm 2014).

While the nations were struggling with food shortages during the Second World War, the US President, Frank De Roosevelt mentioned 'four freedoms' in his 1941 annual address to the US Congress. These freedoms were freedom of speech, worship, freedom from want and fear (State of the Union Address 1941). He did not mention food security per-se but this was inherent in freedom from want. Roosevelt interpreted freedom from want mainly as 'economic understanding' which would allow all nations a healthy life during peaceful years all over the world. Later, in his 1944 'State of the Union' address to the US Congress, Roosevelt called for adopting 'Economic Bill of Rights' These rights included educational rights, protection from old age, unemployment and accidents, right to decent living and recreation (Historic Documents 1944). He went ahead and addressed linkages between freedom and hunger as he famously said:

> "Necessitous men are not free men. People who are hungry and out of a job are the stuff of which dictatorships are made" (Ibid).

In 1945, the League of Nations was replaced by United Nations Organisation (UNO) in international politics. In the same year, UN Food and Agriculture Organisation (FAO) was established with the motto 'fiat panis' meaning 'Let There Be Bread'. The foundation of the organisation was laid in 1943 at the conference in Hot Springs, Virginia by an initiative taken by President Roosevelt. He had linked political security with food security in his speech at the conference saying that political security will be enhanced if every nation could be assured of its food requirements (Food For Peace 2008). World Bank and International Monetary Fund had already been established in 1944 at the Bretton Woods Conference. In 1946, FAO organised a World Food Survey in order to assess if people had enough food and energy (calories) around the world. The survey concluded that around 33 percent of world population lacked required calories to live a healthy life (Simon 2012). The first document at international level to recognise an individual's right to food was Universal Declaration of Human Rights adopted in 1948. Article 25 of the UDHR states that all human beings have a right to living standard which is enough for them and their family's health and welfare including right to food, shelter and clothing (UN Website).

Aided by technological advancements in farming methods, the US and European countries took measures to ensure food for their citizens and soon, there was food surplus in these countries which needed to be managed (Simon 2012). The US had started 'Food for Peace' program, also called 'Public Law 480' in 1954. This program aimed to send surplus food as food aid to the countries that were in severe food crisis (US Food Aid and Security Website). In 1960, the US President D Eisenhower suggested that the food aid should be channelled through the UN. In 1961, the World Food Program (WFP) was instituted on three-year experimental basis. The WFP gave food aid after the Iran earthquake in 1962; assisted the victims of hurricane in Thailand and it also gave food assistance to around five million refugees who were resettling in Algeria in 1962-63. Due to its outstanding work in eradicating hunger, the UN passed the resolution to make WFP a permanent body in 1965 (World Food Program Website). Meanwhile, the Article 11 of International Covenant on Economic, Social and Cultural Rights (ICESCR) asked all the states parties to the convention to recognise 'freedom from hunger' as a fundamental right of their citizens. It also placed the responsibility to improve production and distribution of food on the member states (UN Office of the High Commissioner for Human Rights Website). Another important event from the perspective of food security in international relations was World Food Conference held in Washington in June 1963, attended by around 1,300 delegates from 100 countries. The then Director General of FAO, B R Sen had taken this initiative under his 'Freedom From Hunger Campaign' (FFHC). FFHC was launched in 1960, at a time when efforts to eradicate poverty around the world had been slow and population increase threatened to make the situation worse in future. In March 1963, a week long campaign was run by FAO for freedom from hunger. The attempt was to attract attention of policy makers towards hunger and future threat of population growth outstripping agricultural production (Gibson 2012). The World Food Conference exhorted the developed and developing countries, the UN and its specialised organisations, other international organisations and non-government organisations to fight against the problem of hunger and starvation. The concerns of low agricultural output compared to population growth were based on FAO's projections for agricultural production between 1962 and 1970. The projections showed that demand for food will increase faster in developing countries than the industrialised nations as they will have more population growth and increase in incomes. In comparison, the developed countries were expected to have food surpluses which could be supplied to countries which were food deficit and efforts for food aid were started as explained in earlier paragraph (Shaw 2007).

Between 1950s and 1960s, the food production in the world increased by more than 50 percent while per capita consumption increased by one-fifth or 20 percent, leading to food surplus. This food surplus was a regular feature in the international grain market and brought some 25 million tons of additional grains to it. This was interrupted in 1972 due to adverse climate in grain growing areas reducing the food production (Simon 2012). These food shortages increased food prices which also increased domestic as well as international political interest in issues of food security. A number of factors combined to create food shortages in early 1970s. Along with adverse climatic conditions in grain producing areas, there were changes in Canadian and American food reserve policies, high prices of fertilisers and failure in Peruvian anchovy catch aggravated the food crisis. The crisis was further worsened by the decision of Organisation of Petroleum Exporting Countries (OPEC) to hike petroleum price to new levels, which in turn affected prices of chemical fertilisers and transportation of food. The Soviet Union too started importing grains during this time and made interventions in international grain market, which raised food prices (Hopkins and Puchala 1978). Soviet Union had become food importer in early 1970s and various factors were responsible for this situation. Due to increase in food prices, shortage of good quality food and poor economic conditions, riots broke out in Gdansk and Szczecin, two Polish cities in 1970. The Soviet government feared a domino effect of such riots over other cities and allocated more funds to agriculture. The leadership was apprehensive that Soviet citizens would not tolerate a crop failure in future and started to import grains in 1971 (Atkin 1992). As a result, Soviet Union bought around 3 million tons of grain from the US in November 1971. This was a quarter of total US wheat crop and led to wheat price increase in the US and international market. The Soviet Union had signed a three-year deal with the US in 1971 to purchase large amounts of grains (Markham 2002). Such large amounts of wheat purchase by the Soviets were later referred to as 'The Great Grain Robbery' by some experts,[1] as Soviet Union purchased this grain at relatively cheap prices from the US. As a result, the American farmers were robbed of their due share and received less payment for their produce. Such large amount of food purchase by Soviet Union created food shortage in international market and grain prices skyrocketed once this

---

1   Trager, James (1975), "The Great Grain Robbery", New York: Ballantine Books.

deal was announced. The poor countries dependent on wheat imports too were impacted as they ended up paying more for food purchase from international market (Larsen 2012). That is why; this event was called 'The Great Grain Robbery', mainly in the US media. Soviet grain imports from the US, Canada, France, Australia and Sweden amounted to more than a billion dollars in 1972 (Broening, November 6, 1972). The total grain imports by Soviet Union in 1972 have been pegged at 40 million tons. The Soviet grain crisis was also compounded by factors other than crop failure. Due to obligations of Cold War politics, Soviet Union supplied food aid to fellow communist regimes in Cuba, Poland, Vietnam and Czechoslovakia. A large number of grains were also used in production of beer and vodka. The domestic alcohol consumption in Soviet Union and vodka exports were increasing faster than the average grain harvests in the country (Medvedev 1987). All these factors made Soviet Union a grain importer in early 1970s which created imbalance in the international grain market.

Around half a million people are estimated to have died during the food crisis of 1972-74 due to food shortages, price rise and lack of proper system available for emergency food distribution (Shaw 2007). Keeping this crisis in focus, two important conferences were organised by the UN in 1974. World Population Conference was held in Budapest in August 1974 which discussed demographic growth around the world and its relationship with development. Another related event was World Food Conference held in November 1974 in Rome which discussed food security at the global level in relation to rapidly increasing population. Two new UN organisations were established by recommendations made by the World Food Conference. International Fund for Agricultural Development (IFAD) was an international financial institution and started its operations in 1977. The motive was to financially support rural areas through agricultural projects in developing and poor countries to improve their food production, as these areas have high poverty levels (IFAD Website). World Food Council (WFC) was another organisation that was set up following suggestions of 1974 World Food Conference. It was assigned with the task of coordinating with the agriculture ministries of member states for reducing hunger and malnutrition. However, it was suspended in 1993 (Encyclopaedia Britannica Website). The conference also recognised inalienable right of all men, women and children to be free from hunger and malnutrition. The term 'food security' was used probably for the first time at a global event and was defined at the conference as:

> "availability at all times of adequate world food supplies of basic foodstuffs to sustain a steady expansion of food consumption and to offset fluctuations in production and prices" (UN 1975, quoted in Maletta 2014).

The emphasis was on attaining self-sufficiency in grain production for ensuring food security. This definition was influenced by British economist T R Malthus, who in his 1798 work 'An Essay on the Principle of Population' argued that population, if unchecked increases geometrically while food production increases arithmetically (Malthus 1789). It implies that if food security is to exist, food production should be faster than population growth. Two aspects were needed to be fulfilled for existence of food security according to the definition given at the World Food Conference 1974. One was adequate food supplies and another was stabilising conditions for flow of supplies. This led to international efforts for reducing price fluctuations and financing costs of required imports. At national level, it led to adoption of national strategies for food self-sufficiency (Overseas Development Institute Briefing Paper 1997). The rationale behind this approach was that if every nation was self-sufficient in food production, it would ensure food security for all people around the world. Up to 1980s, the food security concept continued to be defined in terms of self-sufficiency approach. However, this approach did not give due credit to food trade among nations and its role in ensuring food security at national level. It was also silent on issues of food distribution and access to food. Aspects of food quality and nutrition too were neglected by this approach (Maletta 2014).

In early 1980s, a conceptual shift took place in the way food security was understood and defined, courtesy economist Amartya Sen's seminal work 'Poverty and Famines' published in 1981. Sen questioned the 'food availability approach' and demonstrated that famines had taken place in situations of ample food availability, contrary to the belief that famines occurred when there was less food available. According to him, 'entitlement failure' leads to famine. Entitlement failure is related to access to food. He gave two types of entitlements, personal and market exchange entitlements. Personal entitlements include assets legally owned by an individual like land and house. Market exchange entitlements are the one which an individual can access through trade and exchange. Decline in these entitlements can lead the individual to starvation. For example, decline in price of goods produced by the individual reduce his income which limits his/ her capacity to purchase food (Burchi and De Muro 2012). Sen studied Bengal famine of 1943 and Bangladesh famine of 1974 to prove that mere availability of food was not enough to ensure food security. Food availability in Bengal in 1943 was higher than in 1941. However, there was no famine in 1941 while inflation was one of the causes that led to starvation and famine in Bengal in 1943. There was an increase of more than 300 percent in food prices in the period from 1939 to 1943 while the wages of workers increased by only 30 percent (Encyclopaedia Britannica Website). The main victims of the famine were the rural people including the agriculture labourers, fishermen and transport workers (Sen 1981b). During the Bangladesh famine in 1974, there was peak food production in the country but the famine occurred as people's access to food had been hampered by various factors that year (Ibid). He put it in following words:

> "Starvation is the characteristic of some people not having enough food to eat. It is not the condition of there being not enough food to eat" (Sen 1981b).

The linkages between food security and poverty are depicted in the figure 2.2. Poverty leads to hunger and malnutrition which further lead to poor cognitive and physical development of an individual. Weak physical development becomes a cause of low productivity which in turn again leads to poverty. Hence, it becomes a vicious cycle and to break free from it, an individual would require state assistance.

Figure 2.2. Relationship Between Poverty and Food Security.

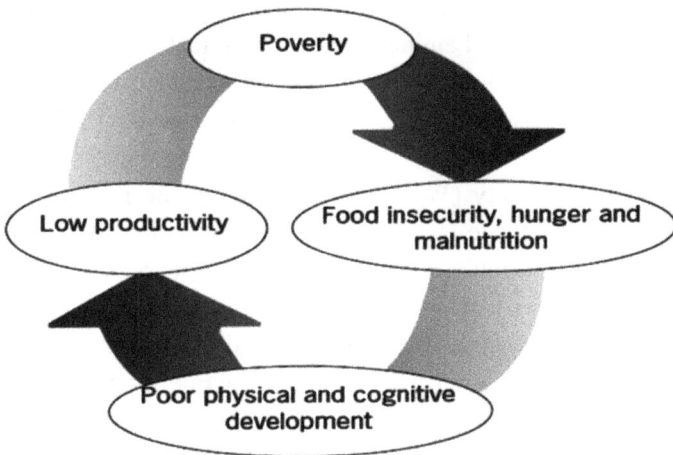

Source: FAO, available at http://www.fao.org/docrep/013/al936e/ al936e00.pdf.

Influenced by the Amartya Sen's work, the Food and Agriculture Organisation included 'access' in the definition of food security in 1983. It defined food security when:

"All people at all times have both physical and economic access to the basic food that they need" (FAO 2006).

This was followed by a World Bank report "Poverty and Hunger: Issues and Options for Food Security in Developing

Countries" in 1986 which again was influenced by Sen's entitlement approach. The report said that two conditions were required for existence of food security – availability of food and people's ability to access the food. Absence of enough ability to access food created food insecurity. There were two types of food insecurity, according to the report. First is chronic food insecurity which is caused by constant consumption of inadequate food either due to lack of ability of a household to access it or to produce it. Second type of food insecurity is transitory, which is short term decrease in a household's ability to access food. It can be caused by fluctuations in production of food, food prices or the household income. Famine is caused by transitory food insecurity in its worst conditions. The report further added that it was not enough to increase food availability for ensuring food security and efforts were needed to enhance purchasing power of the poor sections of society (World Bank 1986). In the period between 1990 and 2005, the UN organised a number of conferences that were related to multi-dimensional concept of food security. The prominent ones were - the UNIDO Conference on Ecologically Sustainable Industrial Development held at Copenhagen (1991), International Conference on Water and the Environment in Dublin (1992), World Bank Conference on Overcoming Global Hunger in Washington (1993), World Food Summit in Rome (1996), United Nations Millennium Summit in New York (2000), Second World Assembly on Ageing in Madrid (2002) and World Summit in New York (2005) (Shaw 2007). Among these conferences, the World Food Summit in 1996 gave a holistic definition of food security as:

"Food security exists when all people, at all times, have physical and economic access to sufficient, safe and nutritious food that meets their dietary needs and food preferences for an active and healthy life" (FAO 1996).

This definition highlights following four aspects necessary for food security.

1. Food Availability: The required food for the population should be available which is ensured by domestic production, food imports, food stocks and food aid from other countries and agencies.

2. Food Access: Physical and economic access to food is ensured by purchasing power of the population and infrastructure for market and transport.

3. Food Utilisation: This includes food safety measures, hygiene and sanitation practices and health care facilities. It underlines role of non-food factors in concept of food security.

4. Food Stability: In order to have food security, people should have unhindered access to food at all times. Price fluctuations, natural disasters and weather variations, political and economic hindrances should not disrupt food availability and access (FAO 2006 quoted on UNICEF Albania Website).

The social dimension of food access did not feature in this definition. There could be social and cultural barriers that affect a groups access to food, for example, women (Simon 2012). Hence, FAO added the word 'social' to access aspect in its food security definition in its 2001 'The State of Food Insecurity' report and defined it as a situation:

> "That exists when all people, at all times, have physical, social and economic access to sufficient, safe and nutritious food that meets their dietary needs and food preferences for an active and healthy life" (FAO 2003). The interplay between the four dimensions of food security is depicted in the figure 2.3.

Figure 2.3. Linkages Between Dimensions of Food Security.

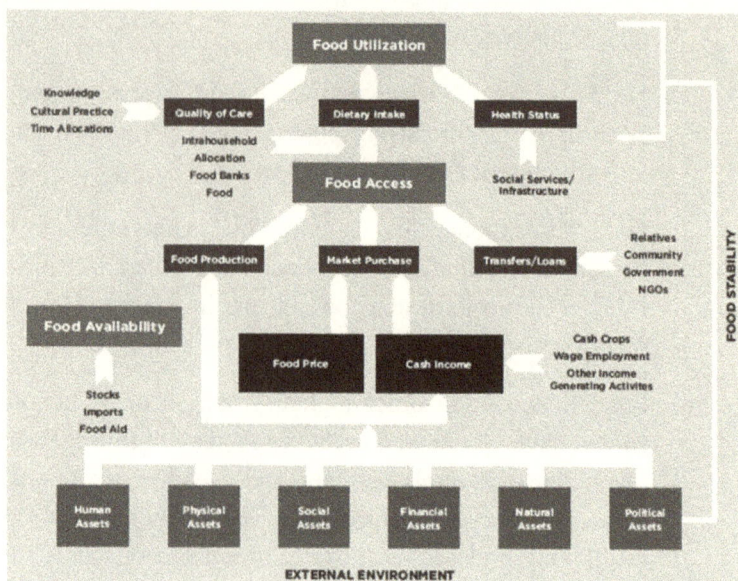

Source: USAID (2011).

Keeping the above multi-dimensional aspect of food security at centre, the present approach to food security focuses on sustainable livelihoods of people. There is no exclusive focus on food security but all the aspects involved in this concept like poverty, health, hygiene and sanitation, clean water etc. are given due importance for ensuring better food security for people. This approach has been more successful among international development organisations like Oxfam, Action Against Hunger and UN agencies. Two features of this approach make it advantageous over the food security approaches in the past. One, it has a long-term perspective and two; it gives due considerations to different contexts like social, political and economic (Burchi and De Muro 2012). However, one of the drawbacks of the food security definition given by FAO in 2001 is that it does not give any consideration for food preferences of the people which play an important role in their diet and caloric intake (Simon 2012).

FOOD SECURITY AND POLITICAL STABILITY

There has been a historical link between food insecurity and political unrest. There is an old saying – "every society is three meals away from a riot", meaning if a big section of population is hungry due to any reason, it will lead to riots and unrest (Shaw 2014).This has been proven right time and again throughout the human history across nations. Indian political scientist, Kautilya (375 BC-250 BC) would be probably one of the earliest thinkers to establish a link between food security and national security. He argued that famine impacts a nation in two ways. One, due to decrease in agriculture output, there is low tax collection by the state. Secondly, low government income due to low revenues will lead to decrease in funds flow to public works. This in turn, would impact income generation in future as state's capacity to spend on infrastructure is reduced. Low revenue also impacts defence preparedness of the country as government spends less on military affairs (Sihag 2014). Roman scholar, M T Cicero (born 106 BC, died 43 BC) had a first-hand experience when his house was attacked by a bunch of hungry people (Patel and McMichael 2009). He concluded that increase in food prices was creating social unrest in Rome (Roston 2012). Roman author and poet, Juvenal, who lived between 1st and 2nd century AD had said that 'bread and circus' are an effective tool for getting support from people and keeping them away from expressing their grievances. A year before the French revolution, France had suffered a bad harvest in 1788 which increased food prices and also led to food riots. Food prices played a role in inciting the French revolution in 1789, since it is due to relative deprivation that people resort to violent behaviour (Brinkman and Hendrix 2011).

America witnessed around thirty incidents where people protested against increasing commodity prices including food during 1776-79 (Smith 2012). Food shortage and high food prices were also responsible for bread riots in Russian cities during the Russian revolution in 1917. Russia was already suffering food shortages due to economic and social impact of First World War and this trend was further worsened by the political instability during the revolution. Food shortages were also reported around the involved countries during the Second World War. In 1998, food prices are believed to have contributed to downfall of the Suharto regime in Indonesia (Symonds 1998). Recently, there was a global food crisis during 2007-08 due to steep rise in global food prices that led to food riots in a number of countries. Former President of Egypt, Hosni Mubarak had even ordered Egyptian army to bake bread for the hungry public. Food price rise was one of the grievances that brought protesters to street during Arab Spring starting in 2010 (Hendrix and Haggard 2009). Mubarak was one of the leaders who were ousted from office during the Arab Spring in 2011. Picture 2.1 shows the major countries that witnessed social unrest due to global food price hike and the countries which banned food exports to shield their own citizens from the impact of food price hike.

Picture 2.1. Protests and Grain Export Bans During Global Food Price Rise.

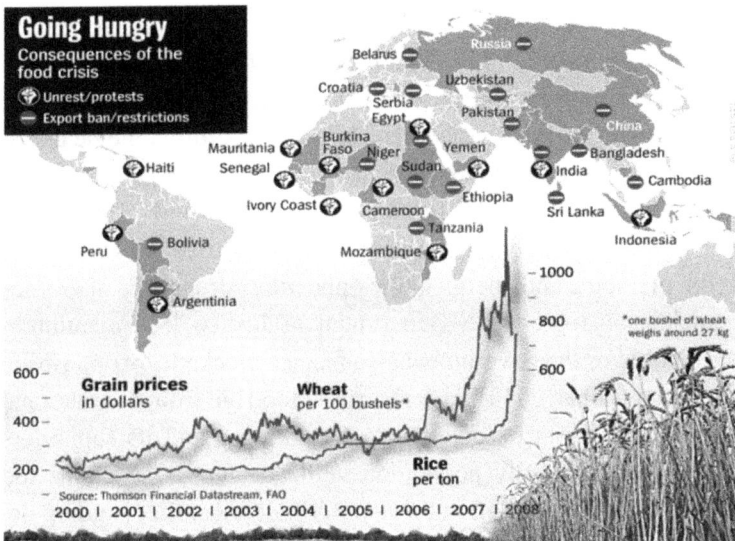

The relationship between political stability and food security is complementary. Political instability and conflict can lead to food insecurity while food insecurity could also contribute to political instability. First, let us study how political instability and conflict lead to food insecurity.

Impact of Political Instability on Food Security

Conflict and political instability lead to food shortages and hunger problems. Conflict damages the rural infrastructure, livestock and displaces people from their homes which cause food insecurity for the affected people. The agriculture and economy suffer neglect and lack of planning, thereby reducing food production (Teodosijevic 2003). Food shortages and famine occur during a conflict when there is a food blockade to starve opponents into submission.

Around 5 lakh Germans lost their lives from hunger and starvation due to blockade of Germany's food imports by Allied nations during First World War (Evans 2012).There are other examples as well when food has been used as a weapon. When the Ukrainians rebelled against Stalin in 1932, Ukraine's borders were sealed to stop food imports while the Red Army ceased all the food available with the people. Also called 'the Holodomor', this strategic use of food as a weapon is believed to have caused deaths of ten million Ukrainians due to starvation and hunger (Kuryliw 2002).Even during the Tajik civil war, the government tried a blockade of food, medicine and energy in the opposition stronghold of Gorno-Badakhshan region (US Department of Justice 1993). Kulob, a stronghold of the government also faced a blockade by opposition forces (Kevlihan 2013). In some cases, food aid from international community could be diverted to the military and its supporters instead of the needy population while economic sanctions too could lead to starvation in the country where conflict is going on. The farming population is reduced due to fear, death, malnutrition, displacement and illness. This leads to decreased food production and food insecurity spreads to other areas as well. Food shortages induced by conflict take time to normalise, even after the conflict ceases (Cohen and Anderson 1999).

Conflict sets the GDP of an average developing country back by around 30 years (World Bank 2011b).Tajikistan underwent a civil war between 1992 and 1997 which had economic consequences for the already poor country. It's gross domestic product decreased by 60 percent between 1990 and 1996 leading to food shortages (FAO 2001). During a conflict, the military expenditure too increases which lowers flow of funds to agriculture, health, education and environmental protection. It also lowers per capita income which makes it difficult for the poor to access food (Bora et. al. 2010). Hence, such a severe impact on the economy of a country is bound to create food problems in a country undergoing conflict. The type of state can also influence food security situation in a country, as demonstrated by economist

Amertya Sen in 1999 in his book 'Development as Freedom'. He opined that a functional democracy has not witnessed famines, as the government has to win public support through periodic elections which is strong incentive to address food insecurity. On the other hand, authoritarian rulers do not need public approval for their rule and they lack incentives to prevent famines and protect their citizens (Sen quoted in Collier et. al. 2003).

Impact of Food Insecurity on Political Stability

Violence also erupts in conditions where people face subsistence crisis and economic conditions take a downward turn. Hunger could lead to violence and conflict when people face severe conditions and fight for their rights. In African countries like Sudan, Ethiopia and Rwanda, governments fell when they could not adequately respond to famines created by their own policies (Cohen and Anderson 1999). During the 2007-08 global price rise, a number of countries witnessed food riots while there was leadership change in Madagascar and Haiti (Brinkman and Hendrix 2010). The governments that have been successful in shielding their citizens from food price fluctuation have reaped political benefits, like Dr Manmohan Singh led United Progressive Alliance came back to power in 2009 in India while President of Indonesia, Susilo Yudhoyono was also re-elected in 2009. In both the cases during election campaign, the winning candidates had highlighted their policies of successfully tackling the global food crisis and not allowing the high world food prices to impact their domestic food market (Timmer 2010). However, even if there is conflict or political instability in a country, it is unlikely that hunger alone could be the cause and there are other factors which should be looked into. Iraq was placed under sanctions after 1991 Gulf war, the assumption being that the Saddam government would be overthrown by the hungry people. The sanctions increased chronic malnutrition in Iraq but the government remained in place (Teodosijevic 2003). By 1995, many people were consuming just 1,000 calories per day provided by government rations. Around

576,000 children died between 1991 and 95, most of them due to malnutrition (Crossette 1995). However, such dire food situation too did not incite people against Saddam regime.

Experts opine that just low level of food insecurity is not enough to cause political chaos and it is important to see how it is distributed among the population (Brinkman and Hendrix 2010). It is not only the level of food insecurity that matters for conflict to arise. The distribution of this insecurity among the population is also important. Relative deprivation rather than absolute deprivation gives rise to violent behaviour. So, it is important to see whether the food insecurity is widely spread or concentrated in certain groups (Reenock et. al. 2007). Even in case of 2007-08 food riots, there were factors other than food prices that triggered protests. The protestors were shouting against injustice, repression, inequality while food prices brought together various sections against their governments. Poverty and governance issues were too responsible for the public outbursts while the politicians ignored the suffering of people (Bush 2010). These events exposed state faults and reflect governance problems in the affected nations. Some of the countries which witnessed these riots had authoritarian or semi-authoritarian governments. These regimes are characterized by inefficiency and widespread corruption (Harsch 2008). Hence, food insecurity does contribute to political instability but other factors like political, social and economic issues determine the intensity of protests. Some factors like climate change have equal impact on both, food security as well as political stability (Maxwell 2012). According to a study by Intergovernmental Panel on Climate Change (IPCC) in 2014, climate change is likely to increase food prices by 3-84% by 2050. This would be a critical situation for those who spend half or more of their earnings on food (Oxfam 2014). This means that 'Low Income Food Deficit Countries' like Tajikistan are going to be at risk of food related unrest in coming years, if they do not take corrective policy measures to tackle the situation. The triggers for conflict could be natural like environmental disasters, economic like change in food prices or political like denial of land use rights and decline in social security spending by states (Bora et. al. 2010). Even increase in population could have impact on both, food security and political stability. While population increase would also lead to increase in food demand, it would also put pressure on governments to provide better governance and employment opportunities for the people so that they have economic access to food.

Correlations between food security and socio-political stability have often existed but not always and everywhere. These linkages vary across time and space and depend on how multiple actors (state and private) respond. That is why; it is difficult to causally point out links between the two. The food riots in response to food price increase rarely occur among most vulnerable, food insecure and politically marginalised people like rural landless and small holding farmers, infants and young children. The rioters, on the contrary, are urban people who are better off than the vulnerable sections. In the overall analysis, food price fluctuations remain a proximate rather than root cause of socio-political unrest. Food price hike is the last nail in the coffin which breaks the patience of people in presence of other socio-economic problems. High food prices could unite people across different sections in the short run, when they think that the state is not protecting them against hunger and it lacks required strength and power to suppress dissent (Barrett 2013). Since democracies allow protests and freedom of expression, such governments are more vulnerable to urban protests and unrest during the times of high food prices (Hendrix and Haggard 2009). Repressive regimes on the other hand deal with dissent with a hard hand and are less likely to witness social unrest due to food insecurity (Hendrix et. al. 2009).According to a recent World Bank report; international food prices impact the local markets and have a bearing on conflicts of all types. It also says that there have been 51 food riots in 37 countries between 2007 and 2014 due to food price rise (World Bank 2014). There is direct correlation between increase in food prices and number of food riots, as shown in the figure 2.4. Experts are already seeing food security linked to national security and are arguing for better policies to ensure food security (Speckhard 2014, McGovern 2011, Suleri 2012). However, food security is not mentioned in matters related to national defence by most countries but it is an integral part of a nation's vital interests (Carles and Montfort 2010).

Figure 2.4. Relationship Between Food Price Rise and Food Riots.

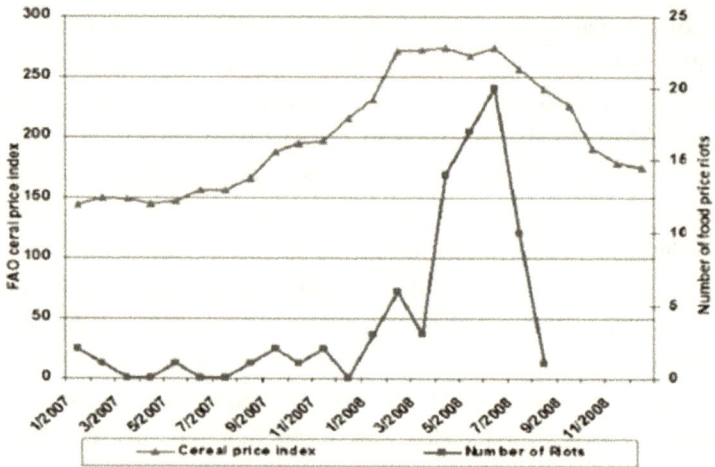

Source: Brinkman and Hendrix 2010: 5.

Food insecurity also contributes in generating a weak state structure which lacks enough capacity to address food problems. Food insecurity could trigger internal as well as external migration from a country. The valuable human resource often leaves a weak country in search of greener pastures abroad to achieve food security. This impacts the economy and agriculture sector of the state as there is lack of human capital to work in these sectors. Neglected agriculture leads to low food production which enhances food insecurity. A weak and food insecure state could also be an attractive destination for the foreign companies to invest. However, these companies could use the weak legal framework of these states to grab large tracts of fertile land and leave marginal land for domestic production (Haberli and Smith 2014). Weak states are economically and politically strained to offer 'public goods' among their masses including food which accentuates migration from the state (Mohapatra 2013). Hence, food insecurity also weakens a state and hampers its political and economic capacity.

FOOD SECURITY AND RESOURCE COMPETITION

Rapidly increasing population and unpredictable weather conditions are leading to increase in food prices. In order to ensure sufficient food availability for their citizens, nations are caught in resource competition (land, water and energy) which again impacts their food security. Competition over land has taken a new dimension as wealthy, food importing nations and private investors, in their bid to guard against future food supply side shocks are acquiring farm land in other countries (often in less developed) (Benjamin 2012). These land acquisitions have also been called 'land grabs' by some experts. The International Land Code (ILC) estimated that by early 2012, land deals totalling to 203 million hectares were under negotiations or approved from 2000 to 2010. An Oxfam study in 2011 claimed that 230 million hectares of land had either been sold or leased since 2001. This land size is equal to that of Western Europe. The US, China, India, Saudi Arabia, Brazil, Libya and South Korea have emerged as the countries which are investing in land resources abroad due to food and energy security concerns. They are growing crops on these overseas lands and send them back home for consumption. These nations are also growing bio fuels on these lands to avoid dependence on hydrocarbons in order to save environment and cut down their carbon emissions (Kugelman 2013: 1-5).

Realists attach highest priority to state security in order to retain their place in anarchic international system. Kenneth Waltz says that security is more than survival in international politics and also includes state behaviour in international system. The land grabs which undermine the interests and survival of the less developed countries at the cost of wealthier nations can be seen as 'state behaviour' for survival in realist sense (Banjamin 2012). Tajikistan too has leased its land to Chinese investors. In 2011, Tajikistan gave away 1,100 square kilometres (around one percent of its territory) to China settling its border dispute with its powerful neighbour. In the same year, Chinese workers started arriving in Tajikistan to work as it leased around 2,000 hectares to Xinjiang autonomous province of China. This has caused local resentment in Tajikistan, as around 1,500 Chinese farmers were expected to work in the districts of Bokhtar and Kumsangir in southern Khatlon (Pannier 2011). In 2015, Tajik government claimed that around 6,300 hectares of land was being cultivated by Chinese investors in Tajikistan (Asia Plus, January 15, 2015).Land grabs have not only led to protests in some countries but there have been political consequences in some cases. In Madagascar, President Marc Ravalomanana lost power after people protested against his attempts to lease 1.3 million hectares, around 33 percent of its arable land to Daewoo, a South Korean company. It is the only example till now where 'land grabs' have led to political instability and overthrow of government (Barrett 2013). The competition is also heating over water resources across different regions. In South Asia, there are water disputes between India-Pakistan, India-China and India-Bangladesh. In Central Asia, the water policies of upstream countries namely Tajikistan and Kyrgyzstan are being seen with suspicion by downstream countries, Uzbekistan, Kazakhstan and Turkmenistan. A United Nations study says that by 2025, 30 countries would be water scarce and 18 of them are in Middle East and North Africa. Another report by Organisation for Economic Co-operation and Development (OECD) says that by 2030, 47 percent of world population would live in high water stress areas (Arsenault 2012).

Land, water and energy are interlinked and they should not be targeted by policymakers in isolation from each other. Their links to sustainable food security are shown in the figure 2.5.

Figure 2.5. Links Between Land, Water, Energy and Food Security.

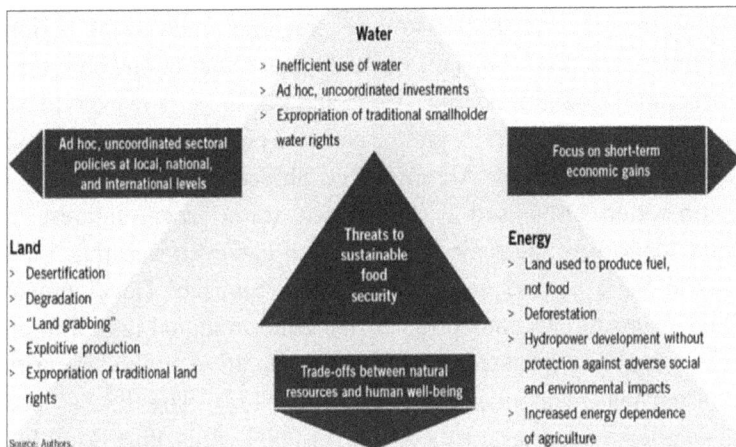

Source: Authors.

Source: International Food Policy Research Institute 2012.

FOOD SECURITY AND REGIONAL INTEGRATION

One of the potential areas to improve food security in a country is by ensuring regional economic cooperation. Regional trade enhances employment opportunities which increase economic growth and income of the poor, thus bringing them better access to food. Regional cooperation could also lead to establishment of a common agriculture and food market, which can offset the impact of global food prices by pooling in the regional food resources in times of crisis (Matthews 2003). Food can be transported from the surplus areas to deficit areas through regional market integration. This ensures that there is less food price variation. Regional economic cooperation also ensures better infrastructure and lower trade barriers which contribute to better food security in the regional countries facing food problems (US State Government Consultant Document 2009). This leads to better regional security as well, as the states can better tackle problems in international trade and agriculture. In Central Asia, Kazakhstan is the regional wheat producer and exporter while other four countries in the region import food stuffs. However, regional trade in the region is hindered by trade barriers while there are restrictions on cross-border movement of people, goods and transport. However, these problems can be solved by mutual action in order to have better food security in the region (Akramov and Shreedhar 2012). Shanghai Cooperation Organisation has shown some recent interest in food security in the region. Kazakhstan has even said that SCO should have a food security program (Eurasian Development Bank Website, December 15, 2014). Other regional organisation which has shown interest in regional cooperation on food security is Eurasian Economic Community (EAEC). The EAEC had developed a food security concept in 2009 (Asia Plus, May 20, 2009). The Central Asian countries can cooperate over the issue of food security, as they stand to benefit from this arrangement. They could also explore the possibility of establishing regional grain reserves, much like South Asian Association for Regional Cooperation has done.

CHAPTER 3

AGRICULTURE AND FOOD SECURITY SITUATION IN SOVIET TAJIKISTAN

HISTORICAL BACKGROUND

There has been human presence on the territory of present day Tajikistan since the early Stone Age. The areas where the ancestors of present day Tajiks lived include Bactria (Bokhtar), Sogdiana (Sughd), Merv and Khwarezm forming the pre-Islamic period in history of Tajikistan. The Islamic period started from 710 AD to 1218 AD under Arab rule. From 1218 to 1800s, the Tajiks came under Turkish rule as Mongols, Timurlane, Timurids and Uzbeks ruled them. The Central Asian territory was divided between three Khanates –Bukhara, Khiva and Kokand in middle of 18th century (Roudik 2007). The territory of present day Tajikistan remained under multiple authorities in 19th century. It was bifurcated between Bukhara emirate and khanate of Kokand. On the other hand, the areas of Khujand, Uroteppa (Istaravshon) and Qarotegin (Rasht) remained disputed and their control kept exchanging hands from one side to other (Nourzhanov and Bleuer 2013). The Russians started to conquer Central Asia in 19th century and eastern parts of present day Tajikistan were the last territories to come under their rule.

RUSSIAN CONQUEST OF CENTRAL ASIA

The three Khanates of Central Asia exhibited characteristics of a slave society and had backward economies. People engaged in cattle breeding and horticulture while small amount of inferior cotton was also produced before Russian conquest (Kaushik 1970). Vaidyanath has quoted Russian orientalist, V V Bartol'd saying that Central Asia was the most backward country in the Muslim world before the Russian conquest due to frequent wars, religious intolerance, illiteracy and its isolation from advanced regions of Asia and Europe (Bartol'd 1927, quoted in Vaidyanath 1967: 6). Major changes in political, economic and social aspects of Central Asia took place after the region was conquered by Russia. There were a number of reasons behind Russian advance in Central Asia. After Russian defeat in the Crimean War in 1856, Russia under Czar Alexander II gave up its focus on the Balkans and showed more interest in Central Asia (d' Encausse, 1994a). In Russia, it was a period of economic transition as feudal-serf relations were making way for capitalist mode of production. Hence, expansion of capitalism in Russia required takeover of new markets. That is why; Central Asia was being seen as a potential market by Russian industrial circles (Kaushik 1970). Quoting N A Khalfin, R R Sharma argues that Russian search for new markets to sustain and promote its capitalist trade led to its conquest of Central Asia (Sharma 1979). The political division of Central Asia in the middle of 19th century is depicted in the map 3.1.

Map 3.1. Political Division of Central Asia in the Middle of 19th Century.

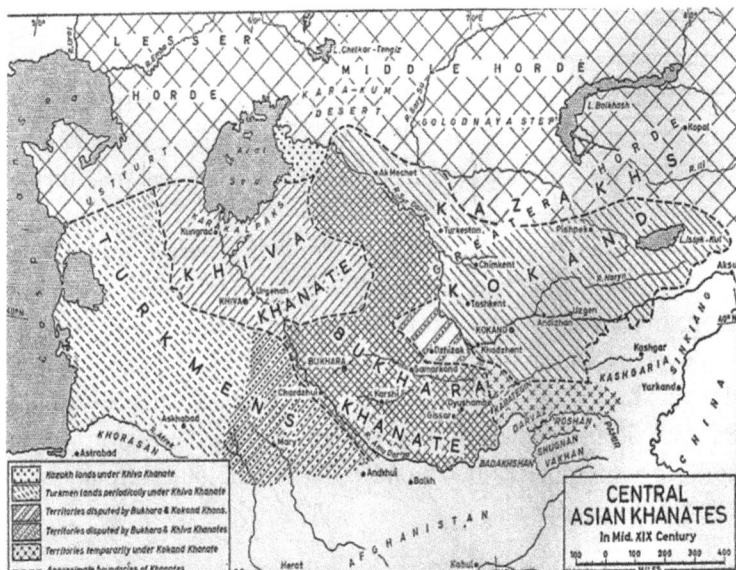

Source: Wheeler 1964: 251.

Russian economy had started moving towards capitalism and Russian trade in Central Asia had capitalist character from the beginning (Lyashchenko 1970). However, the Kazakhs remained a source of trouble for the Russian traders in the region as they would raid Russian trade caravans and hinder trade with the Khanates (Pierce 1960). To secure their trade from notorious Kazakhs, it was necessary that Russia established its control over Central Asian region. Apart from above mentioned reasons, cotton was the main reason that brought Russians to Central Asia. America was main cotton supplier for Russian textile industry. However, it was undergoing a Civil War (1861-1865) and its cotton supplies to Russia were severely hit. Russia desired to secure cotton supplies from Central Asia to replace American supplies (Rakowska-Harmstone 1970). Moreover, the global price of cotton had risen more than five times due to the American civil war. Due to increasing cost of imported cotton, Russia was looking for an alternate source of cheap cotton supply and Central Asia was their first choice as the climate in the region was favourable to grow cotton (Anderson 1997).

The cotton and textile businessmen in Russia wanted government help in securing Central Asian cotton. Around 1860-62, fifteen merchants from Moscow had asked the Russian finance minister to seek Central Asian raw cotton, especially from Bukhara (d' Encausse, 1994a). Lastly, the Russians were also wary of British designs on Central Asia (Pierce 1960, Kaushik 1970) and tried to conquer Central Asia before them. Just before Russian advance in Central Asia, Tsar's Chancellor, Prince Gorchakov used the analogy of 'civilised v/s half-savage tribes' while defending Russian security and commercial interests in the region. In his address to the states with which Russia had diplomatic relations in 1864, Gorchakov said:

> "The position of Russia in Central Asia is that of all civilised states which come into contact with half-savage wandering tribes possessing no fixed social organisation. It invariably happens in such case that the interests of security on the frontier, and of commercial relations, compel the more civilised state to exercise a certain ascendancy over neighbours whose turbulence and nomad instincts render them difficult to live with" (quoted in Caroe 1967: 75).

Russian campaign took off in Central Asia when oblast of Turkestan was separated from Governor-Generalship of Orenburg and was renamed Governor-Generalship of Turkestan in 1867 (Pierce 1960). K V Kaufman was made its first Governor-General and Tashkent became its capital. Turkestan also included areas of Uroteppa and Khujand which became parts of Tajikistan later (Atkin 1997). Russians under General Kaufman made peace with Kokand Khanate but Bukhara was defeated in 1868 (Roy 2000). The emir of Bukhara, Muzaffar-al-Din was forced by Russians to give away eastern part of his dominions, area including Samarkand and Pamirs in 1868. Samarkand had a strategic importance for Russia as far as Bukhara was concerned. Samarkand was an upstream city while Bukhara was downstream on the Zeravshan river. Hence controlling Samarkand meant Russians also controlled water supply to Bukhara. Bukhara's life depended on this water and Russians held this 'life threatening' leverage to control Bukhara's policies (Becker 2004, Ratliff 2010).

Stating importance of Samarkand for Russian interests, Lena Jonson has quoted General Kaufman as saying:

"Our possession of Samarkand, 'the Mittpunkt of the world' and the most important city in Central Asia in historical and religious regards, completely destroyed the dominant influence of the Bukharan emir in this part of the Islamic world, and moreover made the city of Bukhara and its surroundings fully dependent on us with regard to water supply, since by the destruction of dams at Zerafshan near Samarkand we would be able to reduce the city to a ruinous condition". (Jonson 2004: 35).

Bukhara also concluded a commercial treaty with Tsarist Russia in 1868. It was more of a trade agreement. This treaty preserved Bukhara's sovereignty having its own political and economic systems, though with lesser territory. The emir continued to rule autocratically (Rahul 1997). There was a friendship treaty signed between Bukhara and Governor-General of Russian Turkestan in 1873. This sealed the fate of Bukhara as it had to give up its independence and remained a sovereign state in symbolic sense (Martin 2003). Bukhara except Samarkand and Zarafshan valley was placed under the Manghit dynasty (a Turkicised Uzbek tribe) and Russians did not exercise direct rule over Bukhara for some critical reasons. It was a well-known religious centre in Islamic world. Russians feared negative repercussions in Muslim world and decided not to annex Bukhara. Besides, Bukhara also acted as a buffer state between Russia and British controlled

Afghanistan (Atkin 1997, Nourzhanov and Bleuer 2013). There was anti-Russian feeling in the emirate and internal conflict was rife. Hence, conquering Bukhara could have been problematic for the Russians and instead of taking direct control of the emirate;they preferred indirect rule by letting the emir stay on his throne (Jonson 2004).

Russians also added certain areas to emirate of Bukhara. In 1870, cities of Shahr-I Sabz and Kitab were handed over to the emir of Bukhara while the emir, Muzaffar-al-Din had also taken over Hisor and Kulob. After Russia merged Kokand with Turkestan in 1876, Muzaffar added Karategin to Bukhara. In 1877-78, he also occupied Darvaz (Geiss 2003). Russia occupied Chorjui from Khiva and handed it over to Bukhara (Jonson 2006). Russia and the British demarcated their spheres of influence in the Pamir region (south-east Bukhara) in 1895. The areas of Shugnen, Roshan and northern Vakhan came under the emirate of Bukhara in 1896 while southern Darvaz on the left bank of river Pyanj was given to Afghanistan. Russia got the direct control of eastern Pamirs by this agreement and the Russian garrison was placed at Khorog in 1897-98 (Becker 2004). By the end of 19th century, the Russian Turkestan constituted Governor-Generalship of Turkestan (GGT), having five administrative units (oblasts) namely Transcaspian oblast (Ashgabat), Samarkand oblast, Semirechye oblast (Almaty), Syr-Darya oblast (Tashkent) and Ferghana oblast, as shown in the map 3.2. It also included two protectorates of Bukhara and Khiva. Since the boundaries of Central Asia were redrawn after the Russian conquest, the area under contemporary Tajikistan was bifurcated between emirate of Bukhara andoblasts of Samarkand and Ferghana in Russian Turkestan (Rakowska-Harmstone 1970). The northern and eastern areas of contemporary Tajikistan covering cities of Panjakent, Uroteppa (Istaravshon), Nau, Khujand, Isfara and Tashqurghon constituted parts of the oblasts of Samarkand and Ferghana. On the other hand, central and southern areas of present day Tajikistan were parts of Bukhara (Nourzhanov and Bleuer 2013).

Map 3.2. Central Asia at the end of 19th Century

Source: Wheeler 1964: 253.

This division of the present day Tajikistan along the 'north-south' line started under Tsarist Russia, as cited above, had far reaching impact on the political, social and economic aspects of Tajikistan. The northern areas (Khujand, Panjakent, Uroteppa) had a better level of development as these areas were integrated in Russian capitalist market with better industry, railroads, infrastructure, health and education facilities. The southern and eastern areas of Hisor, Kulob, Darvaz and Karategin remained alienated and isolated under the emirate of Bukhara. Eastern Bukhara remained so backward that it did not have railroads and pack animals were used for transportation. Bukhara was treated as a source of raw materials and a market for finished goods by the Russian capitalists (Abdullaev and Akbarzadeh 2010, Nourzhanov and Bleuer 2013).

EMIRATE OF BUKHARA – POLITICAL, SOCIAL AND ECONOMIC ASPECTS

The emirate of Bukhara stretched over a territory of 180,000 square kilometres and its population totalled around 2 million in late 19th century. Tajiks and Uzbeks constituted nearly 80 percent of the population (Abdullaev and Akbarzadeh 2010). The political boundaries of emirate of Bukhara during the early 20th century are depicted in the map 3.3.

Map 3.3. Political Boundaries of Emirate of Bukhara During the Early 20th Century.

Source: Rahul 1995: 1

Tajiks resided in Bukhara and eastern parts of Tajikistan. Uzbeks, on the other hand, lived in the western portion of emirate of Bukhara and controlled political apparatus of the emirate under the Manghit dynasty (Karim 1993). The area inhabited by Tajiks started shrinking due to migrations and Turkic invasions in Central Asia. Forced out of the arable lands of Central Asia, Tajiks shifted to barren and mountainous lands at the time of Russian conquest (Bartol'd 1927, Kisliakov 1959 quoted in Vaidyanath 1967:

13-17). The political order in the emirate of Bukhara has been characterised as 'hereditary patrimonial autocracy' by Paul Georg Geiss (Geiss 2003). Bukhara was a state in the medieval sense of the term. Even Russian conquest could not change his feudal outlook and people of his emirate lived in misery. From 1785, when Manghit dynasty started ruling the emirate to its fall in 1920, Bukhara remained a medieval state (Rahul 1995). The rule of the emir was absolute and despotic when dealing with his subjects but it was bound by Muslim religious laws and customs (Bergne 2007). There were no clear cut instructions about government offices and powers attached to them which shifted according to wish of the emir. The emirate consisted of provinces (viloiats) and begs (hakims) were supreme governors of the provinces.

These governors were usually close relatives or favourites of the emir. However, the central authority (emir) often faced problems in controlling the provinces, especially the more distant ones in eastern Bukhara. Provincial officers were engaged in increasing their own profits through arbitrary tax collection. The political order was fragile in the emirate and whenever an emir died, provinces tried to break off from the emirate (Geiss 2003). Even after becoming a Russian protectorate, the emirate continued to live in seclusion. The emir and the Muslim clergy resisted modernisation which kept the emirate in feudal conditions and things were more complex in mountainous eastern Bukhara (Jonson 2006). Around 90 percent of the population of Bukhara was engaged in agriculture. It meant that three elements – land, water and peasants were responsible for society's economic production (Bashiri 1997). However, the sector was marked by low technical level as peasants used primitive tools to cultivate their lands. The total cultivatable area in the emirate was 2,250,000 desiatinas (1 desiatina = approx. 2.7acres) (Centre State War-History Archives of Russia, quoted in Khan 2003: 27). General level of development was very low in Bukhara on the eve of Russian conquest. The industry was limited to small-scale handicraft production (The Great Soviet Encyclopaedia Online 1970-1979). Periodic floods blocked irrigation channels, making them temporarily unusable. Crops were destroyed by swarms of locusts. Locusts were a perennial problem which could destroy a farmer's produce within minutes. The authorities had effective ways to deal with it but the peasants did not want to offend the God by killing his creatures (Rozevitsa 1908, quoted in d' Encausse, 1994b: 166).

In her other work, d'Encausse has quoted Lieutenant Colonel D N Logofet, a Russian geographer and expert on Bukhara saying that there was a contradiction in Bukhara between the agrarian potential of the emirate and the misery that actually prevailed there, especially in the villages. Land holdingswere abandoned while the population suffered famine (Logofet 1909, quoted in d'Encausse 1966: 14). Conditions were worse in the Pamirs. Only 320 hectares of land could be cultivated there. The grain production was just enough to last until spring season and the Pamiris had to survive on mulberries and grass after it (Khan 2003). Seymour Becker has also noted about a famine in Bukhara in 1971, caused by crop failure of previous fall. Many Bukharans blamed the Russians at Samarkand for not supplying enough water to Bukhara which led to crop failure. General Kaufman had banned grain exports from Russian Turkestan due to high prices. Emir of Bukhara, Muzaffar tried in vain to have the ban lifted in order to provide some respite to his hungry subjects. Kaufman, on his part, thought it enough to send a gift of fifty-four tons of grain to Bukhara However, this was not enough to keep people of Bukhara away from starvation (Becker 2004).

The taxation system was not well defined in Bukhara. The emir did not pay any salary to the officials who collected tax as per their own calculations. Such exploitative was the taxation system that at the time of the harvest, after paying all the taxes from his produce, a peasant was left with just 1 pood (1 pood= 16.38 kg) from his total produce of 8 pood (Pirumshaev, quoted in Bashiri 1997). This system suited the emir, as he neither paid any salary to officials, nor he paid any heed to welfare expenditures like building roads and schools. The tax money was used in foreign trips and lavish parties that lasted for forty days and nights (Bahiri 1997). That is why; famine and starvation existed in Bukhara due to poor economic conditions while health services rarely existed for the people. Pavel Luknitsky in his memoir 'Soviet Tajikistan' recounts that Tajik people could not study science under the emirs and even medicine was dominated by witches and wizards who treated the sick by 'magic spells' and prayers (Luknitsky 1954). There was an epidemic in Hisor in 1897 which wiped out half the population of the province (Ivanov, quoted in d'Encausse 1966: 52). The emirs continued to neglect health services in the emirate despite the Hisor epidemic. Bukhara had only one hospital before the Russian revolution which could not treat diseases like plague, malaria and cholera. These diseases were frequent and widespread among the natives (Mehta 1978).

As a result of poor agricultural situation in Bukhara, there were constant uprisings against the emir. From 1875 to 1890, there were several uprisings against the emir in Hisor and other eastern provinces. There were revolts in Kurghan Tube and Kulob in first decade of the 20th century. Showing the backward nature of the emirate of Bukhara, Nourzhanov and Bleuer have cited Russian geographer L A Perepelitsyna saying, "the economic management of Bukhara is being carried out in a predatory way and has deplorable consequences... The government sucks the blood of poor Bukharans and if some time Bukhara is attached to Russia, we will literally acquire a bunch of mendicant people" (Perepelitsyna 1976, quoted in Nourzhanov and Bleuer 2013: 20).The call for reforms in emirate of Bukhara started becoming louder in the first decade of 20th century. Bukhara saw a revolutionary movement during the reign of Emir Abdul Ahad (1885-1910) in 1905. This was influenced by the first revolution of Russia that started in 1901. The revolutionaries wanted to overthrow the Manghit dynasty and modernise the country. However, the movement failed. Emir Mir Say'id Alim (1910-20), son of Abdul Ahad tried to take a middle path between the conservatives and the reformers (Rahul 2000). The reform movement was sweeping all parts of

Turkestan at that time, not only Bukhara and came to be known as Jadidism. It was derived from Arabic word Jadid, meaning new. Jadid movement in Bukhara was inspired by Ahmad Donish, a Tajik writer, architect, scholar and artist. Another figure of the movement was Sadriddin Ayni, a famous Tajik writer. Between 1910 and 1917, Jadidism remained a movement for cultural enlightenment in Bukhara. It was mainly directed to reform the educational system by introducing new methods. However, the masses resisted this movement as they were under the influence of Mullahs (Abdullaev and Akbarzadeh 2010, Rahul 2000).

CHANGES IN LAND TENURE

The native land ownership system in Bukhara and Central Asia proved problematic for the Russians. The land tenure was based on Shariat law. Private ownership of property was prohibited theoretically and the emirs and khans had the supreme control of the land. There were four types of land. *Miriie* (public domain) was the land at the immediate disposal of the state. *Miul'k* (proprietary) land had hereditary rights. *Amliak* land was the one that was reclaimed from the desert and was not irrigated before. It belonged to whoever irrigated it. *Wakf* land was given by the sovereign and private individuals for religious purposes. Water rights were also governed by Sharia and there was a water controller to manage water distribution in villages (Pierce 1960).

In Bukhara, at least 25 percent of the population was without any kind of land and led a wandering life (Istoriya Uzbekskoi SSR, quoted in d'Encausse 1966: 21). Irrigation was also a problem in the emirate as there was lack of a network of canals to increase the area under irrigation. 57.5 percent of the area was irrigated while 42.5 percent was non-irrigated in the emirate (Nazirat Zemeldeliya BNSR, quoted in Khan 2003: 27). The Tsarist Russia felt a need to simplify this complex system of land ownership which would be uniform and enable collection of land revenue. In 1886, the Russian government expropriated all the land and distributed it among the actual tenets. The land under shops, plantations and houses etc. was made private hereditary property. This land could be sold or disposed as per the wishes of its owner. This was a strategic step as it was 'capitalist' in nature and dealt a blow to the Khans and the feudal aristocracy. Hence, private property became a significant feature of Tsarist land reform and around 90 percent of all the irrigated land in Central Asia was under private ownership (Sharma 1979).

RUSSIAN CAPITALIST EXPANSION IN BUKHARA

The most significant consequence of Russian conquest of Bukhara was that its economy was opened for capitalist penetration, like other regions in Central Asia. Recognising the colonial nature of Russia's Asian regions, Vladimir Lenin in 1899 had described their status as:

> "The South and South-East of European Russia, the Caucasus, Central Asia and Siberia serve Russian capitalism in manner of colonies..." (Lenin 1960, quoted in Heinzig 1983: 426).

Russia's economic policy in Central Asia was akin to its policy in its European colonies. National wealth was confiscated while the valuable raw materials were exported to its industrial centres. Local crafts were dismantled due to influx of Russian goods. Traditional ways of life declined while Central Asia was drawn into new systems of world links through Tsarist Russia (Abdurakhimova 2005). There was rapid development of new economic activities like oil industry and mining in Central Asia. In addition, there was Russian investment in leading sectors like cotton and railways in the region. This transformed the local economy into a colonial economy (Poujol and Fourniau 2005). Central Asia's dependence on Russia was absolute, as the region was economically integrated in the imperial economy of Russia by excluding foreigners, mainly the Britishers from the region (Lloyd 1998).

Transport was required for the final conquest of the Central Asians by the Tsarist Russia. Camel and horse were the main modes of transport before 1880 in the region. There were problems of inhospitable terrain and water supply due to deserts and mountains. All these issued led to construction of Trans-Caspian or Central Asian railway (Ibid). Trans-Caspian railway integrated the Central Asian economy with the capitalist Russian economy and paved the way for its colonial exploitation. Due to this transport facility, the annual trade between Russia and Bukhara more than doubled in the first six years after the opening of Trans-Caspian rail line. The trade tripled between the early 1890s to the eve of First World War in 1914 (Jonson 2004). According to R Vaidyanath, one of the main reasons for constructing the Central Asian railway line was cotton. Russia wanted to smoothly transport the Central Asian cotton to its industrial centres. Gradually, the cotton crop became so important in the economy of Central Asia that it was referred to as 'land of white gold' (Vaidyanath 1967).

COTTON MONOCULTURE IN CENTRAL ASIA

As already explained, securing cotton regular supplies was one of the main motives for which the Tsarist Russia conquered Central Asia. There was a well-planned strategy in place which encouraged cotton production from Central Asia. This led to cotton monoculture (cultivation of a single crop) in the region, to the extent that food stuffs were imported from Russia to meet grain requirements in Central Asia. Russia's policy in Central Asia was similar to British policy in Egypt, where cotton production was increased with a resultant decrease in grain production (Rywkin 1982). Cotton cultivation was a traditional economic activity in Central Asia and it did not differ from any other local industry. Cotton production did not have access to external markets as there were problems of transportation and poor quality (Sharma 1979). Russians were aware of the fact that in order to increase cotton production in Central Asia, they had two alternatives. One was to increase total area under cultivation in the region while second option was to decrease area under crops other than cotton. Since the first option was difficult and involved large economic costs, Russians exercised the second option which was cheaper as well (Pierce 1960). Kai Wegerich also makes a similar argument. He says increased production of Central Asian cotton was not based on expansion of irrigated area. Rather, it was done by shifting area under food crops to cotton crop. This made Central Asia dependent on subsidised wheat imports from Russia (Wegerich 2003). Hence, soon after the Tsarist annexation, Central Asia became a base to supply raw material to metropolitan industries in Russia. Russian policies gave preference to cotton, encouraging it at the cost of wheat and other agricultural crops (Wheeler 1964, Kaushik 1970).

The Russian government was taking all the steps to increase cotton production in Central Asia. In 1870s, Governor-General of Turkestan, Von Kaufman sent two of his representatives, M I Brodovskii and V VSamolevskii to America to study methods and practices of cotton cultivation. Superior quality American cotton was introduced in Central Asia and processing machinery from America was also ordered by Kaufman (Brodovskii 1910, quoted in Pierce 1960: 156). Local guza cotton was very poor in quality and suited preparation of coarsest fabrics only. Hence, American cotton started to replace this cotton in Central Asia (Lyashchenko 1970). According to Alec Nove and J A Newth, the policy of cotton specialisation in Central Asia could have been attractive to the peasants if two conditions were fulfilled – essential goods like grain displaced by cotton were readily available to people and cotton prices remained high to induce people to grow cotton (Nove and Newth 1967). To finance more and more cotton cultivation, cotton firms, banks and informal credit institutions came up in the region. These institutions and many Russian middlemen introduced the system of advance buying which was not in favour of peasants. Since the local textile industry had already been destroyed, this system placed the peasants at the mercy of Russian middlemen and cotton buyers. Peasants were given credit at high interest rates, up to 4 percent per month. Hence, peasants were heavily indebted and as a result, lost the freedom to sow crop of their choice. The moneylenders asked them to grow cotton and the peasants complied, hoping to pay back their debt (Mandel 1944, quoted in Vaidyanath 1967: 46). However, that could not happen as the prices of grain would increase due to scarcity and the peasants sought more loans and credit from moneylenders. It was a case similar to Latin America, where the population benefited from cotton profits but ended up overpaying for food at the same time due to less availability. This increased their debt every passing year (Safarov, quoted in Pierce 1960: 168).

Large amount of state efforts went in encouraging the cotton monoculture in Central Asia. Russians imposed high tariff on cotton imports from abroad. This helped in keeping the market price of cotton advantageous to cotton growers and also allowed the administration to collect high prices in internal market. The tariff was 40-50 kopecks per pood from 1879 to 1884. It increased rapidly to 5 roubles 25 kopecks per pood in 1903. At the same time, equal taxes were levied on land used for cotton and grain cultivation. There was huge difference in market price of cotton and grain on a given area, as cotton was three to four times more profitable than grain. This gave an impetus to cotton cultivation, making it main cash crop of Central Asia by the end of 19th century at the cost of crops needed for food (Kaushik 1970, Pierce 1960). The Russian policy of displacing grain at the expense of cotton was officially expressed by the Tsarist Minister of Agriculture, Krivoschein in 1912:

> "Every additional ton of Turkestan wheat is a competitor with Russian and Siberian wheat, every additional ton of Turkestan cotton is a competitor with American cotton. It is therefore better to supply this region with imported cereals even if they are more expensive and make its irrigated land available for cotton cultivation" (quoted in Wheeler 1964: 157).

An important colonial feature of Russian cotton policy was absence of textile industry in Central Asia while cotton was sent to industries in European Russia. The Tsarist government was influenced by the bourgeoisie interests who favoured Russian metropolitan centres and hindered industrial development in Central Asia. Cotton was sent to industrial centres in European Russia and the cloth made from this cotton was sold to Central Asians at three times the original price (Mehta 1978). Capitalists poured money in industries that yielded maximum profit like cotton while industries which were important for the economy but yielded less profit like manufacturing could not attract investment. Other reason that hindered industry development in Central Asia was that the Tsarist government feared appearance of a proletariat class in outlying areas. That is why; the authorities not only restrained government investment in the region but also did not let the businessmen open industrial units in Central Asia. Hence, the natural resources of Central Asia remained unexplored during the Tsarist regime and capitalists did not invest in areas that were inaccessible (Lavrishchev 1969). Bukhara, due to its feudal nature and mountainous terrain, did not attract any investment from Tsarist Russia. Native manufacturers were prohibited in Central Asia and Russian traders got richer at their cost. The Central Asians, on the contrary, remained 'wretchedly' poor (Hirlekar 1945). The colonial nature of Tsarist regime was not only visible in industrial sector but also in transport sector. Preference was given to construct rail lines that connected the metropolis with the colonies and very few rail lines were constructed to connect the colonies among themselves (Baransky 1956). Lavrishchev has analysed the disparity in distribution of transport between European part of Russia and Asian part of Russia. There was 17.1 km of rail line per 1000 square km of territory in central areas of European Russia while in Central Asia; it was only 1.2 km per 1000 square km (Lavrishchev 1969).

Cotton Cultivation in Bukhara

It is important to mention that before the Tsarist annexation, wheat was the most important crop cultivated in Bukhara, mainly for self-consumption. Agriculture was mainly limited to western parts of the emirate. The eastern part of Bukhara (today's Tajikistan) had mountainous terrain and was neglected for agriculture. The grain production was not enough to support the local population in this part. Hence, western Bukhara was food surplus area while eastern parts were food-deficit (Lata 1989). With construction of Central Asian railway and resultant decrease in freight rates, the cotton import from Central Asia became considerably cheap for Russia than importing it. Central Asian cotton was worth four pence per pound. On the other hand, imported cotton from India, Egypt and America had almost a double cost at seven pence per pound (Curzon 1889, quoted in Lloyd 1998: 104). Cheap freight rates were also applicable on wheat sent to Central Asia from European Russia. This led to fall in prices of grain in Central Asia, compelling natives to cultivate cotton for securing better prices (Pierce 1960). The prices of Central Asian cotton rose by 74 percent in the Moscow market between 1891 and 1914. This was partly responsible for increase in cotton exports from Bukhara to Russia (Luferev 1925, quoted in Becker 2004: 307).

The export of raw cotton from Bukhara to Russia increased more than six times between 1880 and 1915. It was 410,000 poods in 1880 and rose to 2,624,000 poods in 1915 (Holdsworth 1959, quoted in Lloyd 1998: 104). By 1913, land under cotton cultivation in present day Tajikistan had reached 26,700 hectares. It included 13,200 hectares in Khujand, 12,000 hectares in Vakhsh valley and 1,500 hectares in Kulob (Abdullaev and Akbarzadeh 2010). The total land under cotton cultivation in Central Asia between 1886 and 1914 increased 46 times. Central Asia supplied 24 percent of Russian cotton needs in 1900. In 1913, share of Central Asian cotton in Russian industry was 50 percent. Such a tremendous increase in cotton cultivation came at the expense of grain cultivation in Central Asia. The policy to replace grains at the cost of cotton set Central Asia under economic tutelage of Russia in the sense of survival, as it supplied the region with foodstuffs (Caroe 1967). This dependence of Central Asia for food on the Tsarist Russia was not good and it came under strain during testing times of First World War, Russian civil war and the Basmachi movement in Central Asia. The region experienced famine and starvation, killing a sizeable population.

FIRST WORLD WAR, RUSSIAN REVOLUTION AND FOOD SITUATION IN CENTRAL ASIA

The Russian agriculture sector had started underperforming during the First World War. There was a decrease of nearly 10 million dessiatines in the area under crops in Russia. Around 15 million soldiers were mobilised to be inducted as combat soldiers in Tsarist army. This impacted the manpower in agriculture and also shrank crop area. There was reduction in marketable grain while demand kept rising. In 1918, the grain harvest in Russia was just 66 percent of the 1913 level (Mehta 1978). There was also a problem of fertiliser production in Russia during this period which further dealt a blow to agriculture output. Germany was main supplier of mineral fertilisers to Russia but the imports ceased during the war. Russia's domestic production suffered as chemical industry was converted to war industry. Market could satisfy only 8 to 9 percent of the total fertiliser demand in 1916. Meanwhile, food problems were also taking social dimensions and there were food riots in Moscow and Petrograd in April 1915 (Lyashchenko 1970). Urban food shortages continued and food riots again broke out in spring 1917. Crop harvests were short in 1917 and the government's grain collection fell (Davies and Wheatcroft 2004). Such a big reduction in grain production in Russia was bound to create food problems and famines in Central Asia, given its huge dependence on Russia for grain supply. Due to huge fall in production, Russia's ability to supply grain to

Central Asia was severely impacted. The Russian grain supply to Central Asia started to dip from 1914, when priority was given to send food to troops fighting on the Western front (Matley 1994a, Birgerson 2002). The price of grain rose sharply in 1916 in Central Asia, as it went 400 percent above the price in 1913. To further aggravate the situation, war tax of 21 percent was also imposed on the people of Turkestan from January 1, 1915 as the region was not obliged to give military service to Tsarist Russia during the First World War (Pierce 1960). Due to the decreasing food supply, Central Asians had started to grow food crops instead of cotton during the war years (Sharma 1979). However, the Russian army suffered heavy losses on the German-Austrian front. The losses were so heavy that the Tsarist regime had to mobilise the Central Asians for war. The recruitment started in June 1916, a month when Central Asians were preparing for harvest gathering. Peasants were well aware that they would remain hungry if the harvest was not gathered and resisted their induction into the Tsarist army. Hence, rebellions broke out in Samarkand, Tashkent, Andizhan and other places. Russians were able to suppress the rebellions by December 1916 (Peyton and Coates 1951).

Russian Revolution

The food shortages in Russia were politically exploited by the Bolsheviks, as they used food problems to mobilise masses against the Tsarist rule. They were spreading revolutionary ideas among the masses in order to "explain to the masses... that we are in the presence of an historical impellent of the greatest force which generates disaster, famine and countless miseries. This impellent is war" (Leninskii sbornik, quoted in Lyashchenko 1970: 775). Food situation worsened in Russia by the spring of 1918 as the key wheat producing areas like Ukraine, Volga, Urals, Siberia and northern Caucasus were under Whiteguards and the interventionists (Podkolzin 1968). Though food problems started in Central Asia during the First World War, it was mainly during the civil war period that they became serious. The region used to import some 12 to 15 million poods of grains from Russia. However, there was a crop failure in Russia three years prior to the October revolution due to problems in its agriculture explained in last section. A food tax (4 percent of the crop) was collected from peasants and food rationing was introduced. All these issues created a food crisis in Central Asia (Kaushik 1970). There were local voices against displacement of grain cultivation by cotton crops. The issue of grain shortage was discussed at the second Muslim congress held at Tashkent in September 1917. The conference had opposed the intensive cotton cultivation in Central Asia and called for local grain production for self-sufficiency (Roudik 2007).

Policy of war communism was one of the reasons responsible for food problems in Russia and Central Asia. War communism was introduced by the Bolsheviks during civil war in Russia to give the Red Army and Russian cities uninterrupted supply of food and weapons. Private ownership of land was abolished and land was distributed among the peasants. State monopoly of food grains was declared. As the grain production was decreasing in Russia due to drought and effects of First World War, Bolsheviks were requisitioning food and grain by force. Due to this policy, peasants started to decrease sown area to crops, which further created food problems in Russia. The real food crisis began in Central Asia in December 1918, when the region was totally cut-off from Russia due to destruction of bridges and rail lines, especially between Orenburg and Aktyubinsk by the White Armies (Matley 1994a), as shown in map 3.4.

Map 3.4. Orenburg-Tashkent Rail Route.

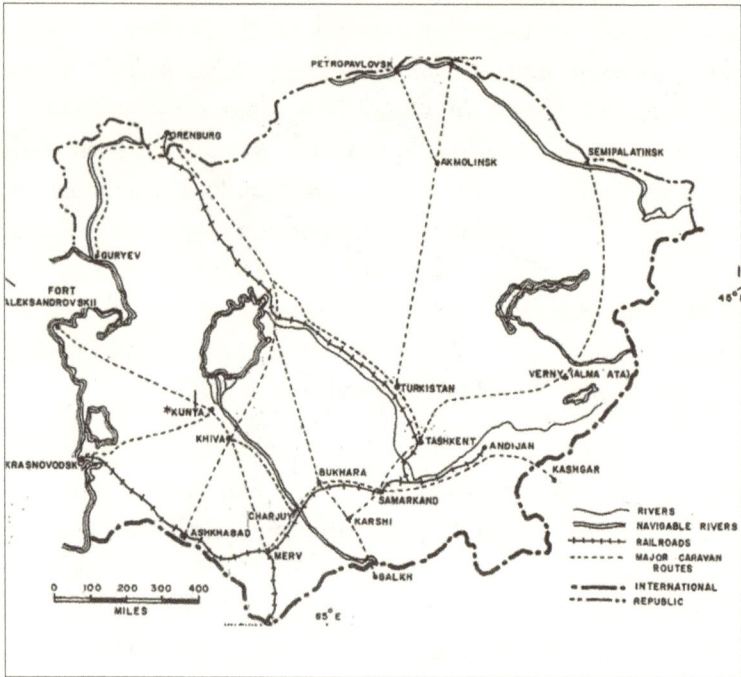

Source: Allworth 1994: 325.

Orenburg-Tashkent rail line was faster, cheaper and a direct link between Central Asia and European Russia compared to the Trans-Caspian line (Taaffe 1962). Destruction of this line was bound to bring famine in Central Asia, as this route was responsible for 76 percent of grain imports to Central Asia in 1914 (N B Arkhipov, quoted in Taaffe 1962: 84). The region was also facing diseases like malaria and typhus (Bergne 2007). As a result of a drought and poor cotton harvest in 1917, Central Asian peasants started growing grains. But, the Bolsheviks started forcible requisitioning (prodraz-verstka) of grains to feed their army. This was a policy they followed in all the areas under their control (Kort 2004). Grain sowings decreased in Russia after the revolution. The grain production in 1920 was 54 percent of the 1909-13 level.

Almost half reduction in grain output led to starvation. Relief measures were not effective due to issues of transportation and disorganisation. Hungry survivors used to roam around in better-off provinces in search of food (Nove 1969). Consequently, the southern Central Asian region faced famines from 1919 to 1923. Over a million lives were lost and the agrarian economy was totally ruined (Matley 1994a). The Tashkent Soviet was reluctant to offer famine relief to Central Asians (Atkin 1997). Russia's indifferent attitude to the dying and starving Central Asians can be explained by the Russian word 'inorodsty' used to describe their official status. It means foreign subjects or alien born (Kort 2004).

Impact on Bukhara

Economic life in Bukhara too had been shaken due to disturbance caused by First World War and the Russian revolution. Import of foodstuffs started decreasing during the war itself. It created conditions of semi-famine in the emirate from the end of 1916. The price of foodstuff increased due to scarcity while that of cotton came down. Decrease in cotton prices also decreased buying power of peasants in Bukhara by 50 to 60 percent. There was a drought in 1916-17 leading to bad harvest. Bukhara was suffering from a severe famine as a result of drop in incomes due to poor cotton harvest (d' Encausse 1966). Nine-tenths of Bukhara's total trade was with Russia. It exported cotton and imported foodstuffs. On the eve of First World War, Bukhara's communication with European Russia was disrupted from summer 1918 to fall 1919. Peasants started to grow grains for self-consumption during this time (Becker 2004). Tajik population living in Samarkand decreased between 1915 and 1920. It was due to a famine in 1917-18 that killed a large number of Tajiks (Rahimov 1989, quoted in Masov 1996).The political turmoil during Russian revolution created famine and food problems in Bukhara. The emir of Bukhara, as usual, ignored public welfare and ruled for his own interests during the times of crisis.

BASMACHI AND JADIDS

Basmachi (Turkic word for robbers or bandits) fighters rose up against the Soviet rule in Central Asia after the Soviet power was established in Ferghana valley in 1918 (Abdullaev and Akbarzadeh 2010). By the spring 1918, Soviet power had conquered main Central Asian regions including the present day northern Tajikistan due to passive attitude of locals (Nourzhanov and Bleuer 2013). Dushanbe and the southern Tajikistan came under the Soviet power in 1921 (Pomfret 1995). The political and social life in Bukhara was witnessing internal churning due to rise of Basmachi and the Jadids. Basmachi fighters emerged in Bukhara and Turkestan due to large scale symptoms of famine, terror, distress and repression in the region during civil war (Marshall 2003). The food requisitioning by the Red Army from the inhabitants of Ferghana valley caused a widespread famine in 1918. A quarter of the population died. Hence, Basmchis comprising of Tajiks, Uzbeks and Kyrgyz became popular and were successful in gaining popular support against the Soviet regime (Bliss 2006).

Another reason for political upheaval in Bukhara was activity of Jadids. Jadidism had taken a political dimension in Bukhara and in March 1917, the Young Bukharan Party had been established. Since the Bolshevik revolution had overthrown Tsar Nicholas II and established provisional government of Duma in Petrograd, the Jadids decided to openly struggle against the emir. Bolsheviks and Jadids pressurised the emir to initiate reforms. Emir Mir Say'id Alim even issued two manifestos of liberal reforms to quell all opposition. However, circumstances did not turn to emir's favour and he decided to repress the opposition of Bolsheviks and Jadids. He even financed the Basmachis and received support from emir Amanullah Khan of Afghanistan. The Young Bukharan Party got support from General Mikhail Frunze, commander of the Red Army on Turkestan front. On September 19, 1920, establishment of Bukhara Khalka Shorlar Jumheriyeti (Bukhara People's

Soviet Republic) was proclaimed, ending the reign of despotic emir (Rahul 2000). The map 3.5 shows political boundaries of Bukhara People's Soviet Republic in 1922. The Basmachi were raising issues of local concern to mobilise public support. They raised concerns against increasing cotton cultivation and resultant fall in grain cultivation. Issues of hunger and starvation were used to drum up support against Soviet authorities. Their slogan was "Hunger is the punishment of God for cooperating with Bolsheviks" (Rakowska-Harmstone 1970). The Basmachi movement received a lot of mass support during its peak days. It stood for definite political goals that sought to preserve old social and economic order (Nourzhanov and Bleuer 2013).

Map 3.5. Political Boundaries of Bukhara People's Soviet Republic in 1922.

Source: Allworth 1994: 240.

That is why, even the emir Mir Say'id Alim tried to take Basmachis help against the Soviets. Famine relief and food were used by both Soviet Authorities and the Basmachis to seek public support against each other. In Eastern Bukhara, people remained loyal to one who was able to satisfy their basic needs. There were many reasons for shortage of food in Eastern Bukhara during this time. Natural phenomena like locusts and drought, disruption of irrigation system and decision of Soviet authorities to collect tax in cash instead of kind were the main reasons. However, Soviet help was seen with suspicion by people and is summed up in the proverb that became popular in those days: 'Soviet power distributes pounds [of wheat], in order to seize poody later' (Penati 2007).

IMPACT OF NEW ECONOMIC POLICY ON BUKHARA

Due to decreased cotton output in Central Asia during this period, purchasing power of the peasants had also fallen and they were not able to buy food. The overall Soviet economy was in a state of ruin due to policy of war communism. To rebuild the economy, Lenin introduced 'New Economic Policy' (NEP) on March 15, 1921. Replacing the strict state control under war communism, NEP allowed foreign investment and some degree of free trade in Russia. Peasants were allowed to sell their remaining produce in market after paying the taxes in order to encourage them to produce more for meeting the demands of the Soviet economy (Peacock 1993). NEP was unable to offer immediate remedy to the economy, as the most fertile areas in Russia were hit by a drought in 1920 and 1921. Volga region was facing a famine. More people died due to famine and starvation than perished in the First World War, Russian revolution and civil war. Many more would have died, had the Americans not offered famine relief to Soviet Union (Kenez 2006).

NEP was instrumental in controlling the Basmachi wave

in Central Asia. The Soviet authorities were aware of the public support for Basmachis and used a carrot and stick policy to turn the tide against them. Conciliatory methods like food grants, promises of land reform and ending agriculture controls led some Basmachis to reconcile with the new government (Atkin 1997). Further, Russian government also lowered taxes, stopped seizing food from farmers and ended anti-Islamic policies. These methods were a part of NEP, aimed to wean away public support from the Basmachi. On the other hand, Bolsheviks skilfully exploited rivalries between different Basmachi commanders (Kort 2004). Bolsheviks were also successful in driving the Basmachi into forcible extortion of corn leading to anti-Basmachi feeling among people. The Bolsheviks gave expensive corn to peasants for eating purpose only and asked them to grow cotton. By doing this, they were able to reduce wheat sowings which forced the Basmachi to extort corn from people, as there was no wheat available in the market. This not only alienated the public from Basmachis but also caused division among themselves (Fraser 1987, quoted in Marshall 2003: 16). Due to decline of Basmachi movement, Eastern Bukhara came under Soviet control in 1926. Basmachis suffered major defeats in 1926 which forced their leader, Ibrahim Beg and his followers to flee to Afghanistan. He was executed in 1931 and by then, the Basmachi movement had subsided and lost popular support due to improving economic conditions in Tajikistan (Abdullaev and Akbarzadeh 2010). Around 200,000 people fled Eastern Bukhara due to the political conflict between Basmachi and Bolsheviks in first half of 1920s (Atkin 1997). During the years between 1920 and 1924, when the Bukharan People's Soviet Republic was in existence, the eastern parts of Bukhara were governed by the 'Extraordinary Dictatorial Commission' which had draconian powers. There was very little time to give attention to socio-economic concerns of the Tajiks residing in the region (Bergne 2007, Rywkin 1982). However, it must be mentioned that Soviet authorities continued their efforts to increase cotton production in Central Asia, despite grain shortages in the region after the end of civil war. It was decided to institute

'Glavkholpkom' or the Principal Cotton Committee on September 22, 1921. Its main task was to increase cotton production to pre-war level, taking all possible measures (Sharma 1979). The efforts to grow more cotton during NEP in Central Asia had an adverse impact on rice cultivation and its cultivation declined considerably (Atkin 1997).

TAJIK AUTONOMOUS SOVIET SOCIALIST REPUBLIC

In 1924, Soviet Union had decided to carve out different republics from Central Asia on the basis of ethnicity. However, Tajikistan was not made a separate republic and it was made an autonomous part of the Uzbek Soviet Socialist Republic on March 15, 1925, called Tajik Autonomous Soviet Socialist Republic (TASSR) (Capisani 2000). With this, first Tajik state came into existence since the fall of Samanids in 999 AD. Tajik ASSR included 12 districts of the Turkistan Soviet Republic, almost whole of the territory of former Bukharan People's Soviet Republic and a part of Uzbek Soviet Socialist Republic. Mountainous Badakhshon Autonomous Veloyat (MBAV) also formed a separate part of the new born republic in 1925. The government of Tajikistan, called revolutionary committee was formed in November 1924. There were six veloyats in TASSR, namely Gharm, Dushanbe, Kulob, Qurghonteppe, Panjakent and Uroteppa (Abdullaev and Akbarzadeh 2010). Although formation of TASSR was important event in Tajik history, the influence of Pan-Turkism halted recognition of Tajiks as a nation in their own right. Tajiks were deprived of their historical cultural centres (Bukhara, Samarkand and Khujand) and not even a single major city or administrative centre was included in the TASSR. Tajikistan without its two cultural centers of Samarkand and Bukhara has been compared toFrance without Paris (Adjari 1994, quoted in Foroughi 2002).A large section of Tajiks continued to reside outside boundaries of Tajikistan. According to Olimov and Olimova, Tajik borders were not carried out on the basis of ethnic lines, but were based on realities of administration, geography, economics and communication (Olimov and Olimova 2002). The newly created republics in Central Asia were called 'backward children of October'. National delimitation was carried out with an aim to establish disputed territories, which was done to ensure permanent role for Russia as an arbiter in the region (Abdullaev and Akbarzadeh 2010).

A small mountain republic with just seven percent of arable area was set up in most backward and sparsely populated mountainous areas of former emirate of Bukhara and the Pamirs. The economy was extremely backward with agriculture suffering from effects of First World War and civil war. Excluding Khujand region, the area under crops in 1924-25 was 46.12 percent of the 1914 level in Tajikistan. The wheat harvest was 51.8 percent and cotton harvest 50.2 percent of the 1914 level reflected agricultural challenges in a republic having limited arable land (Dinorshoev 2005). The most fertile, developed and populated areas of Central Asia were given to Uzbekistan like Samarkand, Ferghana, areas of Syr-Darya oblasts of Turkestan, Tashkent and western Bukhara. Tajiks, on the other hand, received mountainous areas of Eastern Bukhara (Nourzhanov and Bleuer 2013). Neglected and useless areas in mountains were given to them and historical and cultural centres of Tajikistan were handed over to Uzbekistan (Masov 1996). A stark difference between living standard of people living in European Russia and Central Asia had existed during Tsarist period and it continued in initial years of Soviet Union. A Soviet journal, Vestnik Znainy stated before the Russian revolution that Central Asians would need 4,600 years to overcome their backwardness and attain contemporary cultural level of Russians (quoted in Mehta 1978: 449). The decades of Bukharan misrule and civil war had brought economic misery upon the inhabitants of Tajikistan. There was no industry in TASSR while education and health facilities were almost absent (Bergne 2007). Pravda Vostoka highlighted the educational problems faced by Tajiks, as more than five lakh Tajiks had access to just 12 schools (Pravda

Aug 30, 1926, quoted in Masov 1996: 48).

Tajikistan had no modern system of transportation and communication in 1924 and several years after it. There were limited roads through mountains which used to remain closed during winter and cut off the region from rest of the republics. Absence of proper means of transport and communication posed challenge to development of the republic. In 1928, for purpose of transporting 962,095 tons of goods, Tajikistan had only 20 cars, 300 wheeled units, 500 camels and 600 donkeys. Kassymbekova quotes a Soviet worker saying at the Congress of Soviets in 1929 that revolution could not be imported on donkey's back (TsGART 1929, quoted in Kassymbekova 2011: 353). Though Dushanbe was connected to different parts like Khorog and Gharm by air, air transport was very expensive and could not replace cheap transport by road for carrying out economic activities. There was absence of local intelligentsia in Tajikistan and due to poor living standards; it was difficult to attract cadres from outside. Majority of trained technical and political professionals in the republic were Russians (Abdullaev and Akbarzadeh 2010). Soviet Tajikistan had a reputation of hard posting. Even if some cadres came to the republic, they made sure their stay was as short as possible. In 1925-26, short courses were offered by Tajik commissariats of health, education and internal affairs to raise some local cadres. Some Tajiks were sent to schools in Uzbekistan as well (Bergne 2007, Rakowska-Harmstone 1970). Hence, Tajikistan faced uphill task in nation-building. Politically, Tajiks formed a 'disempowered' group in Tajikistan. After the formation of Bukhara People's Soviet Republic, rights of Tajiks who were the largest population group were infringed upon by Uzbeks. By October 1920, only three Tajiks held important administrative positions in Bukhara which shows the level of their marginalisation. Uzbeks kept suppressing rights of the Tajiks living in TASSR under the Uzbek Soviet Socialist Republic. The Turkish tribes used Tajikistan's relative cultural backwardness in comparison to other Central Asian republics to their advantage. They used it as an excuse to scuttle efforts for creating an independent Tajikistan (Masov 1996).

There was also misappropriation of funds meant for TASSR which delayed the socio-economic progress of Tajikistan. Lev Alekseevich Gotfrid, head of Tajik Provincial Committee's Organisation Office in 1928 found that of the 300,000 roubles Moscow allocated for Tajikistan, only 7,500 had arrived by the end of February when he took charge of the post. Due to voices against Uzbek mishandling of funds, a special Commission for the Analysis of Budgetary Disputes between TASSR and Uzbek SSR was instituted. The commission found that funds sent from Moscow were either passed in part or not at all to TASSR. These abuses were happening in all fields – infrastructure, education, poverty alleviation and agriculture (Bergne 2007). The economic fate of the republic, was, however sealed in 1926 when Soviet authorities established the Permanent Expedition for Exploring Productive Forces of Tajikistan. The commission concluded that Tajikistan was an agrarian republic having no industry. It recommended that the republic should focus on mining, hydro-power and cotton growing (Ananiev 1926, quoted in Nourzhanov and Bleuer 2013: 62). This paved the way for massive cotton cultivation to be undertaken in the republic under the Soviet Union.

TAJIKISTAN SOVIET SOCIALIST REPUBLIC

The main reason for Tajikistan's backward nature in 1920s compared to other Central Asian republics was the feudal and despotic rule of emirs of Bukhara till 1920. Under the emirs, there were constant famines in Bukhara and the economy was not in a good shape. Due to Basmachi revolt in Eastern Bukhara, economic development was delayed in Tajikistan and political consolidation too could not take place. In other Soviet republics, these plans began as early as 1921 but in Tajikistan, they started as late as 1927 (Bashiri 1997). On December 5, 1929, Tajikistan was removed from the jurisdiction of Uzbekistan and alleviated to the position of Soviet Socialist Republic, as shown in the map 3.6. It became 17th republic of Soviet Union (Capisani 2000). Areas of Khujand and Tajik lands of Ferghana valley were added to its territory. This increased area of Tajikistan by more than 26,000 square kilometres and population of Tajikistan reached 1.2 million in 1929. TSSR had five provinces – Leninobod, Stalinobod (Dushanbe was renamed Stalinobod in 1929, again renamed Dushanbe in 1961), Kulob, Gharm and Mountainous Badakhshon Autonomous Veloyat (MBAV) (Abdullaev and Akbarzadeh 2010). In terms of area, Tajikistan remained smallest Central Asian republic.

Map 3.6. Political Divisions of Tajikistan Soviet Socialist Republic.

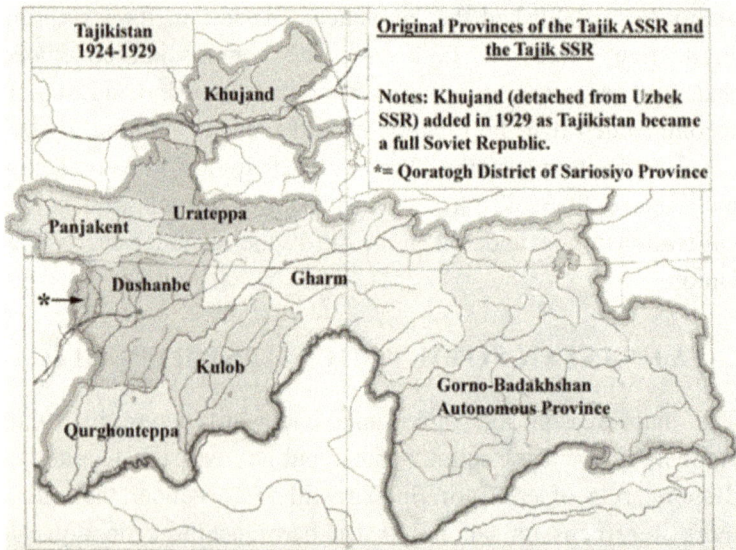

Source: Nourzhanov and Bleuer 2013: 93.

Mountainous Badakhshon Autonomous Veloyat, also called Gorno-Badakhshan Autonomous Oblast (GBAO) was the most backward and isolated area of Tajikistan. It formed majority of the

Eastern Bukhara. The Tajiks of the region belong to Ismaili sect of Shiaism and venerate the Agha Khan while majority of Tajiks are Sunnis. Ismailis form majority of population in Afghan Wakhan, Gilgit (Pakistan Occupied Kashmir) and Chitral in northern Pakistan (Caroe 1967). The languages spoken in the province are eastern Iranian dialects, different from the west-Iranian Tajik-Farsi dialect (Abdullaev and Akbarzadeh 2010). Due to its linguistic and religious differences, GBAO was made an autonomous province within Tajikistan. The province has mainly mountainous terrain and it's inaccessible to the extent that the map of Pamirs was an enigma even for the Russians and it contained mainly blank spaces with the inscription 'unexplored region'.The inhabitants of the region used to struggle for food, often culminating in starvation. They never had access to enough grains. The main food was called 'Attalya', a soup made from peas and grass. Flour was added to it if people got hold of it. People also ate bread made from mulberry. Only the economically well-off (beys and local aristocracy) had access to wheat, tea, coffee and other foodstuffs (Luknitsky 1954). The basic vegetables like cabbage and potato were introduced in the region in 1938 (Monogarova 1949, quoted in Nourzhanovand Bleuer 2013: 102). Market was finally opened in Khorog, capital of GBAO in as late as 1970. Food problems in GBAO were a result of mountainous terrain and lack of arable land.

There are various reasons why Tajikistan was made full republic in Central Asia. Rakowska-Harmstone quotes Stalin from 'Marxism and the National Question'. Stalin felt that Tajikistan fulfilled all the three conditions required for attaining status of a full republic – it was situated on the Soviet border, the leading ethnic group (Tajiks) were in majority and its population had crossed one million after addition of Khujand to its territory (Stalin 1936, quoted in Rakowska-Harmstone 1970: 71). Paul Bergne has drawn attention towards regime changes in Iran and Afghanistan. Nationalist Reza Shah Pahlavi had come to power in Iran in 1925 and Soviet sympathiser Afghan King Amanullah abdicated his throne in 1929. These changes necessitated that Soviet Union recognised Tajik nation and established Soviet model Iranian state in Central Asia (Bergne 2007). The Soviet authorities were also apprehensive about the weak and unstable nature of Tajikistan and the British designs in the region. They thought that Tajikistan could be given up if Soviet grip weakened over it. Hence, keeping that possibility in mind, cities of Samarkand and Bukhara were not included in TSSR and were retained in the republic of Uzbekistan (Ibid).

SOVIET ECONOMIC GEOGRAPHY AND TAJIKISTAN

Soviet economic geography was developed by economic geographers like N N Baransky, N N Kolosovsky, L L Nikitin, A T Khrushchev and well known Soviet economists like N N Nekrasov and M K Bandman. As the name suggests, economic geography determined the type of economy a republic will have based on its geography (climate, terrain, minerals, natural resources etc.). The Marxist-Leninist economic science says that natural conditions form the natural basis of social production (Lavrishchev 1969). The Soviet Union was to be made self-sufficient in all respects but the constituent republics were to carry out economic specialisation based on their geographic attributes that would contribute to the all-Union economy (Cole and German 1961). At the 11th Congress of the Russian Communist Party (Bolsheviks) in Moscow, Vladimir Lenin declared Russia would be divided into regions according to scientific principles and on the basis of climate, economy, fuel availability and local industry (Demko and Fuchs 1974). In terms of area, Soviet Union was largest country in the world. The European part measured 6.5 million square km while the Asiatic part measured 16.8 million square km. The areas of Central Asia, Kazakhstan and Siberia remained industrially backward from the Tsarist times, as almost three-fourths of large-scale industrial output was generated by merely 7 percent of Russian territory. The Soviet territory was divided into 18 major economic areas, depending on regional economic specialisation as shown in the map 3.7.

Map 3.7.Economic Divisions of Soviet Union.

Source: Lavrishchev 1969: 16.

They covered the entire Soviet territory except Moldavian Soviet Socialist Republic (MSSR). MSSR was a separate economic administrative area in the Soviet Union. The economic regions did not have planning bodies of their own; instead they had just constituent units for carrying out regional plans formulated centrally. Though Central Asia had favourable climate for cotton cultivation, still due to uncommonly dry climate and shortage of moisture, cotton was cultivated only on irrigated lands (Lavrishchev 1969). Hence, keeping in view the geographical realities of Central Asia, the region was called upon to free the Soviet Union from dependence on imported cotton (Holdsworth 1952). The Central Asian oasis economies due to their hot climate were seen as having the potential to supply large amounts of cotton to Soviet Union in the context of centre-periphery colonial relations. It meant that the region was to become a part and parcel of Soviet-inter-republican division of labour, focusing on cotton specialisation (Spoor 2000). As a result of its climate, land and water resources, Central Asian economy became the most specialised in the Soviet Union. Subsequently, Soviet Union undertook massive irrigation projects to supply water to cotton fields in Central Asia (Roudik 2007, Mehta 1978). Another factor that could have played a role in development of cotton monoculture in Central Asia was limited availability of arable land in Central Asia, which did not extend beyond 4 to 5 percent of the total land area. This region having mountains, deserts and grasslands was never capable of sustaining a large population (Sharma 1979). Tajikistan too, was a mountainous country having no more than 7 percent of arable land. Soviet planners felt that a region with limited cultivable land should not attempt to grow grains (Deutsch 1986).

Map 3.8. Grain Growing Areas in Soviet Union.

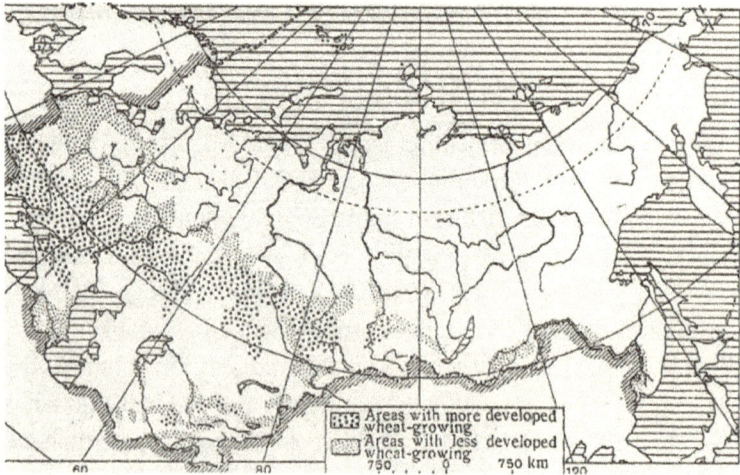

Source: Baransky 1956: 69.

The main grain producing areas in Soviet Union were the Russian Federation, the Ukrainian SSR and the Kazakh SSR, which produced more than 90 percent of the Soviet grains. Central Asia was the region which cultivated less developed grain compared to these regions. This is shown in the map 3.8. Central Asia did not produce enough grains and depended on supplies from Russia. Keeping in view Soviet regional economic planning, Tajikistan was a part of larger economic and political unit (Central Asia) specialised in cotton cultivation to be exported to European Russia, as depicted in map 3.9. In exchange, it received foodstuffs and other necessary agriculture inputs including fertilisers from Moscow. The economic structure of the Central Asian republics was designed to fit the requirements of a larger whole (Soviet Union) and developed differently from that of independent nations (Matley 1981). Hence, Soviet policy of imposing cotton monoculture on Tajikistan was a continuation of the Tsarist economic policy. The government policies limited role of Tajikistan to that of a raw material supplier for the industries located elsewhere in the Soviet Union (Atkin 1997).

Map 3.9. Cotton and Other Industrial Crops Growing Areas in Soviet Union.

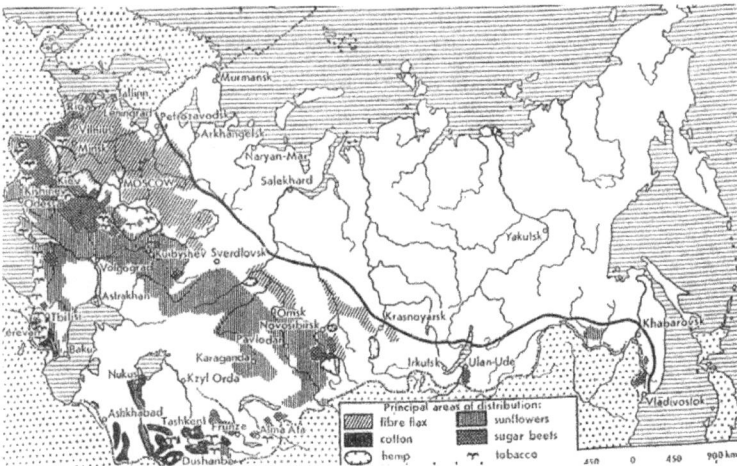

Source: Lavrishchev 1969: 54.

STALIN'S COLLECTIVISATION DRIVE AND ITS IMPACT ON TAJIKISTAN

Joseph Stalin assumed Soviet leadership in April 1922. He was aware of the agriculture crisis in Soviet Union. The agriculture land was divided into thousands of tiny peasant farms in the country. These farms were under performing and there was lack offood to feed the people. Stalin abandoned the New Economic Policy started by Vladimir Lenin and replaced it with his policy of collectivisation. It was forced upon the peasants and their land was taken away to form large state farms. The land, livestock and machinery became state property and Stalin aimed to increase food production by state means (Russiapedia Online Website). Two types of farms were instituted - Sovkhozes were state farms while kolkhozes were collective farms. Government directly managed Sovkhozes while kolkhozes were run by administrative body elected by farm members and duly approved by the regional communist party. Both types of farms were large having more than 1,000 hectares of land, kept under close state supervision. Production plans and targets were set from Moscow and all farms submitted monthly reports on their operations to the state (Porteous 2003).

This social reconstruction of agriculture signified transition in rural areas from private property based on backward farming to large scale socialist farming (Baransky 1956). Large mechanised agriculture production was necessary to meet grain demands of rapidly increasing Soviet Union population. The Soviet planners hoped that collectivisation would lead to large-scale production, reduce labour costs and raise grain yields per hectare due to advanced technology. However, results of collectivisation did not meet these expectations. The total grain output in Soviet Union remained stagnant at 74 million tons from 1930 to 1933 while targets for state grain procurement doubled causing food problems and famines in the country. Around 10 million lives were lost in the 'Great Famine' in Ukraine during 1932-33

(Deutsch 1986). Another devastating famine struck Kazakhstan in 1932 due to Stalin's collectivisation drive. More than a million lives were lost to this famine and the Kazakhs were the largest ethnic group who were victims of the famine (Magauin 2008). Collectivisation in Central Asia started after 1925. Most of the Central Asian republics were in the 'third group' of the Soviet Union areas where collectivisation had to be implemented by 1933-34. In Tajikistan, collectivisation started in 1929 and after a decade, 98 per cent of the land in Tajikistan had been collectivised. There were political, economic and cultural ramifications of collectivisation in Tajikistan. Ideologically, collectivisation aimed to target wealthy farmers (kulaks) to appease the poor peasants, in accordance with the class struggle concept of Marxism. However, there were no class antagonisms in Tajikistan and the idea was doomed. Thousands of people were blamed to be Kulaks and were forced out of Tajikistan to other republics. The Tajiks were frightened by this state led violence and instead of dividing the Tajik society along class lines; it strengthened the tribal, regional and clan loyalties in Tajikistan. People saw these affiliations as a counterbalance to the repressive Soviet regime (Abdullaev and Akbarzadeh 2010).

Economically, collectivisation aimed at increasing cotton cultivation in Tajikistan. However, peasants were not in favour of increasing cotton production in the face of food shortages. The farmers had started growing grain on irrigated land instead of cotton in Central Asia due to grain shortage. According to a report in Pravda, the farmers' slogan in Central Asia during these difficult times was 'the dekkany (farmers) will die of hunger if they sow the irrigated lands with cotton' (Pravda May 15, 1931 quoted in Davies and Wheatcroft 2004: 294). The popular sentiment against cotton cultivation in Tajikistan was evident from re-emergence of Basmachi movement during the collectivisation period in the republic (Birgerson 2002). The Soviet authorities remained unperturbed by these developments and started to explore new ways of expanding cotton cultivation in Tajikistan. The climate and soil were favourable for cotton cultivation in Vakhsh, Gissar and Ferghana valley. However, there were many problems in the republic before aim of increasing cotton cultivation could be achieved. The valleys like Vakhsh where cotton was to be planted were situated on almost unprotected frontier and it was a major security issue. There was lack of soil studies and the soil was known to salify easily. There was also lack of population in the valleys as they had become uninhabitable due to Basmachi raids. Further, the republic did not have enough irrigation channels to support large scale cotton cultivation, as cotton needs large amounts of water not only to feed the crop but also to wash the produce (Luknitsky 1954). Soviet authorities transferred people from mountains to the valleys in order to have sufficient labour employed in the cotton fields.

Before starting big irrigation projects in Tajikistan, the Soviet authorities first suppressed the Basmachi rebellion after executing their leader Ibrahim Beg in 1931. This secured the Afghan border of Soviet Union. The Vakhsh river was diverted into a system of canals which became biggest irrigation system in Tajikistan called Vakhshstroi or Vakhsh valley project (Nourzhanov and Bleuer 2013, Luknitsky1954). All over the Central Asia, canals were made to carry water from Amu and Syr Darya to irrigate cotton fields. This started shrinkage of Aral Sea as it depends on both Amu and Syr Darya for water supply. The Russians did not consider water conservation techniques as it could have led to restriction on cotton production (Roudik 2007). The amount of land under grains which had already decreased under Tsarist Russia further shrank under Soviet Union and was replaced by cotton. Soviet investments also went into production of fertilisers and pesticides to boost cotton yields (Birgerson 2002). Apart from the Vakhsh valley project, the other canals constructed by the Soviet Union included Ferghana canal (90 km), Gissar canal (50 km) and the western terminus of the northern Ferghana canal (45 km) (Lavrishchev 1969). These irrigation projects needed huge amounts of building material which were facilitated by completion of Termez (Uzbekistan)-Dushanbe railway line in 1929 and the needed materials were brought to Tajikistan from other parts of the Soviet Union (Ibbotson and Lovell-Hoare 2013). After one year, it was extended to Yangi-Bazar station (now Vakhdat). The total length of the broad-gauge railway network in Tajikistan was 253 km by 1936. Russians also developed narrow-gauge railways for internal use in Tajikistan. Till 1941, total length of the narrow-gauge railway network was 314 km in the republic (Dinorshoev 2005).

One of the main features of collectivisation in Tajikistan was that the republic was introduced to the Egyptian variety of cotton. Farmers were helped by the agronomists and other specialists to cultivate Egyptian cotton. Though Egyptian cotton was introduced in the republic for the first time after the Russian revolution, the results were not encouraging. In 1939, the area under the crop was 100,000 acres and total yield was 171,000 tons (Peyton and Coates 1951). Egyptian cotton was mainly cultivated in Vakhsh and Panj valleys as they used to receive 180 to 200 bright sunny days in a year and high temperature (Luknitsky 1954). Due to its hot and dry climate, the Vakhsh valley was called as the 'Soviet Egypt' (Baransky 1956). By 1940, the primitive and subsistence agriculture of Tajikistan had undergone massive changes to become specialised agriculture having cotton as a single technical crop. Foodstuffs like grain, fruits and livestock products were subsidiary commodities (Rakowska-Harmstone 1970).

The prices that were being offered to cotton growers were very low and the output was falling. Low prices were a disincentive for the farmers to grow more cotton. The Soviet government tried to compensate by giving the farmers grain, tea, sugar, seeds and fertilisers at fixed prices. When these efforts did not raise cotton production, they were discontinued and the prices of cotton were quadrupled in January 1935 (Khan and Ghai 1979). However, grain prices were not increased. Due to scarcity, the retail price of bread was ten times higher in 1935 than in 1928. The Central Asian peasants were forced to buy more bread than their counterparts in Central Russia as payments in kind were less important in Central Asia (Nove and Newth 1967). Irrespective of frequent food shortages in Central Asia, Stalin was showing dreams of a prosperous life to the Central Asians based on cotton monoculture. Addressing the representatives from Tajikistan and Turkmenistan at a conference in Moscow on December 4, 1935, he said:

> "It looks as if you are going to make good with cotton growing. We shall supply you with machines, you shall receive fertilizers and all the help you need. You are going to make good with cotton growing and a prosperous life is before you" (Stalin quoted in Luknitsky 1954: 99).

Since most of the investments by Soviet Union went in cotton production and induced by high prices, the farmers started growing cotton on irrigated land and cereals were largely cultivated on non-irrigated and marginalised land in Central Asia. Hence, grain yields were lower than they would be if irrigated (Cole and German 1961). The fertile and irrigated areas were under 'white gold' (cotton) cultivation while grain cultivation was carried out on the marginal and rain-fed areas (Spoor 1993).The Tsarist policy of displacement of grains at the cost of cotton thus continued during Soviet Union days in Tajikistan and as a result, it also continued its dependence on Moscow for grain supplies. Huge irrigation and agricultural investments in Central Asia could fructify only if there were constant grain supplies to the region which further depended on transport connectivity between Central Asia and Moscow. Soviet Union planned to supply cheap Siberian wheat to suffice for grains replaced by cotton in Central Asia through Turkestan-Siberia rail line. Construction of this railroad had started from opposite ends in 1912-1913 but was disrupted due to the First World War and Russian revolution. Also called Turk-Sib railway, the construction of the route was resumed during collectivisation drive in Central Asia in 1927 and completed in 1930 (Karl Stahlin, quoted in Pierce 1960: 189). The old Tashkent-Orenburg railway was the main transport artery between European Russia and Central Asia and Turk-Sib rail was constructed to supplement Tashkent-Orenburg route. However, Siberian economy could not meet Central Asian needs for grain and lumber due to low production and this route failed to achieve its motive. The government planned to transport 524,000 tons of grain through the Turk-Sib railway in 1931-32 and 800,000 tons in 1932-33. However, the actual supply was only 64,000 tons in 1931 and 166,000 tons in 1932. Like other regions in the Soviet Union, Central Asia too was receiving less grain than planned and the amount of grain available to the people was relatively less (Davies and Wheatcroft 2004). Eventually, the Turk-Sib line was used as the main evacuation route after Germany invaded the Soviet Union and was later used to ship timber to Central Asia (Roudik 2002) while the grain was brought to Central Asia through the old Tashkent-Orenburg (also called Kazalinsk) line (Taaffe 1962).

The social and economic upheavals caused by collectivisation in Tajikistan soon found a political ramification. Many Tajik communists had been critical of the forcible collectivisation of agriculture. They also advocated interests of their republic including more autonomy. Some also had soft corner for the Basmachis. This did not go down well with Stalin who purged the Communist Party of Tajikistan in 1930s, in his bid to establish national cadres in Tajikistan through his policy of *Korenizatsija* (Capisani 2000). Nearly 70 percent of the party membership in Tajikistan (10,000 people) at all levels of the organisation were expelled between 1933 and 1935. Stalin replaced them with Russians from Moscow. There was another round of purges between 1937 and 1938 after which the Russians or the Slavs dominated all party positions in Tajikistan, including that of first secretary. This continued till 1991 and the Tajik comrades had little influence in the politics of Soviet Union (Atkin 1997). By the end of socialist reconstruction of agriculture in Tajikistan in 1940, it had taken rapid strides in agriculture development. The output of raw cotton increased three fold in the republic from the

1933 level. There were 3,093 collective farms in Tajikistan. The cotton fibre produce rose 97 fold (9,600 per cent) compared to the pre-revolutionary period. There was a ten-fold increase in labour productivity from 1932 to 1940. Some light industries like sewing factories, leather works, knitwear and footwear factory also came up in the republic (Dinorshoev 2005). Tajikistan had become third largest cotton producer in Soviet Union after Uzbekistan and Turkmenistan by 1940 (Abdullaev and Akbarzadeh 2010). The soaring cotton production in the republic was disrupted by the outbreak of Second World War or the Great Patriotic War in 1939. For the Soviet Union, the war began in June 1941 when it was invaded by Germany.

SECOND WORLD WAR AND FOOD CRISIS IN SOVIET UNION

The Soviet agriculture was jolted by the Second World War and the crop pattern was disrupted all over the country. Most of the food-surplus areas of the European Russia were under Germans from 1941 to 1944 (Nove and Newth 1967). Considerable part of western front including Byelorussia, Ukraine and Baltic republics was occupied by Germany. A major part of the harvest in 1941 was lost as about 70 per cent of the arable land was under the Germans. Soviet government was forced to start food rationing all over the country from 1941 (Medvedev 1987). Food supplies to the fighting troops at the front were given priority. The agriculture machinery and livestock were also targeted. The Germans destroyed or shipped home 137,000 tractors, 49,000 combines and 17 million cattle. There was big diversion of manpower from agriculture to war, which decreased agriculture labour force in Soviet Union by 44 percent (Podkolzin 1968). 30 percent grain area was lost due to which food shortages appeared in Soviet Union. Milk, sugar and fats were hard to come while cabbage had disappeared from the market (Briggs and Clavin 2003). Transport and fuel were casualties as well. In 1941-42, over 400,000 tons of bombs were dropped by Germans on key transport hubs in Soviet Union. The total railway length decreased by 40 percent in the country compared to 1941 (Podkolzin 1968). As a consequence, Soviet Union again had a food crisis due to grain shortage. From 1943, the US Lend-Lease Program provided food aid to Soviet Union and high quality products like meat, dried milk and egg powder were supplied (Medvedev 1987). Due to German occupation of Soviet Union's major food-surplus areas, it became impossible to supply grain to cotton growing areas in Central Asia. Subsistence farming rose in Central Asia as a result, especially in grain cultivation. Cotton production fell to 32 percent of the pre-war level in Central Asia in 1943 (Nove and Newth 1967). This downfall in cotton production can be attributed to agrarian disorganisation and reversion of land to much needed food crops. There was an increase of 20 percent in the area under grains from 1940 to 1942 and significant increase was witnessed in winter-sown grain crops (Voznesensky 1948, quoted in Matley 1994a: 291). Soviet authorities had planned to increase winter wheat acreage by 2 million hectares in Central Asia, south Urals and Far East to compensate for grain area lost to Germans on western front. On April 13, 1942, the compulsory minimum of trudodni (number of workday units required to be a member of a kolkhoz) was increased from 80 to 120-150 in main grain producing areas as well as in Central Asia. This was meant to increase production through increasing labour hours in times of crisis (Medvedev 1987).

Impact of Second World War on Tajik Agriculture

In a bid to save Soviet industries from German occupation, many industrial units were shifted to eastern Russia and Central Asia. Tajikistan received light industry and processing plants evacuated from Central Russia between 1941 and 1943 (Abdullaev and Akbarzadeh 2010). The surging cotton monoculture in Tajikistan was halted due to grain crisis in Soviet Union during the war and area under grains was increased in Tajikistan. The total sown area increased by 16,400 hectares in the republic. Cotton was replaced by grain production. 151 rail wagonloads of food and around 2.2

million poods of meat were given to state for helping the Union's food crisis. Some 75 million roubles and 40,750 poods of grain were also collected for the defence fund. The war did not cause any major loss to the republic (Dinorshoev 2005). It is important to mention that cotton cultivation increased in Central Asia due to strong pressure from Moscow. When this pressure was relaxed during the initial years of Soviet regime and Second World War, the native farmers started to grow grains for local consumption at the expense of cotton (Nove and Newth 1967). Unlike during the First World War, Tajikistan's agriculture did not suffer heavily during the Second World War. During the First World War, there were famines and food shortages in Bukhara, whose area later became Tajikistan. Bukhara was undergoing internal political and social instability at that time while Tsarist Russian economy was hit by war damage. However, Tajikistan had achieved internal political, economic and social stability by the time Second World War broke out. There was a proper system in place to manage the economy of the republic while condition of people had improved considerably. Proper planning ensured that Tajikistan did not get affected by the overall food crisis in Soviet Union during the Second World War and agriculture resources were efficiently used. It also ensured that Tajikistan made significant economic contribution to Soviet war effort by donating cash and foodstuffs. Tajiks also contributed to the Soviet Army, as around 260,000 of them joined it during the war (Abdullaev and Akbarzadeh 2010).

POST-WAR AGRICULTURE DEVELOPMENT IN TAJIKISTAN

During the Second World War, regional specialisation in Central Asia was disrupted in Soviet Union due to food crisis in the country. That is why; area under cotton declined while that under grains increased in Tajikistan. The Soviet economy had suffered in the war and there was need to reconstruct it by following the principle of economic specialisation. The time after the Second World War in Tajikistan was officially proclaimed as period of 'struggle for

Communism' and focused on economic development and cultural sovietisation (Rakowska-Harmstone 1970). Economic progress was restarted in Tajikistan under the fourth five-year plan (1945-50). A huge effort was directed into cotton cultivation which was important for the republic. A decree on 'developing cotton production in Tajikistan' was passed in 1945. To ensure better management and efficiency, many smaller collective farms were consolidated into bigger ones. The number fell from 3,093 in 1940 to 453 in 1955 (Encyclopaedia Iranica Online Website). Pesticides and fertilisers were provided by government to increase cotton production. In next five years, the cotton production increased while that of grains decreased (Lata 1989). In 1940, the area under grains in Tajikistan was 567.4 thousand hectares which decreased to 320.5 thousand hectares in 1970 and 195 thousand hectares in 1980. In the same period, the area under cotton in Tajikistan increased. In 1940, 106.1 thousand hectares were under cotton cultivation, which rose to 254 thousand hectares in 1970 and 308.5 thousand hectares in 1980 (Narodnoye Khozyaystvo SSR, quoted in Craumer 1992: 139).

Since there was increase in area under cotton cultivation, this naturally converted to increased cotton production. Raw cotton production increased from 0.17 million tons to 0.4 million tons in 1960. Tajikistan touched 1 million ton mark in cotton production in 1980 (Narodnoye Khozyaystvo SSR 1991, quoted on Encyclopaedia Iranica Online Website). Tajikistan had highest cotton yields per hectare in Central Asia (Khan and Ghai 1979). The population transfers from highlands to valleys were continued to support cotton cultivation in the republic in 1950s and 1960s. Some irrigation projects that were halted due to war were also completed. Qurghonteppe, Kulob, Sughd and Hisor emerged as the leading cotton producing regions in Tajikistan. Since Tajikistan achieved high production of cotton on limited arable land, it showed prevalence of cotton monoculture in the republic having marketing ties with Moscow (Batalden 1997). Pavel Luknitsky has beautifully captured importance of cotton in Tajikistan. He says that not only in valleys but the grain growing collective farms had begun to grow cotton on the unirrigated mountain slopes and this non-irrigated cotton supplements harvest of the region.

> "To grow cotton is regarded as a matter of honour in the republic. Peasants on cotton collective farms try to pick more cotton with every passing day. No task is more honourable than bettering your fellow team, brigade, collective farm, district and region in cotton picking" (Luknitsky 1954: 177).

In Central Asia, cotton procurement prices were kept high compared to grains. In 1952, the procurement price of cotton per ton was nearly 37 times than that of grains in Tajikistan. Hence, the net return on grains was negative and highly positive on cotton. Cotton prices were again increased in 1963 and such increases were at a higher rate than that of grains. Grain procurement price was 99.5 rubles per ton in Tajikistan in 1965, compared to 490.7 rubles per ton for cotton (Khan and Ghai 1979).It was mainly due to such huge price incentives on cotton that grain production remained unimportant to Central Asian republics. The region produced 3,924,000 tons of grain which was a mere 1.8 percent of the total Soviet grain production in 1976 (Matley 1981). Out of this, Tajikistan had a minor contribution of less than 8 percent. Tajikistan also had lower grain yields than the Soviet Union, though other Central Asian republics had yields above Soviet average (Khan and Ghai 1979).

TAJIKISTAN AND ECONOMIC DISPARITY IN SOVIET UNION

Despite having socialism and classless society as its goal, Soviet Union had a hierarchy of classes and income disparity among its population. The economic disparity between Soviet regions and urban-rural areas was aptly summed up by Soviet Premier Nikita Khrushchev, when he once said, "If it's bad in Moscow, its worse in the provinces". However, his successor, Leonid Brezhnev claimed at the 50th celebration of Soviet Union in 1972 that the goal of attaining equal levels of economic development in Soviet Union had been achieved and equity was no longer a priority goal (Fuchs and Demko 1979). That was far from truth and there were regional disparities in per capita income, industrial output and agricultural production. These disparities increased substantially during the 1960s (Whitehouse 1972). Irrespective of all the progress it achieved, the nature of Soviet economic development created fault lines not only between but also within nationalities and between more traditional and radically transformed. The Soviet economic model of social change was uneven and resulted in coexistence of mobile, better educated and urban population with less mobile, less educated and traditional population in rural areas (Sharma 2001). Urbanisation and industrialisation remained unevenly distributed in Soviet Union as large parts of north-eastern and Central Asian regions were far behind the areas west of Urals in terms of development. Living standards of rural and urban areas too exhibited economic disparities (Deutsch 1986). The twin aims of maximum economic growth and regional equality were contradictory goals under Soviet Union. Giving preference to maximum growth strategy would have made Soviet planners to invest in European part of Soviet Union. This would have gone against the principle of regional and socio-economic equality. Conversely, the policies designed for regional and national equality would have favoured non-Slavic southern areas. But, due to their lower levels of capital and labour productivity, it would have worked against goal of maximum economic growth (Liebowitz 1992). In practice, Soviet planners gave preference to maximum growth strategy especially after Second World War due to systemic pressures of Cold War and their efforts to prove Soviet model better than American model. This explains why Central Asian countries like Tajikistan remained less developed in comparison to other republics in European Russia.

Among the Central Asian republics, Tajikistan lacked a rational and unified economy, given its dependence on aluminium and cotton. Tajik economy was dependent on Moscow and received huge subsidy from there which accounted for up to 60 percent of the republic's budget (Cohen and Deng 1998). Tadjbakhsh (1996) argues that the subsidies even went up to 80 percent of the Tajik economy and were instrumental in ensuring food security in Tajikistan. Tajikistan had the highest rate of population growth and lowest employment level in Soviet Union. It explains dependence of its population for their survival on subsidies from Moscow (Rumer 1989). This was a short term measure to raise the consumption level of people in Tajikistan taken by Soviet Union through means of transfers (subsidies) instead of providing them with their own productive means and self-reliant growth (Dellenbrant 1986). Martin Spechler has termed the economic relationship between Soviet Union and Central Asian republics as 'welfare colonialism' due to two factors. First, there were absolute changes in Central Asia that led to long term progress in aspects like social, material and occupational. Second, income transfers from other regions raised standard of living in Central Asian republics ensuring that this region did not become worse off (Spechler 1979, quoted in Sacks 1992). Food supplies were part of the subsidies sent from Moscow to Tajikistan and raised the food consumption level of the masses. Any disruption of these subsidies would have caused food problems in Tajikistan, as happened after 1991.

Though Tajikistan managed to take rapid strides in living standards like education and health under Soviet Union, yet, its economic indicators placed it at the bottom in comparison to other Soviet republics. According to Gertrude Schroeder, the per capita national incomes of Estonia and Latvia were 40 percent above the Soviet average. On the other hand, per capita national income of Tajikistan was less than half the Soviet average in 1970 (Schroeder 1973, quoted in Fuchs and Demko 1979). In 1989, Tajikistan had lowest productive capacity and economic development level in Soviet Union while per capita income was merely 39 percent of the Soviet average (Zokirov and Umarov 2011: 234). Tajikistan was also facing spectre of poverty by 1988, as more than half of its population was living in poverty as defined by Soviet press (Mc Auley 1992, quoted in Stringer 2003: 155). Low performance on economic indicators showed that Tajikistan remained dependent on subsidies from Moscow. Due to poor economic conditions during last years of Soviet Union, people in Tajikistan depended on subsidies from Moscow and lacked proper economic access to food.

FOOD AVAILABILITY AND DEMOGRAPHIC CHANGES IN TAJIKISTAN

Soviet Central Asia underwent big demographic changes contributing to increase in demand of grains under the Soviet Union. The birth rate was slow in Slavonic countries at 15 to 16 per 1,000 but in Central Asia, it stood at 30 to 40 per 1,000. Population grew by 160 percent in Central Asia from 1940 to 1984. At the same time, population growth was merely 29 percent in the Russian Soviet Federative Socialist Republic (RSFSR) during this period. Since Central Asia lacked self-sufficiency in foodstuffs, growing population pressure contributed to food problems. High birth rate over the years added another 20 million people to those who already depended on grain imports and other foodstuffs from Moscow (Medvedev 1987). Population growth had slowed in European Russia to the extent that the Soviet leadership had started to worry about the labour shortage. At the same time, Central Asian population was rapidly growing (Kenez 2006). The population of Qurghonteppe Oblast in Tajikistan grew at more than 200 percent from 1951 to 1987. This rapid population growth was one of the main reasons why Central Asia was not able to produce enough food to feed its people adequately (Craumer 1992). This trend was not limited to Central Asia only and population outpaced growth of grains in Soviet Union as a whole between 1970 and 1986. Soviet Union's population grew at 12 percent during this period while production of food crops (grain, potato, vegetables etc.) rose by 2 to 3 percent only (Medvedev 1987). Susan Senior Nello has quoted Wadekin as he compared growth of population (from end 1983 to end 1987) with agricultural production (the 1986-88 period compared to 1981-85). He found that Tajikistan's production increased by merely 6 percent, lagging behind its population increase which rose at 13.8 percent (Wadekin 1990, quoted in Nello 1992: 861). The increase in Tajikistan's population and main ethnicities living in the republic is given in the table 3.1.

Table 3.1. Total Population of Tajikistan (1926-1989)

Nationality	1926	%	1959	%	1979	%	1989	%
Tajiks	617,125	74.6	1,051,173	53.1	2,237,048	58.8	3,172,420	62.3
Uzbeks	175,627	21.2	455,038	23.0	873,199	22.9	1,197841	23.5
Russians	5,683	0.7	262,611	13.2	395,089	10.4	388,481	7.6
Total	827,083		1,980,547		3,806,220		5,092,603	

Source: Encyclopaedia Iranica Online,http://www.iranicaonline. org/uploads/files/v7f328_t23.jpg.

During the last two decades of the Soviet Union, Tajikistan had the highest birth rate. The 1989 Soviet census put average family size in Tajikistan at 6.1 which was highest in the Soviet Union. Average Tajik women gave birth to seven to nine children. It was because society placed high value on large families and there was absence of birth control measures in Tajikistan, especially in rural areas which accounted for majority of the Tajik population (Atkin 1997). Further, the infant mortality rate had declined in the republic from 80.8 per 1,000 in 1975 to 48.9 in 1988 due to improved health facilities. The Soviet policy of rewarding families having large number of children too proved effective in Tajikistan and the republic's population grew rapidly (Encyclopaedia Iranica Online Website). The increasing population pressure in Soviet

Union had brought the agricultural resources under a strain, inducing agriculture crisis in the country during 1970s and 1980s.

SOVIET AGRARIAN CRISIS

In 1980, US imposed a grain embargo on Soviet Union due to invasion of Afghanistan by Soviet forces in 1979. The US stalled the export of 17 million metric tons of grain to Soviet Union, hoping to create a food crisis in the country. However, this embargo had little impact on Soviet Union food situation, as it was able to buy a record amount of 31 million metric tons of grain from countries like Argentina, European Community, Australia and Canada (Dijk et. al. 2008). Though the Soviet economy had started faltering during 1970s and there were signs of stagnation in 1980s, however, the US embargo could not create food problems in Soviet Union. Apart from internal grain shortages, there were a number of other economic hardships that created and aggravated Soviet agrarian crisis during 1980s. Poland witnessed food shortages while Eastern Europe grappled with foreign debt crisis. The agriculture was increasingly doing worse and food shortages started in Soviet Union. Between 1970 and 1986, the total population growth in Soviet Union rose by 12 percent while production of food crops rose only by 2 to 3 percent which created these food shortages. The grain harvests declined in 1984, 1985 and 1986. Brezhnev tried to address the agrarian crisis and launched 'Food Program' in 1982. However, most of the money was spent on machinery and bureaucratic changes. All the parts of the program were moving except food production (Medvedev 1987). The food crisis deepened in Soviet Union during glasnost and perestroika reforms under Mikhail Gorbachev in late 1980s. The extent of the crisis can be gauged from the fact that before its dissolution, Soviet Union was spending 10 percent of its national income or 20 percent of the government budget on food subsidies (Johnson 1996, quoted in Lerman et. al. 2003).

In the cotton growing republics of Central Asia, the demands of the Soviet state were very harsh. The cotton production increased at the cost of environment. Due to the overall economic decline in Soviet Union, Moscow's ability to provide grants and subsidies to Central Asia decreased (Stringer 2003). At the same time, food problems re-appeared in these republics. The diet mainly remained starch based and Central Asian republics remained at the bottom of Soviet Union in terms of animal products consumption. There was a big gap in per capita consumption between Central Asia and Soviet Union which reflected lower food availability rather than lower demand (Craumer 1992). There were regular complaints in the Central Asian press during the late 1980s that local food prices were higher in the region while availability of foodstuffs were lower than other republics in Soviet Union (Craumer 1995, quoted in Stringer 2003: 156).

GORBACHEV'S REFORMS AND FOOD PROBLEMS IN TAJIKISTAN

Mikhail Gorbachev became General Secretary of Communist Party of Soviet Union in 1985. He initiated political and economic reforms (perestroika and glasnost) across the Soviet Union. Application of these reforms in Tajikistan brought forth the forces that remained hidden during the late Soviet period (Markowitz 2013). These reforms coincided with emergence of religiously charged political movements that started in 1979 due to Islamic revolution in Iran and Soviet invasion of Afghanistan. A sizeable Tajik, Uzbek and Turkmen population lives in Afghanistan and a number of military units from Central Asia refused to fight against their own people in Afghanistan, going against the strict orders from Moscow (Minahan 1998). Encouraged by these developments, the Tajik leadership started asking for greater economic help and political rights from Moscow. Discussion and agitation groups were opened under government control as the government hoped to use them as institutional tools to control opposition. Tajik leadership supported protests against using Tajikistan as a highly chemically treated cotton field (Abdullaev and Akbarzadeh 2010). The different ethnic groups in Tajikistan remained divided and were ruled by officials sent from Moscow under Soviet period. Tajiks were a minority in Tajik Communist Party even in 1990. Gorbachev's reforms started changing this trend. Tajik officials began to recognise the opportunities offered by these reforms and started to implement Tajik solutions to local problems (Shoemaker 2014).

Compared to other Soviet republics, the onset of glasnost and perestroika in Tajikistan was as late as in 1989. Gorbachev's reforms aggravated Tajikistan's economic decline and living standards started falling in the republic during the tenure of K Makhamov as first secretary of the Communist Party of Tajikistan. He tried to initiate marketisation of the Tajik economy which increased poverty and unemployment (Akbarzadeh 1996). The urban intelligentsia quickly organised themselves against corruption by ruling elites, mainly from north and their hold on economic and political power. These groups wanted to reclaim and redefine Tajik identity. Political organisations like Democratic Party of Tajikistan and Rastokhez (rebirth) were established pursuing a democratic, secular and nationalist agenda (Khalid 2007). Tajiks started debating history, culture, language and future of their republic. However, the political and economic divisions also became visible during this time. The main fault line was between industrialised north and unprivileged south (Beshimov et. al. 2011). The policy of *Korenizatsija* pursued by Moscow to establish national cadres in all republics had created political elites among sedentary valley Tajiks in north while highlanders were left out (Gures 2011). This north-south divide had been controlled by Moscow till now, but this divide resurfaced as Moscow's grip loosened over Tajikistan during Gorbachev's reforms. It also became the chief reason for outbreak of civil war in Tajikistan in 1992.

Popular concern was being expressed over perceived injustices like treatment meted out to Tajiks in Uzbekistan and fairness of boundary between Tajikistan and Uzbekistan. Even

Tajik was declared a state language in 1989. The growth of national sentiments in Tajikistan were further fuelled by disputes over water and land rights as well as Tajik claims on the historical and cultural cities of Samarkand and Bukhara in Uzbekistan. Territorial and water disputes with Uzbekistan led to ethnic violence between Tajiks and Uzbeks in 1989-1990 (Minahan 1998). Perestroika started undermining the command system of Soviet Union while it was not replaced with aproper market economy. The trade between the republics was halted and state procurement orders were not being met (Nello 1992). This created chaos in Soviet economy and food situation dwindled all over the country. Along with the overall agrarian crisis in Soviet Union in 1980s, glasnost and perestroika further compounded food problems in Tajikistan. The agriculture output had declined in Soviet Union in 1989 leading to food shortages. Food availability had become an issue among the leaders of different republics who feared consumer backlash and were trying to defend their interests. Tajikistan, along with Turkmenistan and Uzbekistan had the lowest consumption of food per capita in Soviet Union at 2,700 calories, which was 23 percent less than republics like Ukraine and Moldova. International Monetary Fund (IMF) conducted a study in 1991 and found that well over half of the households in Tajikistan had monthly per capita income below 100 roubles in 1988. In Soviet Union, the average of such households was around one-quarter (Severin 1993).

Low purchasing power in times of crisis affects food security of people as the grain prices rise due to scarcity while people lack enough money to buy foodstuffs. Hence, purchasing power of people decreased while prices of food items increased due to scarcity in Tajikistan. Things were even worse in GBAO as there was lack of vitamin-rich food in the province. The children were given vitamin supplements along with their free school dinners. Apart from costly dried fruits, no other vitamin rich food was available on the shops. Milk too was available in short supply as the sovkhozes had to give preference to schools, nurseries and hospitals for milk supply (Bliss 2006). The total area under grain cultivation in 1986 was around 33 percent of what it was before the Russian revolution in 1917. This is depicted in the table 3.2.

Table 3.2. Land Under Grain and Cotton Cultivation in Tajikistan (1913-1986).

AREAS OF CULTIVATED LAND, SELECTED YEARS
(in 1,000s of ha)

Type of Cultivation	1913	1940	1950	1960	1970	1980	1986
Total cultivated land	494	807	837	724	765	764	771
(Irrigated land)	(211)	(n.a.)	(361)	(427)	(518)	(617)	(662)
Cotton cultivation	27	106	126	172	254	308	313
Grain cultivation	438	567	552	361	320	195	151
Fodder crops	13	55	49	131	151	217	258
Oil crops	10	51	96	41	8	4	3
Potatoes, vegetables, and lemons	6	24	13	18	28	34	40

Source: Craumer (1987), Narodnoe khozyaistvo Tadzhikskoi SSR, quoted on Encyclopaedia Iranica Online.

From 1985 to 1992, Tajikistan had an average growth rate of -7.8 percent per annum (Atkin 1997). Its economy was witnessing a bust due to disruption of inter-republican trade. The republic harvested only 5 to 7 percent of its total grain needs which further increased its dependence on Soviet grain supplies. Due to decline in Tajik agriculture and area under grains, Tajikistan had to import more than 80 percent of its grains from 1988 to 1991. The details are given in the table 3.3.

Table 3.3. Grain Availability in Tajikistan (1988-1991)

Year	Cereal Production, thousand tons (without beer)	Cereal Imports, thousand tons	Total Cereal Availability, thousand tons	Imports (% of availability)
1988	303	1320	1623	81
1989	322	1300	1622	80
1990	252	1350	1602	84
1991	286	1250	1536	81

Source: USDA Economic Research, Former Soviet Union Commodity Balances, quoted in Sedik (2012).

Between 1988 and 1991, agricultural output decreased by 17 percent, cereal production by 12 percent, fruits by 15 percent, meat by 19 percent and eggs by 21 percent. The gross domestic product of Tajikistan contracted by 2.2 percent and food scarcity had become a serious problem in Tajik cities (Nourzhanov and Bleuer 2013). Consumer necessities like flour, meat and sugar were in shortage. As a result, per capita consumption decreased in Tajikistan between 1986 and 1989. The government in Dushanbe started food rationing in early 1991 but the consumption of meat and dairy products was at its lowest in last six years. In 1990, per capita meat consumption was 26 kg in the republic, which was around 39 percent of the Soviet average of 67 kg. Per capita milk consumption was 161 kg, which was 45 percent of the Soviet average of 358 kg. At the same time, cotton continued to dominate the Tajik agriculture. 85 percent of the republic's land was under cotton cultivation by 1980s and even the Tajik officials admitted this figure was excessive (Atkin 1997). Riots had broken out in Dushanbe in February 1990 and economic discontent focusing on shortage of housing; food and employment were considered the underlying causes of the riots (Pomfret 1995, Collins 2003). These riots were also called 'Dushanbe Riots' or 'Hot February' which showed that people wanted a change in their economic conditions and state apparatus. Famous poet Iqbal's poem *Az Khobi Garon Khez* (wake up from heavy dream) had become a slogan for the demonstrators (Gures 2011). Table 3.4 shows gross national product (GNP) and per capita food production in Tajikistan in 1990.

Table 3.4. Per Capita Food Production in Central Asia, 1990.

Country	Estimated GNP (US Dollar, 1990	Food Production Par Capita (kg)
Kazakhstan	1,360	1,700
Turkmenistan	1,060	100
Kirghistan	960	400
Uzbekistan	810	45
Tajikistan	750	50

Source: Chen et. al. 1992: 1199.

As the table shows, Tajikistan's GNP was lowest in 1990 and per capita food production was just 50 kg in the republic, very miniscule when compared to 1,700 kg of Kazakhstan and 400 kg in Kirghistan. This further reinforced Tajikistan's dependence on Soviet grain supplies but since Soviet Union too was under an agrarian crisis, Tajikistan faced food shortages. In mid 1980s, an attempt was made to reduce Tajikistan's dependence on cotton, increase employment, food security and self-sufficiency by the idea of 'green bridge' (Capisani 2000). The project aimed to increase production of vegetables, fruits and flowers for exports to Siberian and Ural provinces. In exchange, Tajikistan was to receive mutton, sausage and milk products like cheese and cream (Umarov 2015). However, there was lack of big funds and the economic and political turmoil of 1980s killed the project. Even if realised, it would have faced disastrous communication and supply issues (Ibid). Access to clean drinking water was also a serious problem during this time in Tajikistan, which led to spread of water borne diseases after 1991. During late 1980s in Tajikistan, merely 20 percent of rural population had access to chlorine treated clean water. Rest of the population was forced to use unhygienic water from sources like canals and tube wells which was often contaminated with sewage and pesticides (Sampath 2006).

Detrimental effects of Soviet agricultural policies in Tajikistan also came to fore during the period of glasnost and perestroika. Theharmful impacts of excessive cotton cultivation were exacerbated by the command economy, as it demanded targets based on quantity. Since there were no incentives to improve efficiency in Soviet agriculture, there was excessive use of chemicals and fertilisers to achieve maximum output. The water use was inefficient as well (Rumer 1989). Soviet economic planners did not invest in water saving techniques in Central Asia (Spoor 1993). Water pollution, soil degradation (soil erosion and salinity), deforestation, and biodiversity loss emerged as main environmental challenges in Tajikistan. Per hectare use of pesticides in Tajikistan was higher than the Soviet average. Central Asia used around 20-25 kg of chemicals per hectare compared to 3-4 kg per hectare used in other Soviet republics (Fierman 1991, quoted in Chen et. al. 1992). The humus content of land had reduced massively and was just 30 percent what it was in 1940 (Umarov 1990, quoted in Nourzhanov and Bleuer 2013: 156). Soviet Union had banned use of DDT, a pesticide in 1970. However, 80 percent of the land in Tajikistan was contaminated with its use (Cross and Oborotova 1994). These issues have lowered the productivity of the agricultural land in Tajikistan while soil degradation continues to hamper crop productivity in Tajikistan.

POLITICAL SCENARIO AND INDEPENDENCE FROM SOVIET UNION

In late 1980s, Tajikistan was facing a deep political, economic and social crisis. The authority of communist rule was being challenged by rise of opposition parties due to impact of Gorbachev's reforms. There was absence of a unified political structure to keep them together, as was the case in Soviet Union. There was regional dimension attached to the political opposition in the republic. The Democratic Party of Tajikistan (DPT) had its support base from Qurghonteppe and also had some standing among lower level government officials. Islamic Renaissance Party of Tajikistan (IRPT) represented interests of the deprived people of Gharm and other rural areas (Karim 1993). The core membership of IRPT constituted of people resettled from Gharm in the Vakhsh valley and other Gharmis in their native region. Another party with regional affiliation was La'li Badakhshan Association which was a Pamiri party. Rastokhez, on the other hand was concerned with revival of Tajik culture and language (Abdullaev and Akbarzadeh 2010). These forces stood for secularism and democracy and opposed Communist ideology in essence. The Communist Party continued to receive support from traditional quarters – Gissar valley, Leninabad and Kulob. Gissar valley had accumulated fair amount of resources under Soviet rule, Leninabad was industrial hub while Kulob was an agricultural heartland and supplied personnel for police and army (Olimova 2005). There was an alliance between Leninabadi and Kulobi elite sealed by Khujand-Kulob sister city pact signed in 1990. It was a signal of future competing blocs to be; Khujand-Kulob axis on one hand and Qurghonteppe-Badakhshan on the other (Akbarzadeh 1996). Growing political instability in Tajikistan created fault lines on the basis of religion, region, economic and clan. It was mainly due to this creeping political instability that Tajikistan started experiencing food shortages. The economic and political grip from Moscow that held Tajikistan together started loosening and the economy of the republic started declining. Amid such socio-economic and political chaos, the republican leaders declared Tajikistan a sovereign state within Soviet Union on August 25,

1990. Following the disintegration of Soviet Union, Communist leaders declared Tajikistan as an independent country on September 9, 1991 (Minahan 1998). It must be mentioned that contrary to the Caucasian republics which underwent a wave of nationalist fervour, the Central Asian republics did not want to secede away from Soviet Union. They were not even psychologically, politically and economically prepared to accept independence (Lloyd 1998). Not only the leadership but the people too wanted to stay within the Soviet Union. A referendum held in March 1991 showed that people of Tajikistan overwhelmingly said yes to Soviet Union, as 96.2 percent voted in favour of it (Kommunist Tadzhikistana 1991, quoted in Nourzhanov and Bleuer 2013: 235).

CHAPTER 4

STATE RESPONSE TO FOOD SECURITY PROBLEM IN POST-SOVIET PERIOD

POST-INDEPENDENCE POLITICAL SCENARIO IN TAJIKISTAN

Birth of Tajikistan as an independent nation (Jamuhurii Tojikistan) was one of the bloodiest nation-building exercises among the former Soviet Union republics as it witnessed civil war and redistribution of political power (Abdullaev and Akbarzadeh 2010). Leninobad or Sughd was the region that dominated Tajikistan's political and economic landscape under Soviet Union. Due to modernisation and industrialisation, the people from this region had different value systems than the rest of the country. This led to emergence of regionalism (Mahalgaroi) in Tajikistan. There were many factors behind Soviet support for Leninobad region. Geographically, it was very close to Uzbekistan and did not have a mountainous terrain, unlike other regions in Tajikistan. The province also boasted of large urban, educated cadre that was loyal to Moscow and communist ideology (Tadjbakhsh 1996). The mountainous regions of Kulob, Gharm and Badakhshan were marginalised by Soviet development process in Tajikistan. The initial power struggle was between conservative communists, upcoming democrats and supporters of Islam. However, local, regional and even personal grievances too made their way in the struggle (Akiner 2005). There were four factions that were competing to fill in the power vacuum in Tajikistan created by disintegration of Soviet Union. First was the Leninobad or Khujandi elite from north loyal to the communist ideology. Second was the Kulob clan from central Tajikistan which acted as both, opposition and supporters to communism. While they opposed dominance of Khujandis, Kulobis allied with them to oppose Islamic and democratic opposition. The third faction of Qurghonteppe was associated with the opposition forces. Fourth was made up of Gharm and La'li Badakhshan from Gorno-Badakhshon (US Dept. of Justice 1993). Politically, the opposition forces were represented by Democratic Party of Tajikistan (DPT), Islamic Renaissance Party of Tajikistan (IRPT), Rastokhez and La'li Badakhshan Association.

CIVIL WAR

Tajikistan declared its independence on September 9, 1991. Just two days prior to the announcement, incumbent president, Kakhar Makhamov had to resign from his post on September 7 for his support to the failed coup in Moscow. He was replaced by moderate communist Kadriddin Aslonov, who was soon replaced by hard line communist leader Rakhmon Nabiev in November 1991. Nabiev defeated Davlatnazar Khudonazarov who was opposition candidate and his family belonged to GBAO (Akbarzadeh 1996). The opposition had the backing of democrats in Moscow and they challenged election results. The opposition also brought people from mountains and carried out demonstrations in Dushanbe. Meanwhile, Nabiev started arming his Kulobi supporters and created presidential guard. Civil war started in Tajikistan as armed clashes broke out in May 1992 (Abdullaev and Akbarzadeh 2010). Nabiev had to resign on September 7, 1992 after he was captured and threatened at gun point by opposition forces (Akbarzadeh 1996). Nabiev was replaced by Emomali Rahmon, a former sovkhoz chairman and Kulobi communist elite on November 20, 1992. He chose a Khujandi communist, Abdumalik Abdulljanov as Prime Minister of Tajikistan. Rahmon abolished presidential system and started parliamentary system in the country, apart from announcing ceasefire. The Supreme Court of Tajikistan imposed a ban on the four opposition parties in 1993. The top two positions in Tajikistan were once again occupied by a Kulobi and Khujandi, as was also the case under Soviet days. This further reinforced the opposition unity and they formed United Tajik Opposition (UTO) in 1994 (Gures 2011). UTO may have received support from radical Islamist groups in Pakistan and Saudi Arabia. They also received support from northern Afghanistan leaders and used this area for refuge (Akiner and Barnes 2001). This was akin to the strategy used by Basmachi fighters against Soviet forces during 1920s in Tajikistan. Since Taliban had come to power in Afghanistan in 1996, there were fears that this will further embolden the opposition in Tajikistan.

Analysing the nature of Tajik civil war, Gulash Gures says that there was a famous saying in Tajikistan during the Soviet days as "Leninabad rules, Kuliab guards, Gharm trades and Pamir dances". Tajik civil war was the situation where one of the regional groups tried to alter this division for their betterment (Gures 2011). During the bloody conflict in Tajikistan, different stakeholders were fighting for political ideology which the newly independent state would follow (secular or Islamic, democracy or authoritarian). These stakeholders were as much competing for controlling the state and its resources (Akiner and Barnes 2001). The Tajik economy stopped receiving vital inputs from Moscow after Soviet Union disintegrated. This led to competition over the declining resources culminating in civil war (Tadjbakhsh 1996). Nabiev's election campaign in 1991 demonstrated the political struggle for Tajikistan's resources. He portrayed opposition as 'religious fundamentalists' and 'radical nationalists' and succeeded in securing support of remaining Russian population in Tajikistan. He was also successful in securing support from Uzbek population in southern areas by spreading false rumours that if the opposition won the election, Uzbeks would have to give up their land. Uzbeks living in Vakhsh district were particularly vulnerable to such false rumours, as there was land shortage in the district. There was also a fault line between Uzbeks and resettled Tajiks in the district (Roy 2000, quoted in Hierman and Navruz 2014: 346). The civil war, thus, was also a struggle for wresting control of state resources like cotton and land between the competing forces. There were motivations for controlling the drug traffic too, as Tajikistan is a neighbour to Afghanistan, world's biggest opium producer and remains a transit route for drug supply to other parts of Asia and Europe (Mason 2001). Some analysts agree that Tajik civil war was also fuelled by high fertility rates (population pressure) and prevailing economic problems, besides regional tensions (Olimova 2000, Niyazi 2000 quoted in Roche 2014: 9). The youths in Tajikistan were one of the main groups involved in civil war. The youths did not have a bright future to look up to, as unemployment in Tajikistan just after the independence was estimated at as high as 27 percent and southern regions of Kulob, Qurghonteppe and GBAO were the main affected areas (Narodnaya Gazeta 24 December, 1991 quoted in Akbarzadeh 1996: 1108).

Socio-Economic Impact of Civil War

Tajikistan paid a heavy price for the civil war as the economy started stagnating due to armed conflict and industrial activity was possible only in the northern areas (Capisani 2000). Lives of skilled foreign technicians and specialists working in Tajik industries were threatened due to war and most of them left the country. Consequently, major industries, including aluminium plant at Regar were unable to function at full capacity, since there were less trained specialists who could take over after their departure in Tajikistan. There were problems of fuel shortage which stalled transportation and trade between different regions was hampered. It also created problems in collection of cotton harvests which impacted government earnings (Tadjbakhsh 1996). The economic loss suffered by Tajikistan due to civil war was around USD 10 billion, as per Tajik government (Ministry of Foreign Affairs of Tajikistan Website). The available manpower in Tajikistan was hit by emigration of people to safer places outside Tajikistan and internal displacement. The death toll by the civil war stood at 50,000 while 10 percent of the population (650,000) were internally displaced. The tragedy also struck women and children as the war left 25,000 widows and 55,000 orphans in Tajikistan. Emigration of non-Tajiks like Russians and Ukrainians and refugees from Tajikistan coupled with internal displacement in the country had an adverse impact on services such as health, agriculture and education. This also ensured that Tajikistan began to be more mono-ethnic. In 2000, Tajiks constituted 79.9 percent of the total population compared to 62.3 percent in 1989, witnessing an increase of 17.6 percent in a decade (Abdullaev and Akbarzadeh 2010). The economy started shrinking due to civil war as Tajikistan's gross domestic product was half in 1992 in comparison to 1990 level (Atkin 1997). The worth of real GDP in 1996 was less than 40 percent of its 1989 value. Between 1991 and 1998, government expenditure as share of GDP fell by 66 percent. This reduced government's capacity to shield vulnerable groups and provide them basic facilities of health, food and education during the war (Falkingham 2000). The GDP witnessed a decline by 60 percent between 1991 and 1997 (FAO 2001). So big was the impact of the civil war on Tajikistan that by 2001, the economy was estimated at just half its level in 1990 (Foroughi 2010). The yearly change in Tajikistan's GDP is shown in figure 4.1.

Figure 4.1. State of Tajik GDP Between 1991-2001.

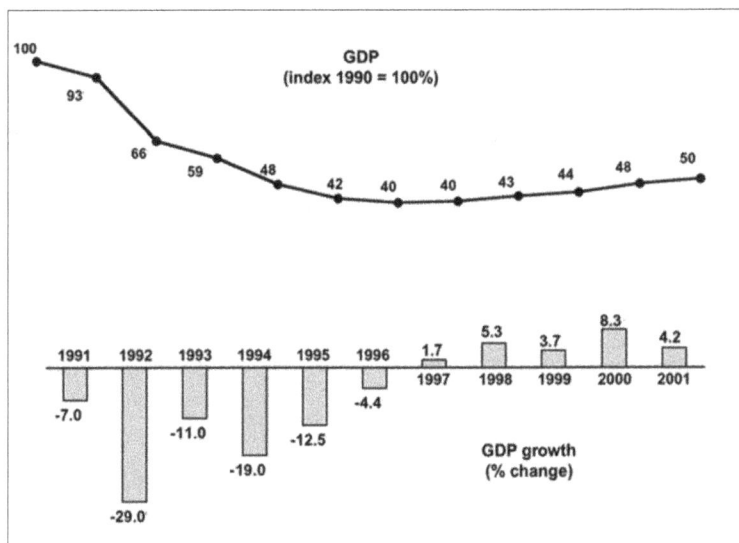

Source: EIU Country Profile: Tajikistan, quoted in Foroughi 2010: 40.

As the figure shows, Tajikistan's GDP witnessed negative growth rate till 1996, the time when the civil war was going on and recovery started in 1997, when the war ended.

Agrarian and Food Situation during Civil War

Civil war in Tajikistan led to political instability which in turn created a food crisis in the newly independent nation. As brought out in the previous chapter, Tajikistan had started witnessing food problems during the last years of Soviet Union. This continued after independence as Tajikistan's economy could not sustain the break-up of Soviet Union. The food supplies from other republics ceased as the inter-republican trade was interrupted. Tajikistan was heavily dependent on other republics, as 80 percent of its trade depended on them (Abdullaev and Akbarzadeh 2010). This situation was similar to what it was in emirate of Bukhara during First World War, when food supplies were cut off from Russia due to transportation issues. Tajikistan lacked enough resources to pay for imported food and hence, a food crisis ensued. As was the case during Soviet days, state continued to dominate the agriculture sector in Tajikistan even after independence as well. State farms and collective farms amounted for 9.6 million hectares of land out of which only 854,000 hectares were arable. This is around 8 percent of the total land. The amount of land under private plots was marginal (75,000 hectares). In 1992, 698,000 hectares of land could be irrigated out of the total cropped area of 812,000 hectares. Grains and food crops continued to be cultivated on non-irrigated land. In the same year, Tajikistan produced 133,000 tons of wheat, which was one-third of the total requirement (Ghasimi 1994). In 1995, the agricultural output had declined by 40 percent of its 1991 level. Since the decline in industry was more than the decline in agriculture, industrial labour moved to agriculture for employment. It is evident from the fact that in 2001, agriculture employed 64 percent (1.2 million people) compared to 45 percent (0.9 million) in 1991 (International Monetary Fund 2003).

Tajik parliament was aware of the unfolding economic and

social situation in the country and had expressed its concerns to Russia just before Tajikistan declared its independence from Soviet Union. In the address, it said, "We face a real threat of food and energy crisis, ecological catastrophe and a new escalation of social and ethnic tensions... We are convinced that alone, deprived of our cooperation of many years, we cannot overcome the present crisis..."(Kommunist Tadzhikistana, 3 Sept, 1991, quoted in quoted in Nourzhanov and Bleuer 2013: 279). Tajikistan was the only country among the Commonwealth of Independent States (CIS) to have a ministry of Grain to regulate bread prices after Soviet disintegration. However, it could not control grain prices due to shortage of foodstuffs, fuel crisis and issues of transportation which increased bread prices. Inflation was soaring in the country, as shown in the table 4.1.

Table 4.1. Inflation Rate in Tajikistan (1991-2000)

Country	1991	1992	1993	1994	1995
Tajikistan	112	1,157	2,195	350	609

	1996	1997	1998	1999	2000
	418	88	28	43	43

Source: EBRD Transition Report, 2004, quoted in Pomfret 2006: 34.

Private businessmen were providing flour bypassing the ministry of Grain. As per the government prices, a sack (50 kg) of flour was to cost 750 rubles when sold by a middleman but it would be sold for more than 5 times at 4,000 rubles. Food prices were lower in the capital than in mountainous areas like Badakhshan, where transportation increased food cost (Tadjbakhsh 1996). The government officials responsible for grain procurement were themselves involved in illegal practices that affected grain supply to the market. Partov Davlatov allegedly directed tons of grain to black market for high profits. Davlatov was appointed as head of cereal procurement authority at Regar by Prime Minister

Abdumalik Abdulljanov. The cities were already witnessing food shortages in Tajikistan. Government resorted to food rationing and limited daily bread usage between 170 and 240 gm per day. The seriousness of the situation could be gauged from the fact that it was just 40 percent of the 600 gm limit fixed during Second World War by the Soviet authorities (Narodnaia Gazeta 1 Nov, 1991, quoted in Nourzhanov and Bleuer 2013: 293).

The Kulob farmers were unable to harvest wheat till September in 1992 due to blockades and fuel shortages during civil war. Some wheat got infected by fungus due to this delay. As many as 24 died due to internal bleeding and liver problems after consuming this wheat. About 1,600 were in hospitals suffering from bloating stomach while another 2,000 victims were in their homes unable to get medical attention (New York Times January 19, 1993). People continued to suffer from food and water borne diseases during the civil war. In 1996, around 100 people lost their lives to Typhoid and another 9,000 were affected by it (Capisani 2000). Bread was the only cheap source of calories and Tajik population started to depend more on it for their needs. Bread is eaten by poor during almost every meal and Central Asia has high consumption of wheat made foods compared to other regions. However, bread prices were soaring due to inflation while people did not have enough purchasing power (World Food Program 2011). State capacity to pay for imported food was further dented as there was poor cotton harvest in 1994 and 1995 which decreased government earnings from cotton exports. That is why; half of the grain imports in 1995 were in form of foreign food aid. Dushanbe and other cities are reported to have experienced social unrest due to shortage of food and flour in 1994 (Clifford 2009). Dushanbe had a single bakery and the queues to buy bread in front of it would start at 5 am since demand was much higher than supply in 1994. Government food stores remained empty due to high prices. In 1995, bread prices rose by 150 percent, as cereal prices rose in international market and Tajikistan's main suppliers of wheat, Russia and Kazakhstan had poor wheat harvests. Food crisis was exacerbating ethnic problems and threatened national reconciliation process aimed to end civil war (FAO 1996).

Amid rising food prices, farmers working on collective farms received low wages compared to other former Soviet republics which limited their access to food. In 1994, they were paid USD 7 per month on an average while payments were delayed for months (Atkin 1997). That is why; poor families struggled to have access to food during Tajik civil war. These families had large number of children who needed food while there were few or no men left to work and earn due to conflict. Food had become a scarce commodity for poor families, especially during springtime when they ran out of their food reserves before the first grain harvest. They resorted to eat small quantities of poor quality food for survival (Gomart 2003). People in rural areas were reportedly eating oil cakes and also bread from corn and bran which was considered inferior. Those in the city were forced to sell their belongings to earn money for buying food. The long lines for food used to start early in morning and would go on till evening. Older people were unable to cope up with this situation and many of them would faint due to exertion. Desperately seeking food, people were looting food supply trucks at traffic lights in Dushanbe (Russian News, May 2, 1995).

However, the government continued to give preference to cotton cultivation on state farms which further limited grain output. Though area under wheat increased but output did not increase much due to inferior quality seed, lack of fuel, spare parts and mechanisation. Cereal import had decreased by 600,000 tons between 1990 and 1995. Government of Tajikistan did not have enough foreign currency reserves and it was forced to use barter system for importing grains. Tajikistan's aluminium and cotton production decreased during this period which limited its ability to barter for grain imports. Between 1991 and 1993, Tajikistan's cotton production fell by 30 percent to 754,000 tons (Atkin 1997). Tajikistan's traditional partners too, wanted delivery of aluminium and cotton before supplying any goods in return.

There was decrease in per capita flour distribution from 120 kg in 1988 to 64 kg in 1994, which shows decline in availability of food and decrease in state capacity to provide food to its citizens (FAO 1996). The food shortages during Tajik civil war should be seen in the context of weak state structure in Tajikistan. Though Tajikistan had a central government in place during the conflict, there was no effective state authority in many parts of the country due to armed opposition. The government lacked economic and political capacity and could not provide basic necessities like food to the citizens. Employees rarely got their salaries and drug trafficking emerged as a main income source in absence of legal employment opportunities (Dadmehr 2003). Kulob faced a blockade from opposition forces during 1992 and the food supplies were cut to the region. In turn, pro-establishment forces imposed a blockade on Qurghonteppe and GBAO. Hence, southern region was cut-off from rest of the country. Blockade of Kulob was a deliberate attempt by the opposition forces to isolate Kulob armed groups from rest of the country. These blockades were mainly aimed at preventing food supplies from reaching these provinces and also deny an exit option to the men who were nearing their fighting age (Kevlihan 2013). There were reports that people died in Kulob due to food blockade and starvation persisted in the region. Hungry people were using tree bark and sorghum for food purposes in the region (Bashiri 1996).

Food situation was worsening in Gorno-Badakhshan as well. A new type of dish had emerged in GBAO as a result of 'post-Soviet hunger' called Samotek. Samotek was prepared by mixing hot water, flour and oil. This dish was eaten in GBAO even after the civil war ended (Niyozov 2004). Situation was so dire that the locals in GBAO were appealing to Dushanbe for help, though they continued to sympathise with opposition forces. Poor economic conditions compelled GBAO local leadership to give up its demand for independence from Tajikistan. Dushanbe-Khorog highway had been blocked due to fighting and by August 1993, there were reports that GBAO population was on verge of starvation (Brown

1998). In 1996, around 620,000 people needed emergency food assistance in Tajikistan, in the provinces of Gharm, Khatlon and GBAO. Some villages had extreme poverty, up to 85 percent of the village population. In some villages, people even contemplated suicide rather than living with hunger and starvation (WFP 1996).GBAO previously depended massively on Soviet Union, as up to 80-85 percent of its food supplies came from Moscow. Food situation was bound to suffer once Soviet Union disintegrated and these food supplies were cut off (Frederik and Haider 2010). This huge dependence on Soviet Union was deliberate, as GBAO was a border area and was scarcely populated. To prevent chances of population migration due to economic hardships, Soviet Union gave huge subsidies and food supplies to the region. A sedentary population in GBAO was a proof of the Soviet sovereignty over the area, necessary to prevent any British misadventure to claim this area during 19th and 20th century 'Great Game' (Middleton 2010). Facing such food shortages, people from different regions came up with their own coping up mechanisms to ensure they received flour and wheat and other eatables. The people living close to Uzbekistan or Kyrgyzstan border would trade their fresh and dried fruits to markets in these countries for flour. Gharm, which was an oppositionist region during the civil war, had large presence of government forces. They created problems for transportations of goods and were hostile to local population. Local Gharm merchants going to Dushanbe often lost their goods at checkpoints. However, some of the personnel in these forces also brought flour with them and exchanged with potatoes from Gharm residents (Tadjbakhsh 1996). Poor households in western Khatlon started to decrease food consumption and ate small amounts of low quality foodstuffs. In war affected and isolated mountainous areas, low quality grain was being used in place of costly wheat. People would gather medicinal plants in highland areas and sell them to ensure food security. In areas of Gharm, Badakhshan, and Khatlon, women would form small groups and beg for food in nearby villages. Stealing was also reported which was triggered by food insecurity during the civil war. It was probably a result of lawlessness during these days. Fruits were being stolen from Gharm orchards while there were incidents of potato being stolen from Vakhsh. To stop thefts, owners of collective farms leased their farms to locals in Gharm so that natives became stakeholders in the farms and stopped stealing (Gomart 2003).

Tajik population would have experienced famine in early 1990s had it not been for the humanitarian assistance given by international community. These organisations tried to fill the food gap in Tajikistan and supplied food aid to vulnerable groups. The details about humanitarian and developmental assistance to Tajikistan from international community are discussed in chapter 5. Amid the political and socio-economic crisis triggered by civil war, the opposing sides started to realise by 1997 that the conflict had gone too far taking their country on the verge of a catastrophe. They also realised that further involvement of external forces like Russia and Uzbekistan in Tajikistan could cost the nascent state its sovereignty (Abdullaev and Akbarzadeh 2010). Consequently, President of Tajikistan, Rahmon and UTO leader Abdullo Nuri signed the 'General Agreement on Establishment of Peace and National Reconciliation in Tajikistan' on June 27, 1997 in Moscow. UTO was given 30 percent representation in the government by the agreement (Gures 2011). The political power sharing agreement was historical one in Central Asia and placed Tajikistan ahead of its neighbours in its efforts to accommodate political opposition. The agreement not only recognised political opposition but also gave it representation in the government (Sharma 2001).However, end of civil war marked a change in the mahalgorai or regionalism system in Tajikistan. The Leninabadi elite, which enjoyed political and economic privileges under Soviet Union, had been marginalised and was replaced by Kulobi elite under president Rahmon (Akiner and Barnes 2001). Exclusion of northern elite from power sharing was successful in ending the civil war but it has not been effective in establishing a better democratic system of governance (Abdullaev and Akbarzadeh 2010).

STATE RESPONSE TO AGRARIAN AND FOOD SECURITY CRISIS

Agriculture in Tajikistan suffered heavily due to the civil war and the government had to take steps to restructure and rebuild the sector. Tajik government responded by initiating land reforms in the country. Land reforms in agriculture are an important means to reduce poverty and increase welfare of farmers and also ensuring their food security. It gives land rights to farmers which incentivises them to produce better as land can be used as private property (Babu and Sengupta 2006). Similar land reform changes were carried out by Tsarist Russia in Central Asia in 1880s allowing existence of private property. It was also similar to New Economic Policy started by Lenin after Russian revolution to improve agriculture productivity in Soviet Union which was hit by First World War and civil war. Lenin allowed certain amount of free trade and private ownership instead of strict state control of agriculture to induce peasants for better production. This was in stark contrast to state owned and supervised agriculture during the Soviet period in Tajikistan. Land reforms were carried out in all the Central Asian republics, as they were dominated by state and collective farms under Soviet Union. State had a heavy interference in agriculture during Soviet days and directed the farmers what to produce, how much to produce apart from providing agricultural inputs and regulating prices (Deshpande 2006). However, newly independent Central Asian states lacked financial capacity to continue state control over agriculture sector and they had to introduce land reforms.

Land reforms were started during the civil war in Tajikistan and have been implemented through a series of laws, official regulations and presidential decrees. Law No 604 was 'Law on Land Reform' passed in March 1992 while another was Law No. 544 'On Dehkan (Peasant) Farm' passed in May 1992. These laws set the stage for division of kolkhoz and sovkhoz farms into dehkan farms. It also gave a property share to all the members of kolkhoz and sovkhoz farms (Mukhamedova and Wegerich 2014). A special land fund was also set up from the excess land that was not being used by sovkhozes/kolkhozes. Individuals were allowed to apply for land from this fund and could start their own dehkan farm (Porteous 2003). Presidential Decree No. 699 'On Organisation of Dehkan Farms' was issued in 1993. It related to the process required to be followed for getting a dehkan farm. It requires a long list of approvals before one can get a dehkan farm. In 1995, two more presidential decrees were passed. Through the decree No. 342, household plots received 50,000 hectares of land from sovkhozes and kolkhozes. Decree No. 621 on 'Restructuring of sovkhozes, kolkhozes and other Agricultural Enterprises' was issued in October 1995. It reiterated the 1992 'Law on Land Reform' and called for restructuring of unprofitable kolkhozes and sovkhozes into dehkan and cooperative farms. Decree No. 522 passed in 1996 further lessened state control over farm land and stated that a farmer did not need permission from the farm management if he/she wanted to withdrawhis/her land share from a kolkhoz. Decree No. 1021 was passed in 1998 which made it mandatory for farmers to have land passports and land use certificates in order to be conferred with right to use land(Duncan 2000). In 1997, another 25,000 hectares of land were allotted to household farms through presidential Decree No. 874. The government revised the 1992 law on dehkan farms in 2003 and replaced it with new law 'On Dehkan Farms'. This law introduced three types of different farms – collective dehkan, family and individual farms (Lerman and Sedik 2008). The land reform remains unfinished and is an ongoing process in Tajikistan. The government has also passed a number of decrees after 2003 to resolve cotton debt of farmers. In 2009, a presidential decree was passed which wrote off USD 550 million worth of cotton debt of farmers. This freed the farmers from debt and allowed them freedom farming, thereby meaning that they were free to decide which crop to cultivate (Asian Development Bank 2013).

Impact of Land Reform on Food Security in Tajikistan

End of civil war and implementation of land reforms arrested the decline in Tajik agriculture and the food production picked up from 1996, as shown in figure 4.2.

Figure 4.2. Cereal Production in Tajikistan (1991-2002).

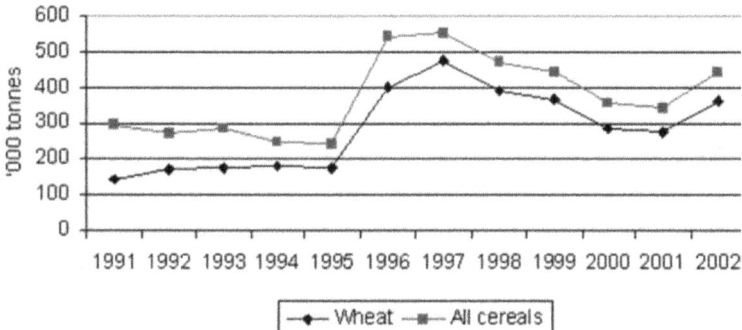

Source: FAO/WFP 2002

Cereal production rose from average 270,000 tons in 1991-96 to more than 500,000 tons in 1996 and peaked at 545,000 tons in 1997. It was around 480,000 tons in 1998 and 450,000 in 1999. However, Tajikistan was hit by a drought in 2000-2001 which brought the production below 400,000 tons in this period. The share of household plots and dehkan farms in Tajikistan's agriculture had gone up and they both accounted for nearly 50 percent of the country's agricultural land. Khatlon produces largest amount of wheat followed by Region of Republican Subordination (RRS), Sughd and GBAO in Tajikistan (FAO 2002). The land reform in Tajikistan has established five types of farms – household plots, private dehkan farms, collective dehkan farms, state farms and presidential plots. From the perspective of an individual and his family's food security, only first two types of farms have been beneficial for them. The land under different types of farms is given in the table 4.2.

Table 4.2. Land Under Different Types of Farms in Tajikistan in 2009.

Farm type	Number	Average size (ha/farm)	% Arable area
State farms	193	322	7.5
Collective dekhan farms	9,000	18	20
Private dekhan farms	18,040	18	39.2
Household plots	740,400	0.3	24.2
Presidential plots	375,000	0.2	9.1

Source: FAO 2009, quoted in Akramov and Shreedhar 2012: 12.

The land under state and collective farms has dropped from 95 percent in the pre-reform period to 27.5 percent in 2009. Around 40 percent of the land is under private dehqan farms while household plots have around 25 percent of the land. Presidential plots account for 9 percent of the total arable land in Tajikistan (Akramov and Shreedhar 2012). Consequently, the share of these farms to gross agricultural output (GAO) also changed. Dehkan farms accounted for nearly 30 percent of Tajikistan's GAO in 2010 while household plots accounted for a record 62 percent. Rest 8 percent was produced by state owned farms (Lerman 2012). Household plots have been instrumental in ensuring food security of the population in Tajikistan. People in Tajikistan were allowed to have 'kitchen gardens or Zamini Bogh' attached to their houses or nearby from Soviet days so that they could grow for their family food needs. The families started growing more than their needs in due time and they started selling it in the market which established first private market system in Tajikistan under Soviet Union. More output meant more profit unlike state farms where salaries were fixed. At the end of Soviet era, around 33 percent of food sold in the market in Tajikistan was grown on household plots. In the times of crisis, these plots become the lifeline of families that own them (Rowe 2009, Amir and Berry 2013). The recovery that began in 1996 with implementation of land reforms brought Tajikistan's agriculture back to pre-transition level by 2007. Due to increase in productivity of household plots, the household income also increased ensuring their food security.

The government has lost its monopoly over choice of crops that farmers will grow over their farms. As a result, the area under grains and horticulture crops has increased while area under cotton cultivation has decreased. Their production too has seen similar change (Lerman and Sedik 2008).

Figure 4.3. Crop Production in Tajikistan, 1985–2011

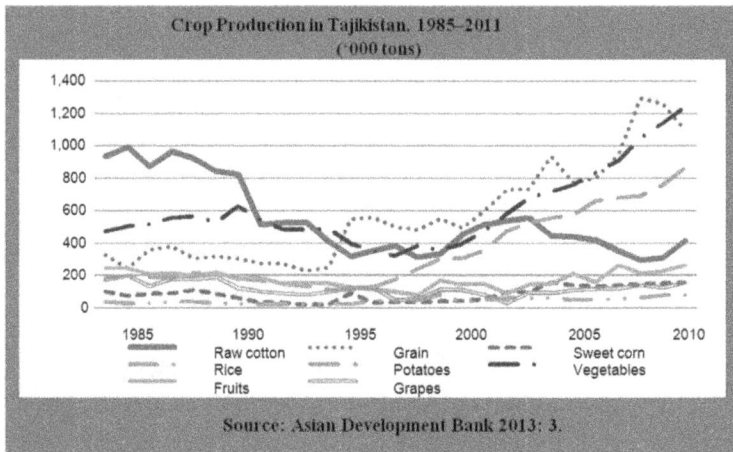

Source: Asian Development Bank 2013: 3.

Figure 4.3 shows that cotton production in Tajikistan was around 1 lakh tons in 1985 but it started to decline from this period and never really recovered after that. Cotton production hit its lowest point in Tajikistan during the civil war in 1996. In 2010, Tajikistan produced around 400,000 tons of cotton. The decline in cotton production has been beneficial for grain production in Tajikistan. In 1985, Tajikistan was producing just less than 400,000 tons of grains which started to rise after the civil war and have been rising since then. In 2010, Tajikistan produced more than 1,100,000 tons of grains. There has been increase in production of potatoes and vegetables as well in the country. However, production of fruits, rice, grapes and sweet corn has stagnated during 1985-2010 period.

Problems in Land Reform and Agriculture Sector in Tajikistan

Tajikistan and Central Asia had a history of communal agricultural, even before the Soviet era. During the Soviet years, agriculture was controlled by state and there was no provision of private farming. The decision making was in the hands of state and farmers were denied this privilege. Hence, it was very difficult to build a case for neo-liberal agrarian reforms in Tajikistan when it gained independence in 1991 (Rowe 2010). However, keeping in view the condition of state controlled agriculture at the end of Soviet Union, there was little choice for the government but to initiate land reforms to reconstruct the agriculture sector. The land reform increased access to land for the farmers and has also increased food productivity in the country. However, the pace of the reforms has been slow, marred by number of problems. Tajik land reforms have been conducted in two phases. First phase kicked off during the civil war in 1992 and finished in 2005. However, the reforms were too slow and did not achieve the desired results, prompting the international lending institutions to recommend another set of reforms. Consequently, the Tajik government had to start second phase of land reforms from 2006. This phase aims to break rest of the state farms and reform corporate enterprises (Hierman and Navruz 2014). Government of Tajikistan has initiated 22-point agrarian reform agenda for the period 2012-20. This aims to facilitate and increase access to agricultural inputs for farmers as well as to teach them better management of resources like water (World Bank CPS 2015-18). The reform process was resisted by elites as they did not want to lose control over economic and agricultural power. The efforts of land reform were contradicted by price increase as price of agriculture inputs increased and subsidies were withdrawn from Moscow (Bautista 2006). The regional divides have resurfaced while implementation of land reform. Original residents of plains resisted land ownership being given to highlanders resettled in plains during Soviet population transfers. Original residents see themselves as custodians of agricultural land and had become local elite during Soviet collectivisation process (Sampath 2006b).

Despite reforms, land continues to remain state property in Tajikistan, as per Article 13 of the constitution. Farmers have hereditary land use rights but the land belongs to the state. In neighbouring countries like Kazakhstan and Kyrgyzstan, land does not belong to the state (Peyrouse 2009, Hierman and Navruz 2014). The land reform remains an ad-hoc process adopted without transparency (Sampath 2006). National targets for cotton production are still followed in Tajikistan implemented by regional officers. That is why; farmers do not have much of a choice in selecting which crop to cultivate and have to grow cotton on their farms. Local officials take away land and revoke land use rights of farmers if land is not used according to their wishes, though legally they do not have this power (Pomfret 2008). The 2003 Law on Dehqan Farms makes it clear that government should not prescribe to farmers what to grow. However, farmers in cotton growing areas are given quotas to be completed according to an unofficial central plan about when to start sowing cotton, when to irrigate and when to harvest the crop (World Bank 2008). The hukumat or the local administration in the Sarband area of Khatlon province asked the dehqan lands to grow cotton on 80 percent of the area. A farmer did not toe the line and grew wheat instead of cotton. The enraged hukumat destroyed his wheat crop with bulldozers. In an another case of official harassment, an independent farm was subjected to as many as 28 tax audits in a single financial year (International Crisis Group 2005). Such official interference is made possible by the fact that land is a state property in Tajikistan.

The land reforms remain incomplete and unreformed farms form a big chunk of the agriculture land. Around 40 percent of the land is under state and collective dehqan farms. These farms have far lower productivity than the household plots. These farms also face debt crisis due to unprofitability. The government intervention in these farms lowers incentive for better production for farmers. The farms makeless profit; generate low incomes for the farmers working on them which have a negative impact on their food security. The agriculture recovery that Tajikistan has witnessed after the civil war is based on narrow base of land resources. Unreformed farms still have around 40 percent of the agricultural land under them. If the state and collective dehqan farms had achieved same productivity level as that of household plots in 2006, agriculture production in Tajikistan would have been more than doubled and seen an increase of 114 percent. Agriculture production would have been 37 percent higher even if these farms had achieved 50 percent productivity of household plots. In this regard, Tajikistan land reform has achieved lower than the other Commonwealth of Independent States (CIS) (Lerman and Sedik 2008). As is the case in other most low-income and food-deficit countries, the problem of food insecurity in Tajikistan can be solved by providing people access to small family farms and increasing productivity of these farms (Amir and Berry 2013). Farmers do not have awareness about the land reform and their land use rights (Sampath 2006). Action Against Hunger conducted a survey in 2003 to assess the impact of land reforms in Tajikistan. 965 houses that did not have a dehqan farm were interviewed in order to analyse their knowledge about land reforms. A staggering 85.1 percent of them expressed their ignorance about land reforms in the country. If people do not know about their land rights, they will not apply and cannot use land for their benefits, mainly food production (Porteous 2003). Process for registration of a dehqan farm is costly and complex, not clearly defined in the laws. Contradictory and overlapping land reform laws differ from district to district and nature of their implementation depends on whims and fancies of local officials (Duncan 2000).

Hidden costs exist in the process of attaining a land certificate. Officially, a farmer needed USD 6 to withdraw his/her shares from a large state farm and start a dehqan farm. However, farmers reported that they were paying around USD 50 for the process. This amount was more than five times the average annual salary of a farmer, which shows amount of corruption involved in the process. Farmers have been paying 17 types of taxes that take away a big chunk of their income (Porteous 2003). Role of hukumats can be checked only when there is accountability fixed for the government which can further be ensured by bringing local democracy but this cannot be done under present political dispensation in Tajikistan (ICG 2005). The cotton sector in Tajikistan is also affected by 'future companies'. During the civil war, when the government did not have financial capacity to support cotton sector, it asked the private companies to provide loans to farmers for agricultural inputs. These companies were backed by foreign lenders and asked for certain amount of cotton harvest at the end of the season from farmers. However, the interest rates of the loans have been as high as 10-20 percent. Many farmers are unable to repay the debt and are forced to grow cotton (Peyrouse 2009). A survey by Food and Agriculture Organisation (FAO) in 2007-08 revealed that almost all the cotton growers (90 percent) in Tajikistan had signed forward contracts for cotton with non-bank financial agents (Lerman and Sedik 2008). There is burden of debt on cotton farms which ultimately is passed on to individual and family farms making the farmers dependent on future companies. In 2001, almost half of the revenues of cotton sector were taken away by the creditors. Khatlon produces 60 percent of Tajikistan's cotton followed by Sughd at 30 percent and rest 10 percent comes from Region of Republican Subordination. The relationship between cotton and food insecurity became clear in 2003 when a Mercy Corps survey revealed malnutrition was mainly found in cotton growing areas of Tajikistan (ICG 2005).Sattar and Mohib have analysed that losses incurred by cotton farms are between USD 163 million to USD 205 million per year. These translate to 10-13 percent of total GDP of Tajikistan. Such huge losses could serve as income for farmers and have negative repercussions for their welfare. These losses create poverty and deprivation among cotton farmers (Sattar and Mohib 2007). The existence of the future companies in Tajikistan to finance cotton cultivation is a throwback to the times when emirate of Bukhara had become a Russian protectorate. The Russian companies, banks and firms used to give credit to peasants in Bukhara at high interest rates to grow cotton. These peasants were not able to repay the debt and were forced to grow cotton which impacted their food security as well. According to World Bank estimates, those who cultivated cotton were worse off than others who did not grow cotton. The average monthly salary of a cotton farmer in 2004 was USD 7 while others who produced anything other than cotton earned 8-13 times more (World Bank 2004, quoted in ICG 2005). Hence, this poverty cycle that cotton cultivators face also impacts their food security as they are unable to buy food especially in times of rising food prices, as happened in 2008 crisis in Tajikistan.

The land reforms in Tajikistan have taken place amid an overall agricultural crisis in the country. The problems in the agricultural sector have further hampered the prospects of land reforms which in turn has a bearing on food security situation in Tajikistan. The prices of agricultural inputs like seeds, machinery and fertilisers remain high and the poor farmers find it difficult to procure them (Babu and Rhoe 2006). The large kolkhozes and sovkhozes had their own tractors and other agriculture machinery for cultivation in Tajikistan during Soviet period. The small dehkan farms lack enough resources to maintain these services while use of machinery on household plots is difficult (Porteous 2003). Though Tajikistan has abundant water resources, these resources cannot be fully utilised as the irrigation system has decayed leaving some of the arable land with almost no water. Irrigation canals and aqueducts require repair but there is scarcity of funds. The condition of pumping stations covering 300,000 hectares of land or 40 percent of irrigated land in 2001 was not good and needed urgent repair. Around 2 million rural residents earned a living from this area (Government of Tajikistan 2002). Well managed drainage can prevent salinisation in arid areas but drainage does not get required attention in Tajikistan (Sharma 2001, Rowe 2010). There are different factors that contribute to poor irrigation system in Tajikistan. Due to low electricity availability in winter, often there are delays in irrigating the crops which impacts their quality and yield. Bad condition of pumps and their frequent breakdowns also contributes to poor irrigation. Damaged channels lead to water wastage and low irrigation efficiency. Almost 70 percent of the water meant for irrigation in Central Asia is wasted which shows severity of the problem (Bliss 2012).

Further, agricultural research and knowledge creation has been neglected in Tajikistan which was not the case under Soviet Union. Tajikistan lacks enough funds to support agricultural research in the country. Due to poor incentives and salary structure given to researchers, the quality of research in agriculture has suffered (Babu and Sengupta 2006). The conditions to exchange agriculture knowledge in Tajikistan are low. There is also lack of effective information sharing with the farmers (Mandler 2011). Tajikistan needs to make maximum use of its agricultural lands to increase food production as it has about 960,000 hectares of arable land which makes up 7-8 percent of its total area. It has only 0.12 to 0.15 hectares of irrigable land per person (Olcott 2014). Almost three quarters of the arable land (720,000 hectares) is irrigated in Tajikistan (Lerman and Sedik 2008). Most of this irrigated land is in the two provinces of Khatlon and Sughd (almost 80 percent) (Akramov and Shreedhar 2012). 16 percent of the total irrigated land suffers from salinity and water logging. This is one of the main factors responsible for low yields of both cotton and food crop, as salinity hampers plant's ability to extract water from the soil. Low yields squeeze the income of the farmer which has a bearing on his ability to spend for his and his family's food needs. Contrary to government's self-sufficiency approach in food grains, Prof K Umarov, Head of Agro-industrial Economy Department, Institute of Economy and Demography, Academy of Sciences, Tajikistan calls for a change in orientation and approach to food security. There should be right combination between what to produce domestically and what to import for food consumption. On the foothills of rain-fed land where wheat is grown, it is possible to grow grapes to create a modern export-oriented industrial orchards and vineyards. The average yield of wheat in these lands is around 7 quintals per hectare which can fetch USD 271.8 in the market. If grapes of different varieties are grown on this land, the average yield would be around 150 quintals per hectare fetching USD 11,650. Hence, viticulture can bring in revenues which are 42.8 times more than the production of wheat. On income derived from each hectare of vineyard, 466 quintals of wheat could be bought (Umarov 2015).

Institutional Framework for Food Security in Tajikistan

Food security, achieving energy independence and finding way out of the communication deadlock are three main strategic goals of Tajikistan, according to President Rahmon (Rahmon's Speech at WTO, Switzerland 2012). Food security also depends on energy availability, communication infrastructure, gender issues, social and environmental issues and the details are discussed in later sections. Tajikistan does not have an exclusive legislative act to guarantee right to food in order to ensure food security. However, food security is ensured in a number of laws and development strategies adopted by Tajikistan. Concept of food security is an integral part of 'National Development Strategy 2015' introduced in 2006, 'National Development Strategy 2015-2030', 'Poverty Reduction Strategy 2010-2012', 'Law on Food Security 2010',

'Food Security Program of Republic of Tajikistan up to 2015' and 'Living Standards Improvement Strategy of Tajikistan for 2013-2015'. Apart from these strategies, Tajikistan has set up a Food Security Working Group in 2006 and a Food Security Council in 2011 to co-ordinate better implementation of policies related to food security in the country. The Article 16 of the 2010 law on food security defines food security as a situation when 80 percent of the main staple food consumed in the country is produced domestically. State is responsible for ensuring physical access to sufficient food through domestic production in order to 'ensure active and healthy life and demographic growth' (Asadov 2013). Food security is also an important part of the National Development Strategy 2015. It calls for ensuring greater purchasing power in hands of public and increasing production and consumption of food products. The strategy aims to decrease food imports as food production is to be increased. It also seeks to establish food reserves for emergency provisions (National Development Strategy 2015). The Poverty Reduction Strategy 2010-2012 seeks to ensure food security and agricultural promotion. Agriculture remains most important sector for the national economy and its promotion is equal to promoting food security, as per this strategy. It also includes livestock, water and land resources in the framework of food security and seeks their sustainable development. The strategy sets its sights on rehabilitation of irrigation services, use of new lands and improving transport infrastructure. It also recommends simplifying the land registration system and strengthening land use rights (Poverty Reduction Strategy 2010-2012).

Food Security Program of Republic of Tajikistan up to 2015 is an exclusive document on food security in Tajikistan. Its main objective is to identify socially, financially and technically feasible measures for attaining food security. It seeks to reinforce state support in areas of food security and safety. The aim of state support is to increase food production to fulfil basic needs of the population. Another important aim is to promote efficient use of water and land use rights for ensuring food safety. It argues that sustainable use of natural resources should be encouraged for achieving food security in Tajikistan (Bliss 2012, Bobodzhanova 2012). Living Standards Improvement Strategy of Tajikistan for 2013-2015 is yet another development strategy adopted by Tajikistan and one of its focus areas is food security. It advocates adopting agrarian protectionism strategy for attaining food security in Tajikistan. This is one of the very few strategies that connect food security and demographic issue. It stresses a need for proper planning to have a demographic policy for sustainable development in the country. Reduction in poverty levels remains a focus point for achieving food security by improving living standards of population and by achieving energy dependence at national level (Living Standards Improvement Strategy of Tajikistan for 2013-2015). President Rahmon had issued a presidential decree and established a food security working group (FSWG) in 2006. It is headed by Minister of Economy and Trade. FSWG has to coordinate and monitor the food security policies and programs in Tajikistan. Different ministries like Ministry of Economy and Trade, Ministry of Finance, Ministry of Health, Ministry of Water, Ministry of Labour and Social Protection and agencies like State Nutrition Centre, National Economic and Agricultural Centre are members of FSWG. It is authorised to use the resources at the disposal of these ministries and agencies. However, in practice, there are differences in priorities and preferences of the FSWG members, lack of communication among involved ministries and departments while there is also lack of manpower and financial resources to devise and implement policies related to food security (Knuth 2008).In 2011, a Food Security Council (FSC) was established with passage of Government Regulation No 359. Its organisational structure is depicted in figure 4.4.

Figure 4.4. Organisational Structure of Food Security Council.

Source: Boymatova 2011: 10.

It is chaired by the Prime Minister of Tajikistan while deputy chair is deputy Prime Minister. Different ministers, chairman of some state committees and heads of some agencies are members of the council. The council has been established according to the Article 15 of 'Law on Food Security'. It is a consultative-advisory body for coordinating activities and adopting strategies regarding continuous supply of food in Tajikistan. It also has to prepare swift plans to deal with food crises and emergency food situations. The council meets once in a month and representatives from international donor organisations and countries can also be invited as observers (FAO 2014a). Food security in Tajikistan is a wide and scattered concept which is an inherent theme in laws on land reforms, food safety, social security and water code of the country. Access to clean drinking water is very important for ensuring food security. Populations which have better access to water suffer less levels of malnutrition as a rule (Bobodzhanova 2012). In Tajikistan, only 33 percent of the total population has access to chlorinated piped water. Around 30 percent rely on spring water while rest of the population depends on river and other sources like open ditch water. Only five percent of the population has been connected to sewerage system (UN Economic Commission for Europe 2012). Due to poor access to water in Tajikistan, a quarter of the children under age of five are stunted (USAID 2014). Water, like land remains state property in Tajikistan under Article 13 and state determines its use in interests of the people. However, the water infrastructure built by Soviet Union has been decaying while Tajikistan lacks financial capacity to repair it. Food safety, another aspect of food security is a neglected area in Tajikistan. Food safety is based on Soviet standards while there is lack of coordination due to involvement of a number of ministries and agencies (Khodjamurodov and Rechel 2010).

As is evident, Tajikistan lacks a specific legislation on food security and a wide range of laws and sub-laws covering food security are in place in the country. The multifaceted nature of concept of food security requires a focused national action. Experts have been arguing that Tajikistan should adopt a food security act which would help in coordinating all the aspects of food security in Tajikistan (Knuth 2008). Such a law is necessary to lay out a conceptual legal framework and fix responsibility for food security in Tajikistan. Since its independence in 1991, Tajikistan has made some good progress in its quest for attaining food security. The area under cotton cultivation has come down while area devoted to grains and vegetables has grown. However, Tajikistan is a weak state which requires help and assistance from foreign countries and international organisations in ensuring food security for its citizens. This has been discussed in chapter 5. Tajikistan continuously monitors food security situation in the country with the help of international and UN organisations. Since 2005, Statistical Agency under President of the Republic of Tajikistan has been bringing out a quarterly report on food security and poverty in Tajikistan. This report covers areas like food availability and accessibility, area under crops, health indicators, water supply, prices and climatic conditions. The report helps in assessing food security situation in Tajikistan and also helps to plan for potential emergencies in future.

IMPACT OF FOOD INSECURITY ON SOCIETY IN TAJIKISTAN

The concerns over food insecurity have direct impact on society in Tajikistan. Better access to food requires employment but Tajikistan lacks such opportunities. Hence, people have migrated to Russia and Kazakhstan in search of employment to keep their families away from hunger and also provide them better education and health facilities. Food insecurity also leads to health concerns among women and children. Food insecurity could also lead to resource competition in Tajikistan, as it is estimated that its population would nearly double by 2050. The details are discussed in succeeding paragraphs.

Relationship between Food Security and Migration in Tajikistan

The Tajik Ministry of Agriculture estimates that around 1.2 million Tajik migrants work abroad, mainly in Russia (Ministry of Agriculture 2012). Unemployment and poverty force youths to seek work abroad. Remittances from such a large pool of migrants have been instrumental in economic growth and poverty reduction in Tajikistan, thereby also directly impacting food security of the households. In 2011, Tajikistan received USD 2.3 billion in remittance inflows which further increased to USD 3.1 billion in 2012. This accounted for 47 percent of the GDP of Tajikistan and covered basic needs of more than half of the country's population (BTI Report 2014). In 2014, the remittances further increased to more than USD 4 billion contributing 52 percent to Tajikistan's GDP (Trilling 2014).

Tajikistan is most remittance dependent country in the world and such a large dependence on remittances makes Tajikistan vulnerable to external shocks. Problems in Russian economy would decrease remittances to Tajikistan which will impact food security in the country. Russia is under Western sanctions over the Ukraine crisis and its economy is in a state of recession. Russian gross domestic product increased by just 0.6 percent in 2014, which is slowest since 2009, when its economy faced contraction (Andrianova 2015). Russian economic crisis is expected to impact the Tajik economy too, as around 400,000 Tajik migrants could return back to Tajikistan from Russia due to unavailability of opportunities this year. The remittances could come down to USD 1.7 billion which is more than 50 percent less than the 2014 level. Such a huge decrease in remittances will have impact on food security and poverty reduction of Tajik households. The impact could be more in villages, as 80 percent of the migrants are from villages (Umarov 2015).

Food insecurity can trigger migration while the remittance sent by migrants can offset and mitigate impact of food insecurity. A study 'Migrants from Badakhshan' was conducted in GBAO by Aga Khan Foundation. 40 percent respondents from the region said that they migrated in search of work due to food problems in their families while 41 percent left due to lack of employment. 17 percent cited reasons like education and housing (Haqnazar 2004, cited in Olimova 2005: 7). The relationship between migration and food security in Tajikistan has been analysed through the conceptual framework depicted in figure 4.5.

Figure 4.5. Impact Of Migration on Food Security.

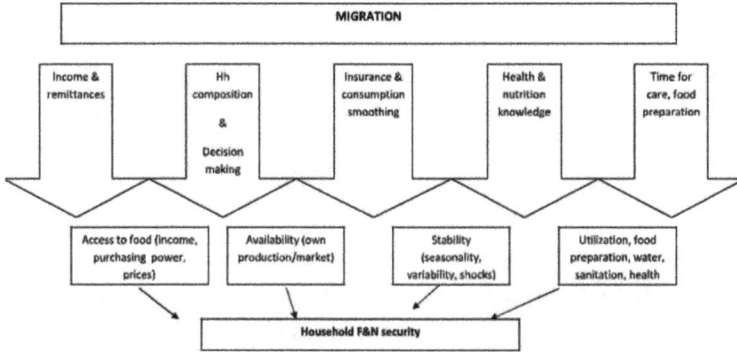

Source: Azzarri and Zezza 2010: 56.

Migration can impact household food security in many ways. Income and remittances alleviate food security as it increase purchasing power and decreases malnutrition. In Tajikistan, those children under the age of five whose family has been exposed to migration have better growth and nutrition levels. Household composition and decision making is also changed as male members migrate for work and family is headed by females. There is better knowledge about health and nutrition requirements as well (Azzarri and Zezza 2010). Olimova (2005) has argued that migration has helped a big amount of population in Tajikistan to keep starvation at bay which is a result of poor economy and lack of employment opportunities. The remittance money mainly funds basic needs of the population, from medicine to food and education. Often, many generations of a family are supported by this money and without this money; they would go back to ranks of poverty and food insecurity (ICG 2009).

However, there are negative impacts of migration as well on food security in Tajikistan. Migration has affected availability of labour in agriculture sector. A large chunk of the male workforce remains out of the country between April and October, the main agricultural season in Tajikistan. This also contributes to low yields as crops require timely care. Remittances can also lower the incentive to work in fields, as households have a fixed source of income. This can further lower productivity in agriculture (Bliss 2012). Male migration from mountainous areas also decreases local food production which cannot be compensated by food supply bought from remittances (Olimova 2005). Politically, migration of such a big scale has been a safety valve and economic salvation for the government of Tajikistan. The youths that could have potentially asked for change and joined ranks of opposition in the country work abroad which gives the government a lifeline to safeguard its interests without much of a social protest (ICG 2009).

Links between Food Security and Health

Health was a state responsibility during Soviet times in Tajikistan but after independence in 1991, the state's ability to provide healthcare to its citizens has been weakened due to economic problems. According to the World Bank, Tajikistan spends USD 55 per capita on health which lowest in Central Asia. The linkages between food and health have an impact on people in Tajikistan, especially the poor. There has been a traditional preference for fatty and animal products in Tajik diet instead of fruits and vegetables. A diet having low content of antioxidants coupled with lack of proper detection and treatment of hypertension contribute to cardiovascular diseases in Tajikistan. The access of vulnerable groups to micro-nutrient rich diet has been hampered due to low purchasing power and health problems like anaemia and iodine deficiency have increased among them (Khodjamurodov and Rechel 2010). Due to lack of iron content in the diet in Tajikistan, there is prevalence of thyroid problems in the country (Mack and Surina 2005). Intake of poor quality food, unbalanced diet and improper child feeding practices by women are main causes of malnutrition in Tajikistan. 26 percent of the children under age of five years in the country are stunted, 10 percent wasted and 12 percent are underweight (Tajikistan Demographic and Health Survey 2012). The malnutrition rate increased in rural areas due to 2008 winter crisis in Tajikistan which reduced food consumption of poor households due to rise in food prices. Another concern is diarrhoea as 19.2 percent of child mortality in Tajikistan is caused by it. Diarrhoea is caused by poor water supply, sanitation and hygiene and these standards are low in Tajikistan (UNICEF 2010). Diarrhoea is also linked to loss of body mass among children (World Health Organisation 2011). It is estimated that under nutrition costs Tajikistan USD 41 million per year, due to enhanced mortality, lost productivity and reduced physical and cognitive development (UNICEF 2012). Hence, health and food issues complement each other in Tajikistan and there is need to improve both sectors in order to increase food security and nutritional intake of people of Tajikistan.

Impact of Food Security on Demography

Tajikistan had a very high fertility rate under Soviet Union and this trend has continued even after independence of Tajikistan. Tajikistan has highest population growth rate among Central Asian countries. Marriage is a universal phenomenon, done at early age in most cases which quickly leads to childbearing (Abdullaev and Akbarzadeh 2010). In 1991, Tajikistan had a population growth rate of 2.2 percent per annum. Population growth rate started decreasing after that due to civil war in the country and touched a low of 1.3 percent in 1998. Clifford has even found positive relationship between food crisis in 1995, drought of 2001 and fertility decline in Tajikistan (Clifford 2009). However, as political and economic stability started after end of civil war, the population growth rate started increasing and touched 2.4 percent in 2013 (World Bank Indicators Tajikistan 2013). Tajikistan does not have a proper policy in place to control birth rate and only one in four women uses modern contraception (Warcholak and

Boboev 2012). Recently revised UN population projections are a warning bell for Tajikistan, as its population is expected to increase by 88 percent between 2010 and 2050, as shown in Table 4.3. The UN projection in 2010 predicted that Tajikistan's population will increase from 8 million in 2010 to 11 million in 2050.

Table 4.3. Future Population Projections for Tajikistan.

	2010 Population	2050 Population Projection (2010)	2050 Population Projection (2012)	New 2010-2050 % Change
Cambodia	14	19	23	64%
Ethiopia	87	145	188	116%
Mali	14	42	45	221%
Mozambique	24	50	60	150%
Senegal	13	29	33	154%
Tajikistan	8	11	15	88%
Uganda	34	94	104	206%

Source: Mogelgaard 2013.

However, the UN revised these estimates in 2012 and predicted Tajikistan will have a population of 15 million in 2050 (Mogelgaard 2013). Tajikistan faces classic Malthusian dilemma, as its population is expected to grow faster than its food growing capacity. Per capita food availability in Tajikistan was 248.8 kg in 2008 and it reduced to 201.1 kg in 2011, a decline of 20 percent. The population increased by 182.3 thousand during this period and population increase seems to have offset growth in food resources (Asadov 2013). This is a worrisome sign for Tajikistan, as per capita cereal demand has been projected to increase by 10 kg in Central Asia between 1995 and 2020 (Lorch 2000). Demographic changes will also impact per capita land availability in Tajikistan. The country has 0.14 hectares land per capita which is around half less than the global average of 0.26 hectares per person. By 2050, since Tajikistan's population will nearly double, the land per capita will be half of what it is now. Keeping in view the ethnic mix of Tajikistan (80 percent Tajiks, 15 percent Uzbeks and 5 percent minorities), the possibility of conflicts over land resources cannot be ruled out (Christmann et. al. 2009). Though there are concerns about future decrease in per capita land in Tajikistan, yet the government of Tajikistan ceded around one percent of its area (1142 square km) to China while settling its border dispute with the giant neighbour in January 2011. Tajikistan also leased 2,000 hectares of land in Khatlon to 1500 Chinese farmers (Hierman and Navruz 2014).

Food Security and Gender

During the Soviet Union, agriculture was managed by menfolk in Tajikistan while women took care of household works. Those women who gave birth to many children were given 'Mother Hero' certificates and received benefits as Soviet Union encouraged big families (Warcholak and Boboev 2012). However, the situation changed for women as Tajikistan became independent and civil war struck the economic growth of the country. Due to lack of manpower during the civil war, women had started to go to market to sell their produce, an activity that was still a man's arena. Women and children started becoming main workforce on agricultural fields (Gomart 2003). This trend has continued in Tajikistan due to migration of more than one million youths, mainly males out of the country in search of work. The migration figure is around one-third out of the total 3 million labour force in Tajikistan. As a result, women and children have been forced to work on fields (Abdullaev and Akbarzadeh 2010). Women have been playing a main role in cotton fields in Tajikistan but receive almost no benefits. In cotton growing areas, they constitute around 85-90 percent of the work force (ICG 2005). Even children work in cotton fields and a report in 2009 said that child labour accounted for around 40 percent of the total cotton harvest in Tajikistan (Eurasianet Website, November 2, 2009). Both women and children face hard and testing conditions in cotton fields like hot weather, poor water and food facilities and lack of medical care.

Large amount of state cuts in social service schemes like health, child and maternal benefits have impacted women and their access to resources like food (Falkingham 2000). The households headed by females have received smaller fraction of land allocated by Presidential decrees for food production. The number of dehkan farms headed by women decreased from 13.4 percent in 2006 to 10.4 percent in 2011 showing lack of decision making capability for women in agriculture sector (Asadov 2013). The troubled market oriented economic transition in Tajikistan has negatively impacted women by inducing personal insecurity, economic hardships and less political participation in Tajikistan (Mirzoeva 2009). According to Tajikistan Living Standards Strategy 2007-09, 23 percent households headed by men were poor, 4 percent more than the 19 percent poor households headed by women (Ibid). Food insecurity also has health impacts on women as 58.6 percent of women faced iodine deficiency in Tajikistan in 2009, compared to 54 percent in men (United Nations Children's Fund 2012). Women are expected to face these issues in future as well, as negative impacts of climate change and population pressures could aggravate overall food situation in Tajikistan, having maximum impact on vulnerable groups of women, children, poor and the elderly.

TRANSITIONAL POLITICAL SYSTEM AND FOOD SECURITY IN TAJIKISTAN

The kind of state that emerged out of ashes of Tajik civil war has not been democratic and inclusive in its approach. However, it has managed to work somehow as a development agent. It remains a hybrid state under President Rahmon whose security approach is undefined and will seek self-preserving methods if government is seriously threatened. In the outlying and remote areas, there is still very less state interference allowing regional divide to exist. The state has turned towards authoritarianism, especially after 9/11 terrorist attacks on the US (Matveeva 2008). In the post 9/11 world, Rahmon has used state security as a pretext to crackdown on opposition and strengthen his hold over power in Tajikistan. The 1994 constitution and amendments made to it in 1999 have concentrated all the power in the hands of the president. In 2003, a constitutional referendum was held to change Article 65 which limited president's tenure to single term of seven years. The referendum allowed Rahmon to be elected for two more seven year terms which reflects exclusionary nature of his policies. Rahmon has been using the informal clan system to hold the state together. He has been courting both Russia and the US and excludes other clans from access to power and politics. Initially, he gave positions to competing clans but did not balance the clan interests while his family has also grown hegemonic (Collins 2006). The West also tacitly approves of Rahmon's secular credentials since it does not support the Islamist parties in Tajikistan (Pomfret 2006).

Tajikistan has been seen as a weak state reflecting its low political and economic capacity. The post-communist states had to make a transition from centrally planned economies to market economies. This was a tough task for a state like Tajikistan having limited economic resources. There was economic and social insecurity and due to resource constraints, some countries like Tajikistan even withdrew from state responsibility in spheres of health, agriculture and education inherited from Soviet era (Tadjbakhsh and Chenoy 2007). Political institutions are weak in Tajikistan while the economy is still struggling to be self-sustaining. More than half of the gross domestic product comes in form of remittances from abroad. Any disruption in remittance inflow will lead to food insecurity among the families that depend on remittances. Due to existence of transitional economy, Tajikistan has lowest development levels in Central Asia along with Kyrgyzstan. In the Human Development Index prepared by UNDP, Tajikistan ranked 133 out of 187 countries in 2013. It is important to note that Tajikistan's HDI value has come down from 0.610 to 0.607 between 1990 and 2013. This corresponds to 0.02 percent decrease per annum (Human Development Report 2014). Poverty rate in Tajikistan was 35.6 percent in 2014, with households earning less than 145 somoni per month rated as poor. 14 percent were extremely poor as they could not earn 104 somoni per month (Chorshanbiyev 2014). Consumption of the richest 10 percent in Tajikistan is six times that of the poorest 10 percent (OECD 2014). Hence, these poor people remain food insecure as they lack access to food. The regional disparity and 'north-south' divide has continued in Tajikistan, as the northern areas are better developed while those in south lag behind, especially GBAO. Some experts have also classified Tajikistan as a neo-patrimonial state. It refers to simultaneous existence of formal democratic structures and autocratic leadership in a country. In neo-patrimonial states like Tajikistan, the agriculture policy mainly serves the political and financial interests of the elites. Strengthening of elite is seen as a way to bolster and strengthen the political dispensation (Peyrouse 2013).

There is widespread corruption in Tajikistan and it is ranked 154th out of 177 countries in the corruption index of Transparency International (Asia Plus December 3, 2013). The International Monetary Fund (IMF) in 2008 had asked for return of USD 47 million loans given earlier to Tajikistan as the government had submitted fabricated statistics about condition of national reserves (Abdullaev and Akbarzadeh 2010). The economic and agricultural reforms have been very slow in Tajikistan which has impacted the living standards of the people. Prof H C Wolf has classified various post-Soviet states according to pace of reforms they adopted. The fastest pace of reforms was followed by Eastern Europe and they are called radical reformers. Gradual reformers had a slightly slower pace and included countries like Poland and Hungary. The slowest were laggards and it included countries like Tajikistan, Ukraine and Russia. These countries were unable to do away with the old order while their basic economic institutions were weak that hampered foreign inflow of funds (Wolf 1999). Though Tajikistan has been witnessing an average growth rate of 6 percent per year in the last decade, experts believe this high growth rate is mainly due to low base than due to real economic gains (Pomfret

2006). It is amid such a political and economic scenario that one has to look at the food security situation in Tajikistan. Food situation was very bad in the country during the civil war. This has improved after land reforms were started but Tajikistan is not self-sufficient in food grains and still depends on food imports to satisfy around 50 percent of its requirement (Umarov 2015). The weak economic capacity of Tajikistan hampers its efforts to create transport, energy infrastructure and mechanisation of agriculture, both of which will have a good impact on food security of the country. Due to transitional nature of Tajik political and economic system, there has been direct and negative impact on food security in the country. Unlike Soviet days, there is no subsidy on food while social security schemes of the government cover a small amount of population since state revenues are not large enough to cover all the food insecure people. The government has also failed to effectively implement land reforms and agriculture modernisation which lower food production in Tajikistan.

CHALLENGES TO FOOD SECURITY IN TAJIKISTAN

Food security in Tajikistan is not a problem limited to agricultural production and there are a number of other issues involved that impact the availability, access and utilisation of food in the country. These are discussed in succeeding paragraphs.

Natural Disasters

Tajikistan faces a number of natural disasters like draughts, floods, earthquakes, avalanches and mudflows which negatively impact its food security. It has also been affected by climate change leading to long drought spells, extreme hot summers and winters, melting glaciers and resultant floods. These natural disasters have been induced by increasing deforestation as well (Foroughi2012). The country is third most disaster-prone in Eurasia behind Russia and Afghanistan. Such a frequent occurrence of natural disasters combined with government's weak capacity to respond impacts food security of thousands of people in Tajikistan (Ibid). A drought in Shurobod district of Khatlon province in 2006 had destroyed 3,680 hectares of grain harvest (Asia Plus July 4, 2006). A serious earthquake could probably trigger market supply crisis in the country which would impact food availability in Tajikistan (Beuter 2007). The frequent incidents of natural disasters make it hard for the policymakers to draft food security policies in the country. According to the UN Office for the Coordination of Humanitarian Affairs (UNOCHA), Tajikistan faces on average 150 small and medium scale natural disasters that affect at least 10,000 people every year. Every year, around 600 families are forced to migrate in Tajikistan as natural disasters make their village and lands uninhabitable (World Health Organization 2009). The UNDP coordinator in Tajikistan estimated that Tajikistan suffers USD 600 million losses annually due to natural disasters (Poverty Reduction Strategy 2010-2012). The 2000-2001 droughts however, remain a painful experience for Tajikistan as it had a big impact on food security in the country.

Droughts

The 2000-01 drought was one of the worst faced by Tajikistan in last 75 years, estimated to have affected 2 million people. There was below average rainfall in Tajikistan in 2000 which lead to drought and affected rain-fed wheat. 172,000 hectares of 200,000 hectares of rain-fed wheat were affected by drought while estimated 50 percent of the cereals produced on irrigated land were affected too (International Federation of Red Cross, July 20, 2001).In 2000, people had no choice and consumed seeds for next year's planting season which contributed to decline in production in 2001 (World Bank 2008). There was decrease of 46 percent in wheat output in 2000 compared to 1999, and it stood at 236,000. There was not much improvement in the second year of drought in 2001 and wheat production stood only at 303,000 tons.Such a large scale scarcity of wheat increased its prices by 63 percent in 2000(FAO 2000, 2001). The situation was very serious and President Rahmon appealed to the international community to provide his country food aid of 500,000 tons in 2001 (Agence France-Presse, April 26, 2001). The impact of the drought was quite severe and people underwent a lot of hardships to secure food. The people living in rural areas were even forced to sell roofs, doors and windows of their houses to buy food. In 2001, they even lacked proper clothes to keep them warm in winter. According to Roger Brackle, former head of Red Cross to Tajikistan, children were competing with rodents in their battle to survive as they were ransacking rat holes in wheat fields hoping to find some wheat hoarded by rodents. Drought also forced people to use water from contaminated sources while it also increased anaemia and malnutrition among children (IFRC, August 21, 2001). Those who resided in remote and mountainous areas were worst affected by food shortages. There were less employment opportunities and problems of transportation compounded food insecurity (FAO, August 14, 2001).According to World Food Program, Tajikistan was on verge of famine in 2001 and the situation was similar to that in Horn of Africa (Agence France-Presse, October 13, 2001). This drought played a major role in increasing people's monthly expenditure on food and the 2003 Living Standards Measurement Survey found that people were spending 67 percent of the household expenditure on food (Knuth 2008).

Food-Energy-Water Crisis in Winter

In 2008, Tajikistan witnessed a new kind of disaster, a kind of compound disaster[1]. It was a combination of severe cold, drought, breakdown of energy infrastructure, locust infestation and increase in global wheat prices that impacted Tajikistan too (Tajikistan Committee of Emergency Situations and Civil Defence 2010). The crisis started with extraordinarily long winter in 2007-08. The temperature ranged between -8°C and -25°C which increased

---

1   A compound disaster involves multiple disasters like inflation, food insecurity, energy and water crisis. The basic services (gas, water, electricity and health) are not able to operate while the economy faces contraction (Kelly 2009).

demand for heating. However, the rivers were frozen while there was less water in dams, leading to decreased electricity production (UNOCHA 2008a). There was lack of coal and gas while rural areas received electricity for not more than two hours per day. Infants and elderly were worst affected and hundreds are believed to have died but no official figures were reported (Matveeva 2008). Even power supply was being cut to restaurants and cafes in Dushanbe and they were asked to use candles instead. There were problems in water supply as well and people were reported to be leaving Taboshar town in Sughd province due to water shortage (Integrated Regional Information Networks 2008).

The poor energy situation in Tajikistan had been in the making after it gained independence in 1991. During Soviet days, each house in Tajikistan received seasonal coal quotas for cooking and heating in severe winter. Coal quotas were stopped in 1991 and people have been using electricity for heating. In winter, there is overloading of as much as 150 percent as demand rises. However, power distribution lines have been damaged while local circuit breakers and fuses do not work. Facing electricity shortage, people have started using firewood (Sampath 2006). Cutting of forests for firewood is decreasing the forest leading to soil erosion. People also use animal waste and biomass for heating. This reduces the supply of organic fertiliser to crops as farmers lack enough access to costly chemical fertilisers. This in turn, has an adverse impact on food production (Amir and Berry 2013). Access to energy reduces food insecurity as food can be refrigerated and its usage period can be extended. Water can be boiled and disinfected by using energy which enhances food security (Robic et. al. 2010).

The 2008 winter was very severe which led to a compound food-energy-water crisis in Tajikistan. Anecdotal evidence suggests that 33 percent of wheat area in Tajikistan could not be cropped due to extreme cold conditions experienced by the country in last 40 years (Christmann et. al. 2009). The combined effect of these hard circumstances on the vulnerable sections was harsh. The prices of bread, major ingredient of Tajik diet and cooking oil more than doubled during the crisis while prices of other basic items increased by 50 percent (UNOCHA 2008). Man and animals are expected to have perished due to cold and hunger. Sughd, Khatlon and Region of Republican Subordination were the hardest hit by the crisis. Between 40 to 45 percent of the autumn wheat in 2007 and 100 percent of winter wheat in 2008 was damaged. The 50 percent increase in global wheat prices kept wheat out of the reach of urban poor and rural households in Tajikistan (Olcott 2014). During rise in global wheat prices, Tajik and Kyrgyz people started using local wheat as it is cheaper but it leads to decreased nutrition as this wheat is less nutritious (Peyrouse 2013).

A joint survey conducted by Food and Agriculture Organisation and Government of Tajikistan in mid-2008 found that 15 percent of urban population was severely food insecure while 22 percent were moderately food insecure. In rural areas, 12 percent were severely food insecure and 22 percent were moderately food insecure. In all, around 2.2 million people were food insecure in Tajikistan in 2008due to the compound crisis (FAO 2009). As if it was not enough, around 220,000 hectares of land were affected by locust infestation in 2008 and army was mobilised to fight the infestation, as poor farmers were unable to afford cost of pesticides (Pannier 2008). According to Saidjalol Saidov, director of Research Institute of Crop Production in Tajikistan, the country loses up to 30 percent of its harvests every year due to pests (Asia Plus June 14, 2008). The hard conditions of 2008 crisis tested patience of otherwise calm Tajik citizens and protests broke out in the capital Dushanbe and other cities of Kulob, Panjakent and Khorog. The Tajik government did not use force to quell the few protestors acknowledging their failure in allowing the crisis to reach this level (Matveeva 2008). Tajikistan's economic growth rate dropped from 7 percent in 2008 to 3 percent in 2009. Due to global economic slowdown, inflow of remittances decreased from USD 2.6 billion in 2008 to USD 1.6 billion in 2009 (Amir and Berry 2013). During the crisis period, Tajikistan was forced to use one-fifth of its export earnings for food imports, which is more than double the world average. Half of the households in Tajikistan had to reduce their food consumption, 15 percent higher than the Central Asian average of 35 percent. Regions of Khatlon and GBAO witnessed an increase in poverty due to the crisis between 2007 and 2009. In Khatlon, poverty increased from 47 percent to 53.9 percent while in GBAO it increased from 42.9 percent to 61.9 percent during this period. Overall, Tajikistan poverty stood at 47.2 percent in 2009 (Akramov and Shreedhar 2012). The government estimated that Tajikistan had lost USD 850 million in damages and lost revenue due to the crisis in 2008 (UNOCHA 2008a). This crisis once again underlined Tajikistan's weakness in dealing with aspects of food security in the country by itself and also highlighted its dependence on foreign countries and agencies to feed its population.

Lack of Social Security

The food security of vulnerable groups remain at risk and it is up to the state to ensure that these groups have state protection and get access to food. The vulnerable groups in Tajikistan have been identified by a survey conducted by the National Social Investment Fund of Tajikistan. These groups include – families having a woman head, families with young children, families with five or more people and old age people. The most vulnerable include – families having a sick head of family, unemployed members and farmers having no assets at all (Amir and Berry 2013). Social protection and security have been enshrined in the 1994 constitution of Tajikistan. Article 34 calls for the state to protect mothers and children (Son 2011). Article 39 provides for economic access to food as it advocates social assistance in old age, illness, disability or in case of loss of provider (Knuth 2008). Tajikistan also has a law 'On Pension Provision of Citizens of Tajikistan' which guarantees monthly payments to elderly, disabled and special merit individuals like World War II veterans etc. In 2009, Tajikistan government allocated 685.5 million TJS (Tajik Somoni) for social protection constituting 3.3 percent of the GDP (Son 2011).

Tajikistan has failed to continue non-contributory social protection system that was followed by Soviet Union. In this system, state bears all the burden and employees do not contribute to it. However, this system was sustainable during Soviet times as the state had huge funds at its disposal. Tajikistan is a financially weak state and lacks enough resources to continue this system. In August 2010, the government owed around USD 11.8 million in salary and pension arrears to people. The arrears were highest in Khatlon which had a negative impact on the food security in the region (UNDP 2010). Only one percent of Tajikistan's poorest quintile is properly covered by state social assistance schemes. According to the Poverty Reduction Strategy of 2007-09, Tajik government can support only 43.71 percent of the most basic needs in this sector (Olcott 2014). According to the World Bank, the social assistance budget in Tajikistan is lowest in Europe and Central Asian region. These programs are poorly targeted. Government lacks financial ability to increase the social security budget while international donors do not support the social security program as Tajikistan does not have institutional mechanisms for financial control, auditing and monitoring (World Bank 2011). In the wake of weak financial resources at the disposal of Tajik government, social security is expected to play a limited role in food security of vulnerable groups.

Environmental Degradation and Climate Change

The environmental degradation in Tajikistan started under Soviet Union, when Soviet economic planners disregarded the agricultural ecosystem in the country and gave utmost importance to increasing cotton production at any cost. The chemical fertilisers and pesticides were used in abundance while massive irrigation was carried out for cotton. This depleted the water tables all over Central Asia and soil salinized (Mack and Surina 2005). The main environmental degradation concerns in Tajikistan relate to deforestation, soil degradation, air pollution, poor availability of chemically treated drinking water, losses due to natural disasters and lack of environmental awareness. Deforestation results in loss of topsoil as land becomes vulnerable to landslides and mudflows. This is mainly applicable in spring when soil defrosts and rains take place. The soils that are washed away further lead to silting in water streams and rivers (Sampath 2006).

Farmlands in Tajikistan have reduced by 4 percent in Tajikistan in last ten years due to environmental issues (Poverty Reduction Strategy 2010-2012). Agriculture experts believe that erosion affects around 60 percent of the irrigated land in Tajikistan. One of the worst examples is Yavan valley, where 20 percent of the 6,000 hectares of irrigated lands cannot be cultivated due to erosion limited food production in this isolated area. Soil erosion is a consequence of improper soil and land management due to overgrazing and deforestation etc. (World Bank 2007). A World Bank study conducted in 2008 had shown that environmental damages in Tajikistan amounted to 9.5 percent of its GDP in 2006. Highest losses are due to land degradation (soil erosion and salinity) accounting for 3.7 percent of the GDP, followed by loss due to natural disasters at 1.6 percent, costs from poor water supply and sanitation issues amounted to 1.5 percent, air pollution accounting for 1 percent and rangeland degradation costing 0.7 percent of the GDP. The details are shown in the figure 4.6.

Figure 4.6. Impact of Environmental Damages on Tajik GDP.

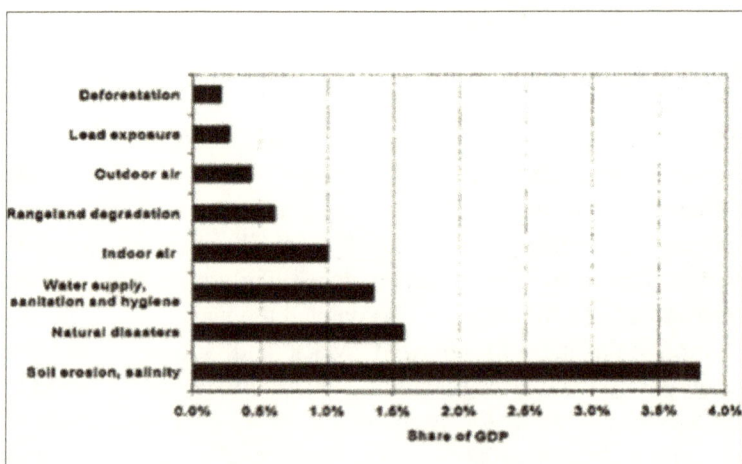

Source: World Bank 2008a: 24.

Climate change poses a big challenge to Tajikistan and will impact food security in the country. The abundant water resources in Tajikistan have been shrinking since the 1950s due to global warming (Abdullaev and Akbarzadeh 2010). According to the Intergovernmental Panel on Climate Change (IPCC), the temperature in Central Asia and Caucasus region will rise by 3.7° C till 2100, which is way higher than the global average of 2.8° C. Around 32 percent of glaciers could melt by 2050 while some glaciers would completely disappear in the region by 2050. The crop yields could decrease by 2.5 to 10 percent in the region up to 2020 and by 5-30 percent by 2050 (IPCC 2007, quoted in Christmann et.al 2009: 9). The melting of glacial ice will pose serious threats of floods while in the long run there could be water shortages. There will be food security risks due to rising food prices and the women, children and urban poor would be vulnerable to such risks. Increased temperatures will also increase the risk of heat stress and crop failure (World Bank 2014a).

These risks are going to come for Tajikistan at a time when its population is expected to nearly double by 2050. Decreasing crop yields and increasing population will trigger competition for resources like land, water and food not only in Tajikistan but among the Central Asian Republics who are already bickering for resources like water. Tajikistan already faces a number of natural disasters per year and climate change will further compound the impact on food security in the country. Climate change could also increase chances of malaria in Tajikistan, as warmer temperatures are expected to push the carrier mosquitoes to higher elevations (Scott et. al. 2008). The change is evident from the fact that the hot weather days between 1940 and 2005 have already doubled in Tajikistan while the glaciers have melted by 33 percent on average during this period (State Agency for Hydrometeorology of the Committee for Environmental Protection 2008). According to Fay and Patel (2008), Tajikistan is most vulnerable country to climate change among the countries of Eastern Europe and Central Asia, as shown in the figure 4.7. They also argue that

Tajikistan has the least adaptive capacity among these countries to respond to climate change (Fay and Patel (2008), quoted in World Bank 2009: 7). However, Tajikistan needs sustainable growth and management of its agriculture resources in order to cope with the climate change impact. Land and water management should be done to increase efficiency of land and increase crop yields. Proper land management can increase land productivity by 20 to 30 percent (Christman et. al. 2009).

Figure 4.7. Impact of Climate Change on East European & Central Asian Countries.

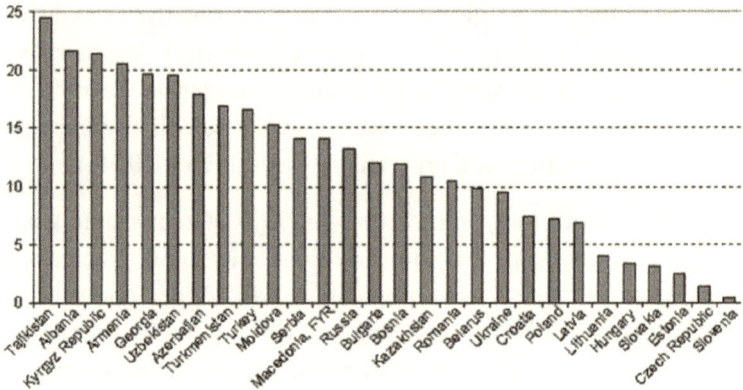

Source: Fay and Patel (2008), quoted in World Bank 2009: 7.

Poor Transport

A well connected transport system ensures market integration and smooth supply of foodstuffs all over a country. Tajikistan, a highly mountainous country lacks proper transport network to facilitate inter-regional trade. Since Tajikistan is a landlocked country, poor transport network also hampers Tajikistan's access to world markets.

Road Network in Tajikistan

Due to overwhelming mountainous terrain, roads are preferred to railways in Tajikistan. The condition of these roads is poor and does not meet the requirements of international standards which increase fuel consumption. This also increases food prices in the isolated mountainous areas. The government lacks substantial funds to repair these roads. From 2002-08, only 362.8 km of roads were repaired and renovated by foreign and government assistance (Poverty Reduction of the Republic of Tajikistan for 2010-2012). Mountainous terrain of Tajikistan fragments its smaller markets into further smaller markets. Reaching the highlands becomes difficult in winter, when roads are closed due to heavy snowfall. Breaking the communication deadlock is one of the strategic goals of Tajik government but the progress in the transport sector is slow. Roads between Dushanbe and Khujand (340 km) go through Anzob pass in north which remains closed for seven months in winter. Another option is to take a long detour through Uzbekistan which is 940 km long. The transport costs between the two cities can even triple in winter as trucks use Uzbekistan route taking 2 to 3 days travel time (Beuter 2007). Anzob tunnel through the Anzob pass has been completed through Iran's assistance but remains dangerous due to poor lighting and ventilation inside. There are two routes that connect Khorog, capital of GBAO to Dushanbe. One is the Pamir Highway that passes through Gharm valley, Kalaikhumb and goes along Pyanj river. Another route passes through Osh in Kyrgyzstan and connects Khorog through Murghob. Due to higher transport costs, goods cost 27 percent more in GBAO than in Dushanbe. However, in winter, the difference can be up to 46 percent (Ibid). High transport costs increase cost of foodstuffs, especially in times of crisis. Physical access to food in mountainous areas in Tajikistan is hampered by poor roads, fuel costs and long distances. Around 17 percent of the population in Murghob district does not have proper access to food items (WFP 2013). These factors make mountainous people more vulnerable to food insecurity than those living in valleys in Tajikistan (Sampath 2006).

Rail Network

Main distribution of the rail network is in south Tajikistan which connects commercial centres of Gissar and Vakhsh with the outside world through Uzbekistan, as shown in the Map 4.1 (Website of Embassy of Tajikistan to Geneva). The northern Tajikistan is connected to southern region through Uzbekistan which is 1,340 km long route. Railways are used by Tajikistan mainly for its international trade. Most of the foreign food aid reaches Tajikistan from Baltic port of Riga through railways via Uzbekistan. Over 80 percent of the Tajik foreign trade relies on railways and a big chunk of its grain and wheat flour imports rely on railways to reach Tajikistan (WFP 2005). However, Tajikistan is dependent on Uzbekistan as its food imports and aid pass through Uzbek territory. Uzbekistan had blocked rail traffic to Tajikistan during critical months of winter in December 2011. Even the humanitarian aid sent by World Food Program was not allowed to reach Tajikistan leading to food price rise in Tajikistan due to shortage (Radio Free Europe Radio Liberty, December 14, 2011).

There are serious concerns about Tajikistan's ability to cope up with a major crisis if its food supplies are interrupted by Uzbekistan as around 90 percent of all imported foodstuffs pass through Uzbekistan (WFP 2005). Uzbekistan-Tajikistan relations have been historically strained as brought out in chapter 3. After 1991, both the countries have been contesting their demarcated border and Uzbekistan has raised concerns over construction of Roghun dam by Tajikistan, as it feels it will lessen flow of water to Uzbekistan. President of Uzbekistan, Islam Karimov has even warned of a war over water issues with Tajikistan (The Economist September 29, 2012). Like Tajikistan, Uzbekistan too, needs water for its food and cotton crops. It is also pursuing policy of food self-sufficiency for which it requires water for irrigation. Hence, water needs for agriculture could trigger conflict between the two countries in future. Tajikistan totally depends on Uzbekistan for natural gas supplies but Uzbekistan has been cutting off the gas supplies as well. In January 2009, Uzbekistan had cut 50 percent of its gas supplies to Tajikistan saying that Tajik gas debt had reached USD 9 million (Central Asia Online, January 6, 2009). In January 2012, Uzbekistan had completely cut off its gas supplies to Tajikistan (Khovar, January 5, 2012). Gas and electricity shortages also increase food prices in Tajikistan. Such shortages had increased bread prices by 50 percent in northern Tajikistan in November 2008 (Asia Plus November 30, 2006). Hence, Uzbekistan controls vital leverage over energy and food supplies to Tajikistan and a major conflict between these two countries could create a humanitarian crisis in Tajikistan.

Cotton v/s Grain Dilemma

Central Asia was traditionally a grain growing region before the Tsarist conquest of the region in second half of the 19th century. Grains were replaced by cotton cultivation by Tsarist Russia and it also continued under Soviet Union. The grains were supplied to Tajikistan by Moscow while the Tajik elite grew rich due to cotton profits and their economic well-being got intertwined with fate of cotton. However, as brought out in chapter 3, Tajik farmers have switched to grains in times of crisis, whether during First World War or collectivisation. This shows that given a choice, they aremore likely to grow grains for self-consumption. This historical importance of cotton and grain for Tajik agriculture has also been reflected in national emblem of the country which depicts cotton branches on left and wheat branches on the right. Wheat and cotton growing areas in Tajikistan are shown in map 4.1.

Map 4.1. Wheat and Cotton Growing Areas in Tajikistan.

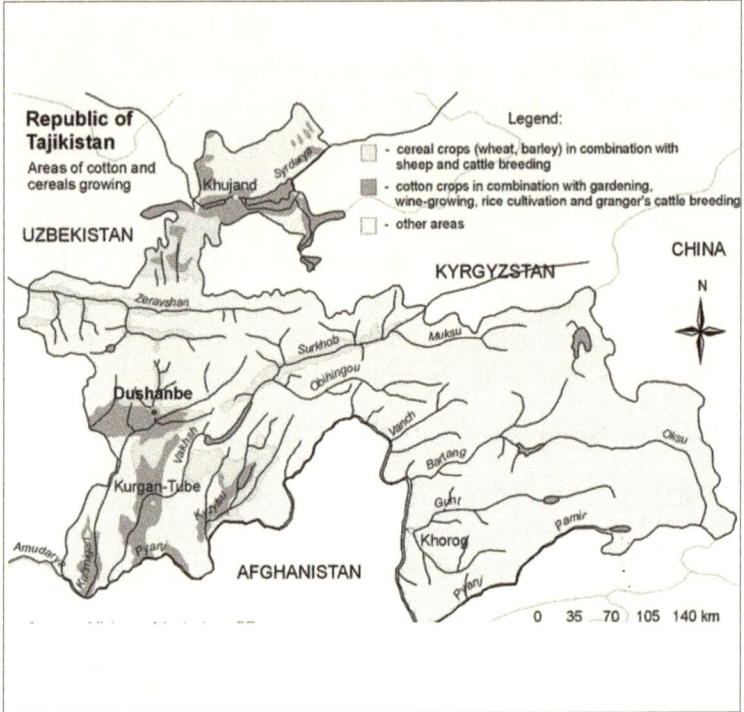

Source: Lerman and Sedik 2008: 12.

Khatlon is the main wheat producing area in Tajikistan, accounting for nearly 56 percent of the total production in the country. Region of Republican Subordination is next with 24 percent followed by Sughd at 20 percent (Beuter 2007). Cotton, on the other hand is cultivated in hot river valleys, Ferghana in Sughd valley, Vakhsh, Kyzlysu and Panj valleys in Khatlon and Hissor valley (Abdullaev and Akbarzadeh 2010). The area under cotton has come down considerably since 1991 considerably in Tajikistan. It stood at around 300,000 hectares in 1991 (Von Atta 2009). In 2012, it stood at 191,000 hectares (FAO 2014). However, there are various factors that continue to make cotton a favoured crop in Tajikistan. Cotton has been mentioned in the laws that govern water and agricultural operations according to the constitution of Tajikistan. Article 59 of the constitution makes it clear that primary agricultural role of water is to increase productivity of cotton and other agricultural operations. Since cotton is the only agricultural crop that fetches government foreign reserves, it has been given a constitutional protection (Rowe 2010). Hence, it is not a surprise that irrigation is done as per the water needs of the cotton plant and most of the cotton is cultivated on irrigated area (World Bank 2008). Food crops are cultivated on rain-fed area which lowers their productivity due to lack of proper irrigation.

Government of Tajikistan maintains influence over all the stages of cotton production and marketing in the country. Cotton exports are levied a ten percent tax which increases incentives to grow cotton (Pomfret 2008). There was drop in global cotton prices in 2009-2010 which decreased cotton production in Tajikistan but when the prices rose in 2011, farmers resumed cotton production. Farmers grow cotton as there is a ready market for the crop to produce income and allows for debt discharge. A survey done by the Asian Development Bank in 2008 concluded that pressure from local officials and problems in arranging independent financing were the reasons why cotton dominated food crops. Survey was done in Khatlon and Sughd, main cotton growing areas in Tajikistan (Olcott 2014). The government earns far more money by controlling cotton sector than it could earn through profits from grain and vegetable production, as these profits are minimal and hard to control privately (Peyrouse 2009). Cotton also needs less elaborate facilities for storage and transport, unlike the foodstuffs which require large investment in storage (Christmann et. al. 2009). State in Tajikistan is inflexible and protects the interests of the elite. Effective food security steps would mean more food crops and less cotton, which is a large source of revenue for the elites. The government has no interest in truly providing for good food security policy (Bleuer 2014). However, Tajik farmers have started intensive food crop cultivation since 1991 and the consequent food crisis during civil war. This is similar to the state of agriculture in the country before Russian conquest in 19th century. This pattern picked up during the last years of Soviet rule and has increased due to better land access to people provided by land reforms. People do not view cotton cultivation as an economic means to ensure their food security (Olcott 2014). According to FAO, cereal production in Tajikistan was 264,000 tons in 1992 which has increased to 1.2 million tons in 2012. Wheat production has increased from around 150,000 tons in 1991 to 789,560 tons in 2012 (FAOSTAT calculator). This increasing wheat production shows increasing food self-sufficiency in Tajikistan. Due to increasing population pressure, Tajikistan has to import 50 percent of its required wheat and flour, 30 percent of its beef and 80 percent of poultry and almost all the sugar (Peyrouse 2013). Though food availability has increased in Tajikistan, concerns still remain about food security in the country. People living in mountainous areas require more calories than those living in plains but they lack access to nutritious food. Households still spend two-third of their income on food and majority of this expenditure (40 percent) is spent on bread. There are no food reserves in Tajikistan to face emergency situations (Asadov 2013). Not only the government but the private traders too do not keep food reserves in their stock. Since around 90 percent of the internal transport is by road in Tajikistan, any glitches in fuel imports or breakdown of a major road could cut off food supplies (Beuter 2007). Almost half of Tajikistan's food is imported and such a big reliance on imports exposes the people to global food price rise. Food prices started picking up in Tajikistan in 2007 and kept rising till 2011. Between 2008 and 2010, food prices in Tajikistan were even higher than the global food prices, as shown in figure 4.8.

Figure 4.8. Food Price Trends in Tajikistan, Globally

Food price trends in Tajikistan, globally (2007–2010)

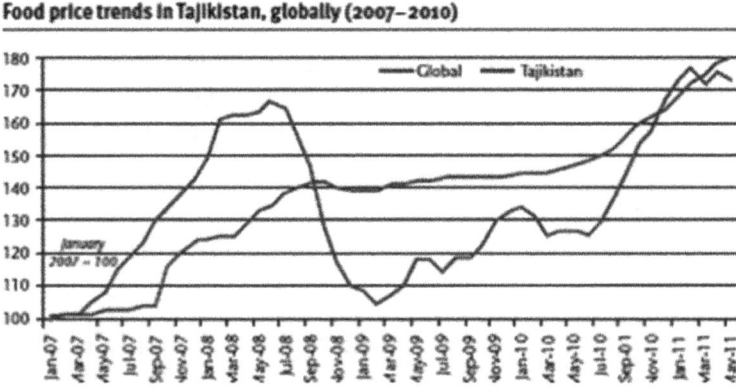

Source: Welthungerhilfe (2012).

Tajikistan's wheat imports are not diversified and most of it comes from Kazakhstan through Uzbekistan. Any fluctuation in food production in Kazakhstan has a direct impact on food security of Tajikistan. Wholesale prices of wheat and flour increased in Tajikistan by USD 8 in 2011, due to increase in prices of Kazakh wheat (Asia Plus January 25, 2011). This is a result of high import dependence and also due to the fact that Uzbekistan had raised tariffs on Tajik goods passing its territory by as much as 74 percent in 2011. Along with the food prices, prices of seeds, fuel and fertilisers also rose. As a result, small farmers need to invest more in food crop inputs before they are able to grow any crop (Welthungerhilfe 2012). Households use a variety of coping up mechanisms to adjust their food needs during times of price rise. Food consumption strategies include eating less expensive food, small portions of meals while also consuming seeds meant for next season sowing. Livelihood diversification strategies include relying on friends for help, food purchase on credit and increase in labour migration (WFP 2012a). Tajikistan is classified as a 'Low Income Food Deficit Country' (LIFDC) by the Food and Agriculture Organisation. Since LIFDCs have low per capita income, they remain vulnerable to threat of food insecurity, especially in times of volatile global prices. Tajikistan is not self-sufficient in food while its self-reliance remains at risk, as its export earnings highly depend on cotton and aluminium exports. Self-reliance means Tajikistan should be able to earn enough through exports to pay for its food import bill (Asadov 2013). In 2011, 34.5 percent of the total population in Tajikistan was food insecure. Out of this, 17.13 percent were severely food insecure who could not meet minimum 1830 kcal per person per day requirement (Ministry of Agriculture of Tajikistan 2011).

There are a number of problems why Tajikistan is not able to attain food self-sufficiency. Average wheat yields per hectare in Tajikistan were around 2.5 metric ton in 2010. Yields depend on type of irrigation; rain-fed wheat yields 1.5 MT while irrigated wheat yields 7-8 MT. Other factors that influence wheat yield are use of fertilisers, pesticides and machines (KOC 2012). Even the land taxes for cotton are about half of that for other crops (Hofman 2017). Though high yielding variety (HYV) cereal crops are being introduced in Tajikistan, there are concerns about them in the long run. Tajik farmers abandoned their own varieties in favour of HYVs during Tajik civil war. After two years, it came out that this new wheat moulded if left to dry in fields and it had a bad taste. Some farmers crossed over to Afghanistan and recovered their ancestral wheat varieties. The new varieties of food are ill-adapted to mountainous areas, more vulnerable to pests and diseases (Frederik and Haider 2010). Better land and water management and input supply is expected to increase yields better than the HYVs (Christmann et. al. 2009). The cotton vs grain dilemma though still continues in Tajikistan, the food crops have started to get more land for cultivation while land under cotton has come down. Food crops in Tajikistan require better inputs and water management which can raise their yields and hence the total production.

FOOD SECURITY AND POLITICAL STABILITY IN TAJIKISTAN

Tajikistan has witnessed both political instability as well as food insecurity. There are linkages between the two which could be found in the country. Whenever there has been political instability in Tajikistan, it has created food shortages and starvation in the country. This was evident during the days when First World War and Russian revolution took place, as brought out in chapter 3. When Tajikistan got independence from Soviet rule in 1991, a bloody civil war ensued in the country, though a government was in place but there was no political stability in the country due to war. This again created food problems in Tajikistan. Hence, we can say that political instability and conflict in Tajikistan lead to food problems in the country. However, as was witnessed during the global food crisis of 2007-08, food insecurity played a role in ouster of some governments like in Haiti and also in Arab Spring. Tajik journalist Dododzhon Atovulloev has said that there is need to organise Tajik 'Tahrir' as Rahmon will not leave office voluntarily and would cling on to power (Google Translation of Dododzhon Atovulloev's interview with Maria Yanovska for Ferghana News, January 31, 2012). Is there a possibility of political instability due to food insecurity in Tajikistan? The Food and Agriculture Organisation in 2011 had hinted at the possibility of food related unrest in Tajikistan, saying expensive food imports could become a 'major burden' for Tajikistan (Asia Plus February 16, 2011). However, that did not happen and there are a number of factors which point out that Tajikistan is unlikely to witness this eventuality.

Threats of political instability are nothing new to the Central Asian countries, as they have already witnessed 'colour revolutions' during 2005 (Uzbekistan and Kyrgyzstan). In the threat perception of the Tajik government (due to Russian influence), West inspired revolutions are the main threats to socio-political stability in their country. Consequently, the government harbours deep suspicion for civil society organisations, all types of media and the opposition political parties which could destabilise the government. In its efforts to preserve present political 'stability' in Tajikistan, the government exercises strict controls over these actors. The Tajik political system is not balanced while power is centralised in the hands of the President. Even the economy is largely dependent on remittances from Russia. Since Tajikistan has already witnessed a bloody civil war between 1992 and 1997, the 'post-war syndrome' survives and is an important factor in the social lives of the Tajik citizens. That is why; the Tajik society would tolerate any social hardship in order to avoid outbreak of yet another bloody conflict (Mullojanov 2014). There are three dimensions how the people perceive present regime in Tajikistan. One, they see it as a successor of Soviet state. Since Soviet Union had a good character, its successor also has to be good when it acts like Soviet regime. Two, the bitter experience of civil war makes people to see the present regime better than the past and three; the people find themselves in a better position than the neighbouring Afghanistan where the state is in doldrums. President Rahmon is viewed as a peacemaker while the opposition has no experience of governance. The Islamist hardliners are not viewed favourably by people while the northern elite have been out of power for far too long to be considered as a potential contender for power in Tajikistan (Matveeva 2008). The Tajik government is aware of the potential impact of Arab Spring on Tajikistan. President Rahmonhas been explaining to people the reasons behind the severe compound crisis of 2007-08, in a sign of his acknowledgement of the problem (Tahir 2011). It seems that the authorities have already learnt their lessons from the Arab Spring and protests would be violently suppressed by the Central Asian governments (Muckenhuber 2013).

Organising Arab Spring type protests in Tajikistan would be difficult, if not impossible. President Rahmon has support among the officials in bureaucracy who receive support from their respective clans. Rahmon would also get support from his region, Kulob while the drug mafia is also happy with the status quo in the country. Even if the opposition is able to organise public protests, there will be resistance against them. The situation would be closer to what it was before the civil war in 1992. Even the important external stakeholders, Russia, China, the US and Uzbekistan do not want to see a regime collapse in Tajikistan (Malashenko 2012). Political instability in Tajikistan could have a domino effect in Central Asia while it could also embolden radical elements in Afghanistan and none of these countries wants that to happen. The opposition and media play a big role in mobilising people. However, both these agencies are weak in Tajikistan and face government control. Tajikistan lacks daily newspapers while the provincial newspapers publish once or twice in a month. Most newspapers have a circulation of 3,000-4,000 while they are not able to reach the rural areas. Media agencies are placed under heavy burden of taxation as they have to pay 15 national, regional and local taxes to make them follow the government diktats. There is provision of imprisonment for five years for publicly insulting the Tajik President under the Article 137 of Tajikistan's penal code (Abdullaev and Akbarzadeh 2010). The independent publications face high pressure from government as they face penalties if found guilty of libel, a charge which is used by government for its own purposes (Olcott 2014). The power of internet to initiate organised protests and unexpected events has been well recognised in Central Asian states. That is why; cyber security is viewed as fifth danger to national security apart from drug trafficking, separatism, terrorism and extremism (Huasheng quoted in Zikibayeva 2011: 4). The criminal code of Tajikistan has been amended in order to make character defamation on internet a punishable offence, attracting up to two years prison term, Social network sites like Facebook and YouTube have been blocked by the government in the past in its efforts to control internet content (Olcott 2014). Opposition essentially has been weakened in Tajikistan. In the recent parliamentary elections in March 2015, the main opposition party, Islamic Renaissance Party of Tajikistan (IRPT) could not receive even 2 percent of total votes polled while it also lost two seats it had in the Tajik parliament. The number of seats held by IRPT has been halving with each successive election. They had 8 seats in 2000 which reduced to 4 in 2005. In 2010, the party got 2 seats while in 2015; it has none (Vinson 2015). The Tajik government has even used the foreign assistance to marginalise the opposition in the country. The international assistance to Tajikistan has led to emergence of new elites giving them opportunity to reorganize state structures. They have used foreign aid for their own benefit to control state institutions and finances. The appointments reserved for the opposition parties have been either forfeited or implemented partially by the Rahmon regime (Nakaya 2009). Even the civil society is weak in Tajikistan further denting hopes of public mobilisation against government. In the aftermath of 2005 'colour revolution' events in Uzbekistan and Kyrgyzstan, the Tajik government has been tightening the noose around international organizations, local civil society organisations, and foreign offices. The Foreign Ministry of Tajikistan has been asking the international organisations about their planned events in advance; while the local civil society organisations face tough conditions for organising events (Mullojanov 2005). Owing to all these factors, it is very difficult for food insecurity to create political instability in Tajikistan.

CHAPTER 5

INTERNATIONAL RESPONSE TO FOOD INSECURITY IN TAJIKISTAN

TAJIKISTAN'S DEPENDENCE ON FOREIGN ASSISTANCE

Since gaining independence in 1991, Tajikistan has struggled to keep its population food secure as the country is making a transition from centrally planned to market-oriented economy. The agriculture sector faces a number of problems as explained in previous chapter and needs financial and technical assistance to increase food production. Other than the agriculture sector, food security is also related to transport, energy, infrastructure, water and sanitation, health, gender, climate change and governance. The interplay between food security and these sectors has been brought out in chapter 4. Tajikistan needs assistance in all these sectors to improve its food security and pursue the path of sustainable development. Promotion of sustainable development requires foreign aid and assistance transfer to Tajikistan. The country required a total amount of TJS 30 billion to finance its Living Standards Improvement Strategy (LSIS) 2013-2015. Out of this, Tajik government was able to contribute TJS 12 billion (40 percent) while TJS 18 billion (60 percent) came as foreign aid (Tajikistan Development Partner Profiles 2014).

There are around 80 development partners in Tajikistan from the international community which are playing an important role in alleviating the food crisis in Tajikistan through their developmental assistance. These organisations not only bring in much needed financial assistance to Tajikistan but also provide technical assistance to the government and help its capacity building for tackling the food insecurity in the country. The food situation in Tajikistan was very critical during the initial years after independence in 1991. Tajikistan was facing a humanitarian crisis during these years and it received humanitarian as well as structural aid from international community. Humanitarian aid was directly distributed to the affected people in the civil war damaged areas. The structural aid was provided by the US and European countries through the government channel, namely the Ministry of grain. The most effective aid distribution program was carried out by the Aga Khan Foundation in GBAO named 'Program for Relief and Development of Pamir'. This program made sure that all households in the Pamir had access to flour, tea, dry milk and salt (Tadjbakhsh 1996). The international assistance to Tajikistan during the civil war was in sync with the international humanitarian law which establishes that the non-combatants in intra-state and interstate wars have a right to food and should not starve due to conflict (Cohen and Anderson 1999). Food aid was part of humanitarian assistance which was directly given to affected people in Tajikistan during civil war, as most of the local production resources were fully or partially damaged (Yao and Ruffer 2005). These were the times when wagons and wagons of humanitarian flour, oil and sugar were sent to Tajikistan by the international agencies (Imomberdieva 2015).

Another international organisation that provided crucial food and medical aid to Tajikistan during the civil war was the International Committee of the Red Cross (ICRC). ICRC provided relief supplies to the internally displaced persons between December 1992 and May 1993 in Dushanbe, Gharm valley and southern areas of Khatlon province. 2,100 tons of aid was given to 860,000 beneficiaries in these areas. Some 30,000 people who had taken shelter with their relatives in these areas too benefited from ICRC aid. Around 270,000 displaced people living near the Afghan border in the Kumsangir region too benefited (Bornet

1998). It was not only the civil war but also the natural disasters like earthquakes and floods that had struck Tajikistan in 1990s and impacted its grain production. The declining agricultural productivity over the years and low revenue resources made it difficult for the Tajik government to respond to food shortage, especially in times of emergencies. External assistance was also extended by countries like Russia, Turkey, India, Saudi Arabia and China (Pomfret 1995). Between 1988 and 2002, Tajikistan had received 1,305 thousand tons of food aid. In 2001, 22 percent of total available food in Tajikistan came from food aid (US Dept. of Agriculture, May 2004). Tajikistan imports around 50 percent of its cereals that it consumes (FAO 2013). The share of food aid has declined considerably and Tajikistan needs it only in times of crises like 2000-2001 droughts and 2008 winter crisis. In 2013-2014, Tajikistan received only 15,000 tons of food aid from WFP out of 2,186 thousand tons of cereals available in the country (FAO 2014).

TYPES OF INTERNATIONAL ORGANISATION HELPING TAJIKISTAN'S FOOD SECURITY

The international organisations and different nations have played a crucial role in ensuring Tajikistan's food security since its independence, particularly by providing humanitarian assistance in times of civil war and other crises. Tajikistan's international development partners include international financial institutions like the World Bank and Asian Development Bank, UN agencies like World Food Program (WFP) and Food and Agriculture Organisation (FAO) and international non-government organisations like German Agro Action, Mercy Corps and Aga Khan Development Network. Different states like the US, Russia, Japan, China, India and European Union too help Tajikistan in its development efforts. It is important to briefly examine how some of these organisations deal with food insecurity in Tajikistan and how is their assistance going to help Tajikistan in strengthening its capacity to tackle food crises in future.

ROLE OF INTERNATIONAL FINANCIAL INSTITUTIONS IN TAJIKISTAN'S FOOD SECURITY

International Financial Institutions (IFIs) help the developing countries to overcome their social and economic problems by extending loans and grants. They also provide policy guidance and technical assistance to manage their economy and development strategy. The role of main IFIs helping Tajikistan in its development and alleviating its agriculture and food security is discussed below.

World Bank

Agriculture is the most important sector in Tajikistan for improving livings standards, reducing poverty and ensuring food security as 70 percent of the population directly or indirectly depends on it and this sector contributes 20 percent to the GDP of Tajikistan (Ministry of Agriculture, Tajikistan 2012). Keeping this strategic importance of agriculture in view, World Bank has been focusing on it to improve living conditions in Tajikistan. In June 1993, Tajikistan joined the World Bank as a member state. World Bank initiated Farm Privatisation Support Project (FPSP) in 1999 to help land reform initiative of the Tajik government. The aim was to improve agriculture efficiency and contribution of agriculture sector to GDP (Sampath 2006b). It also aimed to develop institutional mechanisms and procedures to transfer land from state farms to private individuals and groups. It was required to create sustainable family farming practices so that individuals could operate in market conditions without state interference (World Bank Farm Privatisation Support Project 1999). The project lasted up to 2005 and cost World Bank USD 23.5 million. This project was critical in rebuilding Tajik agriculture after the ruinous civil war. As people were given access to land, they started growing food crops and food production picked up. The World Bank supports the agricultural sector in Tajikistan by investments in agricultural reforms and also by policy recommendations. Its efforts are also targeted at reducing food insecurity, repair irrigation networks and helping water management efforts. World Bank improves access to agriculture credit to ensure flow of better inputs for crop cultivation. It also ensures capacity building of the agriculture sector ministries by providing them technical assistance. Capacity building also focuses on climate change and its potential impact on the agriculture ecosystems. World Bank also comes out with periodic evaluation of its projects which serve as a lesson for future projects in the country (World Bank 2011).

The World Bank formulates its policies in Tajikistan through Country Partnership Strategy (CPS) which it brings out once in four years. This document serves as a guideline framework not only for the World Bank but also for the government of Tajikistan. It covers aspects like poverty, banking, food security, agriculture, energy, connectivity, gender, governance and climate change. The emphasis of the strategy was shifted from increasing agricultural productivity to increasing food security. A comprehensive reform strategy was launched with the government to cover land and water reforms, cotton debt, rural development and agriculture credit. The strategy also helped Tajik government in effectively dealing with the 2008 winter crisis and the economic slowdown in Tajik economy (World Bank CPS 2015-2018). During the CPS 2010-2013, three important projects for food security, Fergana Valley Water Resources Management, Land Registration and Cadaster for Sustainable Agriculture and the 2nd Public Employment for Sustainable Agriculture were completed. These three programs are very important for food security in Tajikistan. The water resource management project in Ferghana valley aims to increase agriculture productivity in Ferghana valley by making improvements in land and water resources of the area. The project for land registration and cadastre system aims to increase farm privatisation to increase land access for rural population. The third project focuses on temporary public employment for sustainable agriculture in twelve districts of Khatlon province. The project is expected to benefit around 770,000 people by increasing crop yields and better incomes through increased employment opportunities. These districts have been witnessing high levels of food insecurity and include Rumi, Jilikul, Rudaki, Vose, Pyanj, Hissor and Nosiri (World Bank Website). The overall portfolio of World Bank in Tajikistan has 13 projects estimated at USD 220.56 million. The largest share of this goes to agriculture and rural development (46 percent) as shown in figure 5.1. Next is energy with 16 percent, Public sector, governance and economic policy with 11 percent, Health and social protection with 8 percent, education and water both with 7 percent and private sector with 5 percent. Average age of World Bank projects in Tajikistan is 3.78 years. The new World Bank CPS for 2015-2018 was approved on June 10, 2014 with a funding of USD 280 million. This strategy will help Tajikistan in achieving better growth by increasing private sector investment and also improve employment opportunities for the poorest 40 percent of the population which will ensure their economic access to food.

Figure 5.1. World Bank Portfolio in Tajikistan.

Source: The World Bank Group-Tajikistan Partnership Program Snapshot: 2014

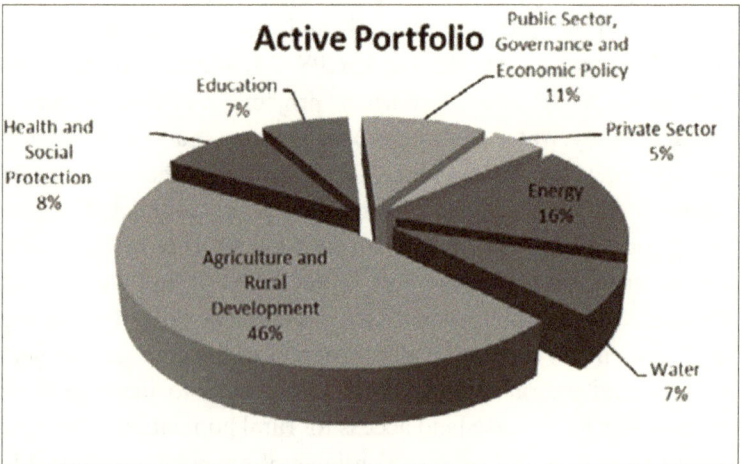

Social inclusion would be achieved by improved access to education, health, water and sanitation facilities. Another aim is to improve Tajikistan's access to regional and international markets by building better infrastructure (The World Bank Group-Tajikistan Partnership Program Snapshot 2014).Tajikistan is expected to suffer due to economic recession in Russia, as Tajik migrants send almost 50 percent of Tajik GDP in remittances.

World Bank assistance to Tajikistan comes with certain conditions of structural adjustment program which seeks to liberalise Tajik economy and open it to market reforms. The World Bank has been holding policy dialogues with Tajik government on poverty reduction, agriculture reforms, governance, fiscal policy and sustainability of debt. This broad and comprehensive approach is implicit in World Bank projects on agriculture, health, energy, transport and other sectors (International Monetary Fund 2004). Tajikistan is also a beneficiary of 'Governance Partnership Facility' which focuses on transparency and accountability in main sectors like energy and agriculture (World Bank 2012).Tajikistan has set an ambitious agenda for it to be achieved by 2020 – to double its GDP and reduce its poverty to 20 percent. Achievement of this target requires good economic growth. However, according to World Bank estimates, Tajikistan will have an annual growth rate of 6 percent between 2015 and 2018. Tajikistan needs to have better investment environment, reduce state control, expand private sector and connectivity to regional and world markets to double its GDP by 2020 (World Bank CPS 2015-2018). Keeping in view Tajikistan's weak economic capacity, it would continue to require assistance from the World Bank for achieving better levels of food security.

Asian Development Bank

Tajikistan joined the Asian Development Bank (ADB) in 1998. The initial focus of ADB in Tajikistan was on post-conflict and natural disaster rehabilitation activities and projects. It was the time when Tajikistan needed reconstruction assistance after five years of civil war. The later programs were more diversified in approach and focused on economic growth, infrastructure, regional connectivity, energy and agriculture issues. During the span of 15 years from 1998 to 2013, ADB has approved 38 projects worth USD 1.035 billion in Tajikistan and 61 percent of it was on grant basis. Transport sector in Tajikistan has received maximum funds from ADB, as it accounts for 42 percent of the total funding till 2013, as shown in the figure 5.2. This is followed by energy with 24 percent, agriculture with 9 percent, public sector management allocation with 8 percent, disaster and risk management operations with 6 percent, social sector with 4 percent, industry and trade with 3 percent, multi-sector 3 percent and finance receiving one percent of the total ADB funds (ADB Country Assistance Program Evaluation 2014).

Figure 5.2. Asian Development Bank Portfolio in Tajikistan.

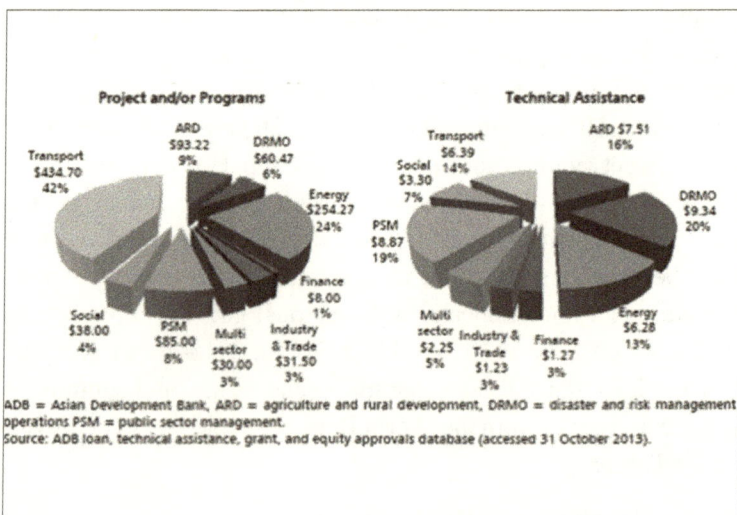

Project and/or Programs · Technical Assistance

ADB = Asian Development Bank, ARD = agriculture and rural development, DRMO = disaster and risk management operations PSM = public sector management.
Source: ADB loan, technical assistance, grant, and equity approvals database (accessed 31 October 2013).

Source: ADB Country Assistance Program Evaluation 2014: 15.

Every year, ADB prepares, evaluates and updates three-year rolling plans for Tajikistan. It consults other donors like World Bank, IMF and also the government of Tajikistan. ADB held these consultations while developing country partnership strategy 2010-2014. This strategy was in sync with the national development strategy of Tajikistan 2006-2015 as both of them aim to remove constraints of sustainable economic growth in the country. As per ADB Country Partnership Strategy 2016-20, the critical focus areas are energy and transport, access to clean water, social security, increased private sector role, gender, governance, climate change and regional cooperation. ADB has played an important role in improving food security situation by a number of measures in Tajikistan. It has supported programs and projects for rehabilitation of irrigation facilities covering 17.5 percent of total arable land amounting to 130,000 hectares. It has been committed to river basin approach for food security and water resource management in the country. The bank has completed a USD 35 million project for agriculture rehabilitation. The project aimed to provide improved seeds and farm machinery to farmers. It also trained farmers on soil fertility and crop husbandry. ADB was also at the forefront of efforts to get the cotton debt waived off in Tajikistan, as it hampered farmers' decision about what to cultivate. Due to debts, farmers were forced to grow cotton which had an impact on their food security. In 2009, a presidential decree abolished the USD 550 million cotton debt which allowed the farmers to grow food crops on their farms (ADB Country Assistance Program Evaluation 2014, Tajikistan Agriculture Rehabilitation Project 2014). ADB connected more than 90,000 new households to clean water supplies between 1998 and 2013 (ADB Development Effectiveness Brief 2013).

ADB has also taken lead in the Central Asian Regional Economic Cooperation (CAREC) program. It was started in 1997 to increase regional cooperation among Central Asian countries. The initiative has 10 members – China, Pakistan, Kazakhstan, Turkmenistan, Tajikistan, Kyrgyzstan, Uzbekistan, Afghanistan, Azerbaijan and Mongolia. The program intends to build six transnational corridors (rail and roadways) that will link these countries and facilitate trade and energy linkages. Apart from the ADB, five other donors – IMF, World Bank, European Bank for Reconstruction and Development (EBRD), Islamic Development Bank (IsDB) and United Nations Development Programme (UNDP) support this program. ADB has extended funding of USD 5.1 billion to the project between 2001 and 2011 (CAREC Website). Tajikistan had joined CAREC in 1998 and corridor 1, 3, 5 and 6 will transit Tajikistan, as shown in the map 5.1.Being a landlocked country, Tajikistan will benefit immensely from CAREC, as it will get connected to other countries by good quality roads. This will open up these markets for Tajik exports and will also facilitate import of foodstuffs at reasonable prices.

Map 5.1. CAREC Transport Corridors in Central Asia.

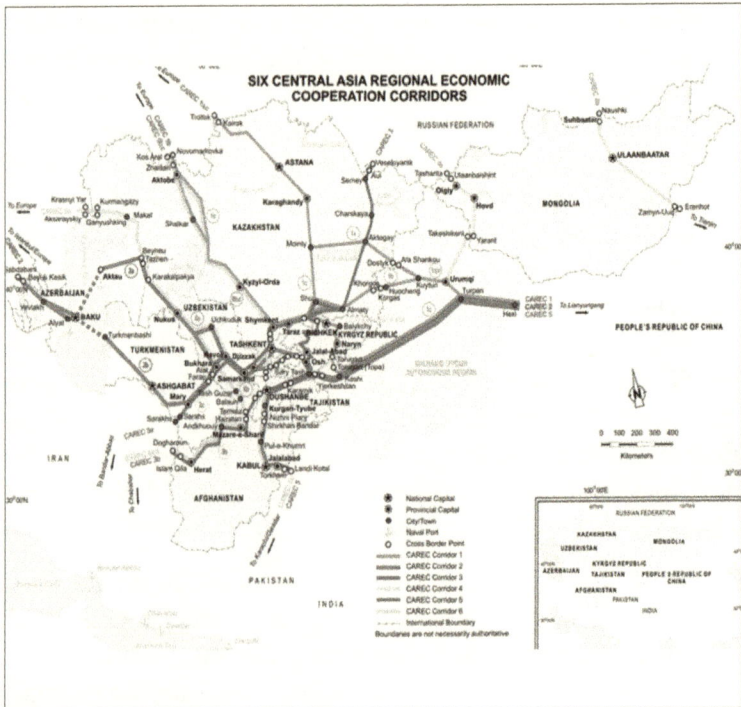

Source: CAREC Website.

The transport and transit costs are likely to come down which will decrease costs of its food imports. This will also lessen its dependence on Uzbekistan for transit of its food imports.

European Bank for Reconstruction and Development

European Bank for Reconstruction and Development was instituted in 1991 to help newly independent states of Central and Eastern Europe in their nation-building process. Tajikistan became a member of EBRD in 1992. The bank has implemented 89 projects in Tajikistan with an investment of € 384 million (EBRD Website). The financial institutions account for 41 percent of the total EBRD funding, industry, commerce and agriculture account for 40 percent while 19 percent share goes to infrastructure projects. The main focus of EBRD remains on development of private sector, strengthening financial sector and extending support to critical infrastructure with focus on municipal facilities and services (EBRD Strategy for Tajikistan 2012). It has granted USD 2.5 million loan to the Khujand water company to repair and rehabilitate an existing wastewater treatment plant. The bank has also initiated water projects in Khatlon, Sughd and Khorog. A USD 8 million project has been sanctioned in January 2015 for better water supply facilities and treatment of waste water in 20 cities of Tajikistan (New Europe Online January 30, 2015).

Ensuring access to water is one of the main tenants to guarantee food security. EBRD is also focusing on repairing the electricity infrastructure and restructuring the state power company, Bariki Tojik. Better access to electricity, especially in winters, helps in keeping houses warm and contributes to food security of people in Tajikistan. EBRD has also provided USD 770 million towards the CAREC program, which will help Tajikistan break its communication deadlock (CAREC Website). EBRD had collaborated with Schiever Tajikistan and started € 5 million discount hypermarket in Dushanbe. The project is expected to bring better standards in food quality and hygiene. It will also partner with local food suppliers to create food value chain (Pyrkalo 2014) and create jobs for people, thereby giving them income earning opportunities and strengthen their food purchasing power. At the same time, the local food cultivators, mainly vegetables and fruit growers, will have a place to sell their products which will encourage them for better production. EBRD has expressed concern over lack of genuine pluralism in Tajikistan as it hampers political and economic reforms in the country. The bank feels that possibility of social unrest cannot be totally ruled out in Tajikistan due to widespread unemployment and poverty, energy shortages and rising food prices (EBRD Strategy for Tajikistan 2012).

Islamic Development Bank

Islamic Development Bank (IsDB) was established in 1973 at Jeddah in Saudi Arabia at the first meeting of the Organisation of Islamic Cooperation (OIC). It has 56 member countries and the main members include Saudi Arabia, Iran, Turkey, Libya, Egypt and Kuwait (IsDB Website). Tajikistan was the third Central Asian country to join the IsDB in 1996, after Kyrgyzstan and Kazakhstan (Eurasianet July 12, 2007). The bank gives loans for 25 years with 7 years grace period at the interest rate of 2.5 percent per annum. At the end of 2013, the total development funding extended by IsDB to Tajikistan stands at USD 124,931,000. The highest allocation goes to transport with 31 percent, energy gets 22.2 percent, education 14 percent, agriculture 12.7 percent, water and sanitation 12.2 percent and health 10 percent (Tajikistan Foreign Aid Report 2013). In agriculture, Dangara valley irrigation project is the main investment by the bank. It includes development of the irrigation systems in the project area by constructing canals, tertiary canals, flood drains and drainage structures. There is also a water rehabilitation project in Dushanbe to repair municipal waterworks in the city at the cost of USD 2.4 million (Asia Plus December 11, 2013). The allocation of funds from the bank to different sectors in Tajikistan is shown in figure 5.3.

Figure 5.3. Islamic Development Bank Portfolio in Tajikistan.

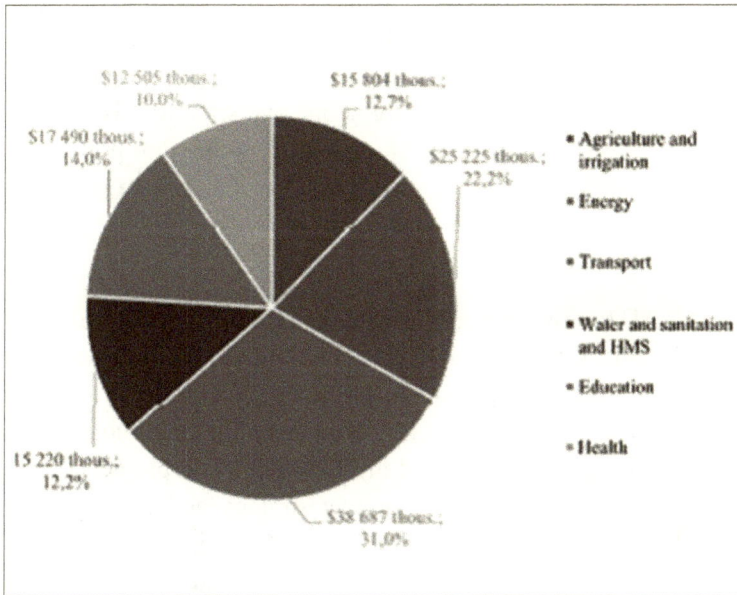

Source: Tajikistan Foreign Aid Report 2013

IsDB is also funding the Central Asia South Asia (CASA) – 1000 project that will allow export of summer surplus electricity of 1,300 MW from Kyrgyzstan and Tajikistan to Afghanistan and Pakistan. Other major financer of the project is World Bank and the IsDB has agreed to finance the funding gap in the project left after WB funding (Bhutta, October 29, 2014). The project will allow Tajikistan to generate necessary revenue to cover its energy needs in the winter months, when it faces severe energy shortages which also impact its food security. The 2008 winter 'compound crisis' explained in chapter 4 is a case in point.

International Fund for Agriculture Development

International Fund for Agriculture Development (IFAD) is an international financial institution and UN agency that was established in 1977. It was constituted as a result of the World Food Conference that was held in 1974 due to food shortages in Africa. Its aim is to provide financial assistance to agricultural programs mainly for food production in developing nations. The establishment of IFAD reflected the fact that food insecurity was not a function of production alone and structural issues like poverty too were important. The majority of the poor population was concentrated in rural areas of the world and there was need to address their poverty in order to ensure better food security for them (IFAD Website).

IFAD has two ongoing projects in Tajikistan worth USD 30.7 million and are benefitting 41,150 households in Khatlon province. Drought-resistant crops will be tested in these projects and they will increase incomes and nutrition intake of the target households by enhancing productivity of the livestock. The projects are in sync with the national development strategy and food security priorities of Tajikistan (Ibid). Khatlon has highest poverty in Tajikistan and that is why; IFAD has focused its activities to improve food security of the poor households in this region. IFAO will also invest over USD 30 million in Tajikistan to lessen poverty and propel economic growth in poor rural areas like Rasht and Tajikobod. Apart from the international financial institutions, there are UN agencies operating in Tajikistan providing it food aid and development assistance. Their role in ensuring food security in Tajikistan is discussed in next section.

ROLE OF UN AGENCIES IN TAJIKISTAN'S FOOD SECURITY

United Nations started its operations in Tajikistan in 1992 with establishment of the UN Tajikistan Office for Peace Building launching peace efforts during the civil war. There are 23 specialised agencies of UN that are assisting Tajikistan in matters of food security, gender, health, child rights, climate change, natural disasters, trade and economy etc. (United Nations in

Tajikistan Website). The role of the major UN agencies in alleviating Tajikistan's food security situation is discussed in succeeding paragraphs.

United Nations Development Program

United Nations Development Program (UNDP) has been present in Tajikistan since 1994. The goal of the organisation is to improve quality of lives in Tajikistan, especially of the poor and vulnerable sections and provide them equal opportunity and life of dignity. The UNDP focuses on local solutions to developmental problems and makes efforts to reduce poverty in Tajikistan. It also aims to meet Sustainable Development Goals (SDGs) targets, ensure accountability of the government and make efforts for sustainable development in the country to mitigate impact of climate change (Ibid). The UNDP has successfully undertaken a rural growth program in Sughd region. It also helps Tajikistan in facilitating better aid coordination among different donors and comes out with yearly 'Foreign Aid Report' in collaboration with UK Department for International Development and State Committee of Investments and State Property Management, Government of Tajikistan. Health initiatives include programs to tackle HIV/ AIDS, Malaria and Tuberculosis. It has also been working to increase natural disaster preparedness in the high-risk areas of Tajikistan. UNDP played an important role in responding to 2010 Kulob floods and Rasht earthquake in 2007. It is also assisting areas of south-west Tajikistan in combating land degradation and improving land management practices. UNDP is assisting the Tajik government in devising another national development strategy (NDS), as the current strategy ends in 2015.

UNDP harmonises efforts of all the UN agencies in Tajikistan. The UN Development Assistance Framework (UNDAF) regulates work of different UN agencies in the country. It has four pillars namely, poverty reduction, food security, clean water, energy and sustainable environment and better quality of basic services (UNDP Tajikistan Website). Poverty reduction strategy is one of the main solutions to food insecurity, as poverty alleviation increases access to food. UNDP has used community approach for ensuring food security in mountains of Gissar, thereby ensuring sustainable means of livelihood. Around 10,000 people have benefited from the project (Ibid). Keeping Tajikistan's low developmental levels in view, the UN agencies are expected to continue their developmental assistance to Tajikistan in near future including food security.

World Food Program

World Food Program (WFP) is one of the two UN agencies completely dedicated to providing food security in Tajikistan, other being Food and Agriculture Organisation. The UN established WFP in 1963 with the mandate of eradicating hunger in the world. There are two ways by which WFP fights hunger. In times of disasters like earthquake, drought, civil strife, failure of crops, WFP gives emergency food aid to the affected people. Secondly, it gives food assistance through programs like food for work in situations where people are chronically hungry. The contributions made to WFP are voluntary from donors. WFP remains the biggest international agency in Tajikistan possessing capacity to undertake projects in all the areas of Tajikistan (United Nations in Tajikistan Website).

WFP had played an instrumental role in tackling food insecurity in Tajikistan during the civil war, as the grain production had reduced due to conflict and there was shortage of food stuffs even in Dushanbe, as brought out in chapter 4. WFP started its Tajikistan operations in 1993. Between 1993 and 1999, WFP distributed humanitarian aid amounting to USD 60.6 million equalling 116,623 MT of wheat and flour. Around one million people benefited from WFP program during this period. Between July 1999 and July 2001, around 500,000 people benefited from WFP's food assistance program. During the 2000-2001 droughts and the compound crisis of 2008 winter, WFP provided humanitarian aid to people in rural and mountainous areas in

Tajikistan. In total between 1993 and 2013, WFP has given 762,000 MT of food worth USD 264 million to Tajikistan (Development Partner Profiles 2014).WFP had launched Protracted Relief and Recovery Operation (PRRO) 200122 in 2010 in its bid to alleviate food security situation in the country after the 2008 winter crisis. The program was to end in 2014 but has been extended up to December 31, 2015. The project supports food security of most vulnerable among the total food insecure estimated at 1.4 million in Tajikistan. It includes victims of recurrent natural disasters, children under the age of five suffering from acute malnutrition and also the patients of Tuberculosis (WFP Website). WFP gets food aid into Tajikistan through the Baltic port of Riga via Uzbekistan. Sometimes, the agency uses UN fleet of trucks to move the food consignments into far-off rural and mountainous areas. These are small trucks that can reach remote areas. Such services are needed when large amounts of food are to be transported, like during the 2000-2001 droughts (FAO/WFP 2000). WFP also comes out with periodic reports and food security bulletins for Tajikistan. These reports highlight monthly status of food security situation in Tajikistan which helps to plan for the potential future risks. In its February 2015 bulletin, WFP has said that depreciation of Tajik currency and high food prices have hampered access to food in the country while households have reduced food stocks due to low wheat and potato harvest. Tajik food security has been impacted by increased return of migrants from Russia. Remittances were main income source for 27 percent of households in November 2012 but in December 2014, this came down to 15 percent.

The areas that are vulnerable include Khatlon, Rasht valley, Ghonchi, east Pamir, and Istaravshan area (Asia Plus March 20, 2015).The importance of WFP assistance becomes clear when we see that in August 2012, cost of minimum food basket per person was USD 28.09 per month in Tajikistan (WFP 2012). This translates to USD 337.08 per person per year. However, Tajikistan had a per capita GDP of around USD 1,000 in 2013 (Asia Plus July 26, 2013). This means that around one-third of an individual's expenditure goes to food. But, one will struggle to make the ends meet if he has a family of four, as the food expenditure per year for four persons will be more than USD 1,000. That is why; WFP is playing an instrumental role in Tajikistan as it targets the vulnerable people who need food security assistance.

Food and Agriculture Organisation

Food and Agriculture Organisation (FAO) was established in 1945 with the motto 'Fiat Panis' meaning 'Let There Be Bread'. Food security is central to efforts of FAO as it strives for getting people access to good quality food to lead a healthy and active life. FAO has three goals – to eliminate hunger, malnutrition and food insecurity, eradication of poverty and sustainable management of the natural resources like water and land (FAO Website). FAO collects; analyses and disseminates information related to food security. It also shares its expertise with different countries and serves as a platform where nations can meet and discuss food security issues. In crises, FAO works side by side with organisations like WFP and other agencies to protect lives from hunger (UN Tajikistan Website). Tajikistan became member of FAO in 1995, when the food situation was getting worse in the country due to civil war. Tajik President Rahmon attended World Food Summit in 1996 at Rome organised by FAO. He spelt out Tajikistan's efforts to increase food self-sufficiency including land reforms during his speech at the summit. He also suggested that the developed countries should set up a fund at UN level to facilitate subsidised food purchase for the countries that are poor and undergoing transition (Rahmon's Speech at the FAO Summit 1996). The earliest engagements FAO handled in Tajikistan were related to emergency situations like helping refugees who were coming back to Tajikistan as the conflict was sliding down, assisting drought victims and rehabilitating ex-combatants. Owing to these developments, FAO opened its Emergency Coordination Office in Tajikistan in 1996. FAO changed its portfolio in 2002 and started focusing on developmental projects from emergency assignments. The organisation has been assisting Tajikistan in food security research and information. It also helps in development of early warning systems so that Tajikistan can prepare in advance for emergency food insecurity situations. The 2005 household budget survey was prepared through FAO assistance. FAO also trains Tajik officials and consultants in matters of food security (FAO 2009).

FAO has been gradually expanding its functions in Tajikistan as it classifies the country as the one facing protracted food crisis due to three conditions. One, Tajikistan has faced 11 food crises, man-made or natural between 1996 and 2010. Two, out of the total official development assistance (ODA) received by Tajikistan between this period, more than ten percent has been in form of humanitarian aid. Lastly, Tajikistan is a 'Low Income Food Deficit Country' with 30 percent of its population malnourished (Amir and Berry 2013). FAO has 20 operationally active projects in Tajikistan worth USD 17,965,032. They are related to phyto-sanitary control services, developing seed sector, management and disposal of pesticides, strengthening management of national food security system and providing small farmers access to good quality seeds (FAO Technical Cooperation Department Website). FAO has also launched a USD 400,000 project in the country for pest management services. Participants will exchange practical experiences that will facilitate local adaptation to pest management (Asia Plus February 9, 2015). In a major food security initiative, FAO has also started promoting quinoa in Tajikistan, A USD 50,000 project has been launched in Tajikistan for providing technical assistance to promote and introduce quinoa. FAO wants to make it a food for local populations as quinoa is nutritious food and can withstand dry and salty environs (Charles August 21, 2014). Hence, promoting quinoa will also enhance community adaptability to climate change in Tajikistan. Apart from UNDP, WFP and FAO, there are other UN agencies like UN Population Fund (UNFPA), World Health Organisation (WHO), UN Office on Drugs and Crime (UNODC), UN High Commissioner for Refugees

(UNHCR), UN Children's Fund (UNICEF), International Labour Organization (ILO), International Organization for Migration (IOM) and UN Women etc. These agencies provide assistance to Tajikistan and look after different aspects of food security in the country.

INTERNATIONAL NON-GOVERNMENT ORGANISATIONS

There is a big presence of international non-government organisations (INGOs) in Tajikistan which carry out socio-economic activities in the country and help its development strategy. These INGOs include Oxfam International, Action Against Hunger, Deutsche Welthungerhilfe or German Agro Action, United States Agency for International Development (USAID), Mercy Corps, Aga Khan Development Network and Save the Children. The role of some of these organisations in Tajikistan's agriculture and food security is discussed below.

United States Agency for International Development

United States Agency for International Development (USAID) started working in Tajikistan in 1993 and has been assisting Tajikistan in areas of health, water and sanitation, agriculture and food security and democratic institutions. It has helped in building 57 water systems providing clean drinking water to around 190,000 people in provinces of Sughd and Khatlon. USAID has also helped to vaccinate 95 percent children under the age of five for polio and helped Tajikistan in stopping spread of the deadly disease (USAID Website). Since 1993, USAID has allocated more than USD 360 million to developmental assistance in Tajikistan. It also works in close cooperation with the different ministries, other INGOs, donors and communities to raise the living standards of Tajik population (Development Partner Profiles 2014). Initially, USAID provided emergency food aid in Tajikistan during the civil war years when there was a humanitarian food crisis in the country. However, now USAID focuses on efforts to increase food productivity in Tajikistan (Addleton May 20, 2014). USAID has been focusing on the agriculture sector to enhance food security in Tajikistan. US government's initiative 'Feed the Future' focuses to reduce poverty and hunger in around 20 countries all over the world and Tajikistan is one of them. The initiative aims to reduce poverty and malnutrition among children under age of five in its areas of operation by 20 percent. In Tajikistan, Khatlon province has been selected as the area of operation due to high poverty and malnutrition rates in the province. Around 200,000 vulnerable households will get food security assistance in this area. In 2011, USAID helped in increasing productivity of farmers and agribusinesses by USD 2 million (USAID Website). USAID has also initiated a project worth USD 5,400,000 named 'Land Reform and Farm Restructuring Project' in Tajikistan to increase food security of farmers. The project provides legal assistance to farmers through local NGOs to get land use rights and make them aware of their land rights. It also provides assistance to government to bring a better land policy and legislation (Mennen November 5, 2014).

Aga Khan Development Network

Aga Khan Development Network (AKDN) is a private non-denominational organisation working in 30 countries all over the world. It is run by Aga Khan IV, spiritual leader of the Shia Ismaili Muslims all over the world. The initial activities of AKDN were related to Ismaili Muslims in South Asia and East Africa but gradually, the activities have spread to areas where Ismailis do not live and AKDN also works for a cross-section of population (AKDN Website). Most of the inhabitants of GBAO are followers of Aga Khan's branch of Shia Ismaili Islam in Tajikistan. The residents of this region have been Ismailis since 11[th]century. Persian philosopher and poet, Nasir-i-Khusraw became devout Ismaili in Egypt. However, he feared persecution and left Egypt to settle in Pamirs in 11th century, laying the foundations of Shia

Ismaili branch of Islam in the region (Capisani 2000). GBAO was an autonomous region within the Tajik Soviet Socialist Republic under Soviet Union and it continued to be so after Tajikistan's independence in 1991. Around 85 percent of the food supplies for the region came from outside during Soviet period. These supplies were hit by the civil war and due to cessation of food supplies from Russia as USSR disintegrated. There was a threat of famine in GBAO in 1991 when the Aga Khan Foundation (AKF) initiated an emergency food aid program. This was followed by an immediate long-term development strategy for the region focusing on agrarian reform. A policy for land and herd privatisation was quickly started in the region. The individuals were given access to land by privatising it and the foundation gave them technical assistance and financial help for better quality seeds and fertilisers. This proved to be a big boost to food self-sufficiency in GBAO, which increased from 15 percent at the end of Soviet Union to 50 percent in 2002 (Middleton 2013).

AKF had signed a memorandum of understanding with the government of Tajikistan to set up Pamir Relief and Development Programme (PRDP) in 1993 to distribute food aid in the region. The food situation in GBAO was made worse by inflow of around 70,000 internal refugees to the region from Dushanbe and Khatlon due to civil war. In 1997, name of PRDP was changed to Mountain Societies Development Support Programme (MSDSP) and its operations were expanded to Rasht valley and mountainous eastern districts of Khatlon as well. MSDSP uses village organisation in its socio-economic development efforts for sustainable development of these regions in Tajikistan. This is also a model of building a vibrant civil society in Tajikistan and empowering people to set their own development agenda (Tetley and Jonbekova 2005). Food security is central to activities of MSDSP and it helps farmers to increase their income. It focuses on increasing production of vegetables and fruits and also gives attention to livestock rearing. Rehabilitation of forests in mountainous areas is done to support wood and fuel supply in these isolated areas. Access to fuel in winters is important for ensuring food security (AKDN Website).

The AKDN has a developmental agenda in Tajikistan which is not merely limited to food security and ventures into fields of health, education, infrastructure development and energy etc. AKDN along with the World Bank and government of Tajikistan in a public-private partnership (PPP) model has established the Pamir Energy project and 70 percent of the total consumers get access to electricity in GBAO in the severe winter months by this project (World Bank Website). University of Central Asia has been started in 2000 by AKDN and the governments of Tajikistan, Kazakhstan and Kyrgyzstan. The health care projects involve training community health promoters, providing affordable medicines and rehabilitation of hospitals in GBAO (AKDN Website). GBAO has been a politically unstable region in Tajikistan and even slight fears of political instability pose a risk to food security of the mountainous areas. Food prices rose immediately after the 2012 military operation in Khorog. Cabbage prices doubled while those of potatoes and flour rose by more than 30 percent (BBC Monitoring Global Newsline - Central Asia Political August 4, 2012). That is why; there is need for the presence of international NGOs like AKDN in mountainous areas to respond to such events which impact food security in the remote areas.

Mercy Corps

Mercy Corps is an international non-government organisation which aims to alleviate poverty, suffering and oppression and help communities in overcoming these challenges. Mercy Corps has been working in Tajikistan since 1994. It focuses on bringing innovation and sustainability while dealing with local problems (Development Partner Portfolios 2014). Mercy Corps deals with conflict through better governance by building community cohesiveness through improvements in land, water and energy rights. It helps the remote villages in Tajikistan and prepares them in dealing with natural disasters. It also works for health and women rights. Mercy Corps in collaboration with the Xylem

Watermark Inc. has started Disaster Risk Reduction Initiative (DRRI) in Hisor district. The project aims to increase access of people to clean and safe drinking water by solar disinfection technology. Seasonal floods and mudslides limit access to clean water in the area. Around 5,000 households including 30,000 people will benefit by this project (Long, March 7, 2013). The organisation is also helping food insecure houses in Rasht valley in improving their living resilience. These houses are given training to increase their food production.

Welthungerhilfe or German Agro Action

German Agro Action (GAA) is a Germany based international NGO which seeks to eliminate global hunger with sustainable food security efforts. The organisation promotes agriculture which suits local needs and conditions, provides access to clean water, innovative and environment friendly energy solutions and also improves health and education standards (Welthungerhilfe Website). GAA opened its operations in Tajikistan in 1994. The initial focus of the organisation was on rehabilitation and emergency aid due to humanitarian crisis generated by the civil war. These were the times when wagons and wagons of flour, oil and sugar were sent to Tajikistan by international community. Between 1994 and 2000, GAA was also focusing on infrastructural rehabilitation works like building the destroyed bridges, irrigation channels and drinking water systems in Tajikistan (Imomberdieva 2015). The focus has now shifted to sustainable approach as Tajikistan's economy has started progressing and food situation too has improved in the country. GAA follows the LRRD (Linking Relief, Rehabilitation and Development) approach in Tajikistan. Since 1994, GAA has implemented more than 90 projects in Tajikistan worth € 90 million. The beneficiaries of the projects are rural houses lacking access to natural resources, poor farmers, women and marginalised sections. The poor and food insecure people in 12 districts if Sughd, Khatlon and Region of Republican Subordination are focus of GAA projects (GAA Tajikistan

Program Factsheet). GAA works for food and nutrition security of the people in Tajikistan through giving them assistance in agriculture. The priorities are the agricultural extension activities, good quality seed provision, and education of the farmers who very often lack knowledge about agriculture management. The organisation is using innovative methods like honey processing and local tourism as income generating sources for the people. A communication system to be used in emergencies has been installed in around 20 villages in Zeravshan and Rasht valley. These areas are prone to flooding and earthquakes and an efficient communication system in these villages during natural disasters can save a lot of lives and can minimise damage (Development Partner Profiles 2014).Apart from the international financial institutions, UN agencies and international NGOs, Tajikistan also gets foreign aid and investments from countries like US, Russia, European Union, China, Saudi Arabia and India among others. The details are discussed in the next section.

FOREIGN AID TO TAJIKISTAN FROM DIFFERENT COUNTRIES

Tajikistan had been receiving food aid and developmental assistance from different countries since 1991, however, aid flow and strategic importance of Tajikistan increased after the US invaded Afghanistan in 2001 as Tajikistan shares border with Afghanistan. Tajikistan received USD 162.55 million worth of financial assistance from the US in 2002, compared to USD 78.39 million in 2001 (Gures 2011). Tajikistan has been supporting US-NATO operations in Afghanistan and since it shares border with Afghanistan, it becomes important to keep Tajikistan stable and away from influence of extremists. Instability in Tajikistan could have further spill over effects on other Central Asian countries too. That is why; Russia, China, India, EU and the US have been providing large amounts of aid to Tajikistan to help its economy. The external aid and assistance has shifted to supporting reforms and development in Tajikistan from initial focus on humanitarian aid. Donor countries had given Tajikistan USD 2,527,388,000 through bilateral mechanism in aid between 2002 and 2013. Highest amount of aid (40 percent) came from China and stood at USD 1,000,430,000. Other major donors include the United States of America (12.2 percent with USD 307,234,000), Japan (10 percent with 251,498,000) and Germany (7.4 percent with 186,871,000). Bilateral donor aid reached its peak in 2008 when Tajikistan was undergoing a compound food-water-energy crisis, totalling to USD 388,749,000, as depicted in figure 5.4. However, due to global economic slowdown after 2008, the amount of aid to Tajikistan has also gone down between 2009 and 2013 (Foreign Aid Review 2013).

Figure 5.4. Flow of Foreign Aid and Assistance to Tajikistan (2002-2013).

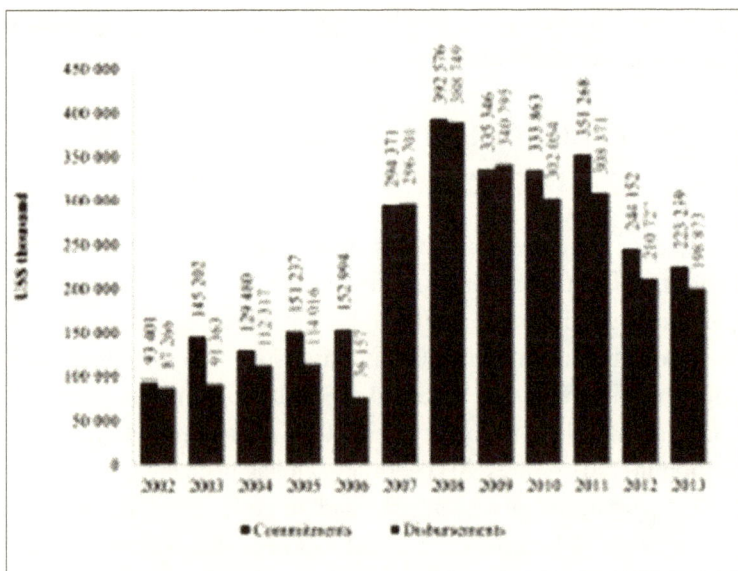

Source: Foreign Aid Review 2013.

Figure 5.5 shows foreign aid given by bilateral, multilateral sources and the NGOs in the agriculture and irrigation sector between 2002 and 2013.

Figure 5.5. Aid Given to Agriculture Sector in Tajikistan by Different Sources.

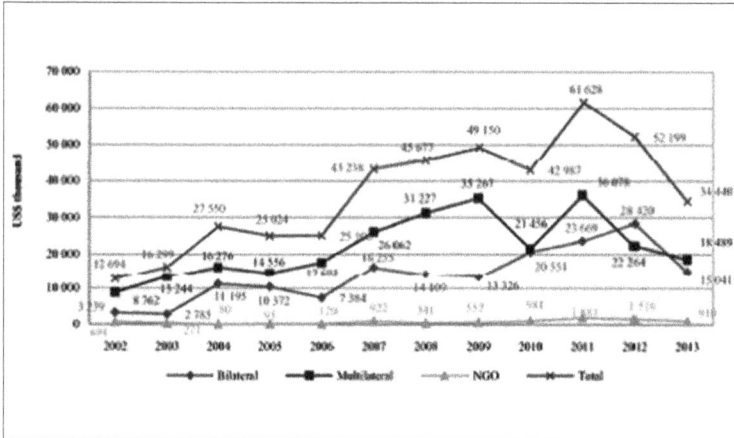

Source: Foreign Aid Review 2013.

After peaking in 2011, the amount of aid to agriculture and irrigation sector has come down in 2012 and 2013 (Ibid). The gradual increase in overall foreign aid to Tajikistan after 2001 is due to the fact that Tajikistan pursues an 'open door' foreign policy, as President Rahmon himself has acknowledged it (Asia Plus April 26, 2013). He seeks to engage the West and also other important countries like Russia, China, India, Japan, South Korea, Iran and Saudi Arabia. His efforts have been successful as the share of foreign aid given by non-DAC countries to Tajikistan has increased substantially. Non-DAC countries are the ones which are not members of Development Assistance Committee of the Organisation for Economic Co-operation and Development (OECD) nations. Around 45.7 percent of the total USD 2, 527,388 thousand aid received by Tajikistan between 2002 and 2013 has come from the non-DAC countries which include India, Iran, China, Russia, Kuwait and Saudi Arabia.[1] However, China dominates among this group with 40 percent of the total

---

1   Calculations based on the data from Foreign Aid Report of Tajikistan, 2013.

aid. This is explained by the fact that China has launched its 'Go West' policy to engage with the Central Asian and European countries. China's energy trade with the Central Asian countries has increased many times and it is also investing in transport infrastructure in Tajikistan. Tajikistan is looking for Chinese investments in the wake of economic slowdown in Russia due to Western sanctions. China is expected to invest USD 6 billion in Tajikistan till 2017 (Farchy, October 10, 2014). Non-DAC aid is usually unconditional unlike Western aid, which emphasises democracy and human rights along with economic reforms in Tajikistan. Hence, Tajikistan favours such type of aid (Save the Children, May 2009).

STATE RESPONSE TO INTERNATIONAL AID IN TAJIKISTAN

Given such a large presence of aid providers in Tajikistan, it becomes necessary to coordinate the aid so that there is no duplication of efforts and less time is required for the recipient nation for achieving its developmental goals. There are different aid coordination mechanisms that exist in Tajikistan. Tajikistan's State Committee on Investment and State Property Management (SCISPM) brings out an annual issue of Foreign Aid Report. The technical assistance is given by UNDP while financial assistance is given by UK's Department for International Development (DFID). The aim of the report is to bring out all the relevant information regarding foreign aid in Tajikistan which can help donors to better formulate their policies. It aims to make cooperation easier between the stakeholders, prevents duplication of projects and also gives a glimpse of aid effectiveness in the country (Foreign Aid Review 2013). SCISPM was established in Tajikistan in 2006 to focus on coordination of foreign aid. 12 main donors like World Bank, ADB, UN agencies and Aga Khan Foundation signed 'Joint Country Partnership Strategy 2010–2012' with the government of Tajikistan in 2009. Under the strategy, regular meetings were held by the food security cluster for streamlining and better coordinating food security policies in Tajikistan (FAO 2011). Under the Joint Country Partnership Strategy 2010–2012, the government of Tajikistan has agreed to lead the foreign aid received by Tajikistan and also see if it is aligned with its national development strategy or not. The development partners have agreed to boost government's capability for aid coordination (Joint Country Partnership Strategy 2010–2012).

Development Coordination Council (DCC) was established in Tajikistan in 2007 to facilitate better aid coordination and interaction among the donors and between the government and the donors. Heads of all the development organisations are members of the DCC (ADB, June 1, 2011). The heads of the 26 donor agencies constitute the membership of the council (UN Tajikistan Website).Tajikistan has been moving away from humanitarian assistance towards development assistance. Between 1991 and 1996, it required emergency and rehabilitation aid, post-conflict reconstruction assistance between 1997 and 2001 and developmental assistance after 2001. The international community has responded positively, as Tajikistan received USD 16 million in aid in 1992 (Aminjanov et. al. 2009) which reached around 198 million in 2013 (Foreign Aid Review 2013).

LIMITS TO INTERNATIONAL AID EFFORTS IN TAJIKISTAN

There are problems regarding aid coordination and effectiveness in Tajikistan. There is lack of clear and detailed legal framework to attract foreign aid to Tajikistan. On one hand, the government is attracting the foreign donors while on the other hand, it uses tax regime to extract maximum from the donors in form of taxes. That is why; aid effectiveness suffers as part of the aid is used for payment of taxes rather than on the projects. Tajikistan lacks proper capacity to monitor aid, as it lacks trained professionals in this regards. No university in Tajikistan trains students in this regard (Aminjanov et. al. 2009). In an ideal situation, the government of the recipient country should determine its development priorities while the donors should use government institutions wherever needed. Some donors including the World Bank feel that Tajikistan's institutions are weak and it has a poor governance record. Some donors see commitment of Tajikistan government to its development strategy as mixed. Some feel that government views its national development strategy as a means of securing foreign funds as it carries a price tag which is twice the budget of the government (Save the Children, May 2009). Lack of cooperation from the government and corruption are two issues cited by the European Court of Auditors as reasons for failure of EU aid in Central Asia. The court suggested that EU should be tough while managing aid programs in Tajikistan and should tie them to anti-corruption provisions (Euractiv, January 21, 2014). There is widespread corruption in Tajikistan and it is ranked 154th out of 177 countries in the corruption index of Transparency International (Asia Plus December 3, 2013). The International Monetary Fund (IMF) had ordered in 2008 that Tajikistan should return USD 47 million loan as the authorities had secured it by submitting false records about status of national reserves (Abdullaev and Akbarzadeh 2010). A FAO evaluation report had found that it was difficult for the international donors to engage the Tajik government on issues of policy, even in cases where it was part of the strategy. There was limited demand from the government for development of policy and often, the government was content with large and ambiguous legal frameworks related to important issues like land reform. The government lacked the will to come up with clear and precise laws (FAO 2009).

Despite these shortcomings, the support of the international community to Tajikistan's development is evident from the fact that per capita foreign aid increased from USD 35.9 in 2002 to USD 57.4 in 2013. It had even increased to USD 78.3 in 2009, when Tajikistan was facing the compound crisis of water-energy-food problems (Foreign Aid Review 2013).The international donors and the government have been trying to enhance food security by aligning their activities. The land reforms launched by the Tajik authorities have received financial and technical support from the international donors. The international community complements efforts made by government of Tajikistan for ensuring food security of the masses. The UN agencies help the Tajik government in formulating its development strategy while other development partners devise their policies in Tajikistan according to this strategy. Efforts have been made to coordinate foreign aid through the Development Coordination Council. However, some donors are suspicious of Tajik government's commitment to reform and governance record. Corruption is also an issue of concern for them and they seek more openness in the Tajik economic and political system. However, this has not stopped the international community from helping Tajikistan in its development efforts. They provide technical assistance, capacity building and financial support to Tajikistan for achieving its food security. Tajikistan needs foreign assistance in its efforts to achieve its three strategic goals – energy security, food security and to solve Tajikistan's communication deadlock. The Development Coordination Council has announced its support to Tajikistan for assisting the country in achieving goals of its National Development Strategy between 2016 and 2030 (Development Coordination Council February 10, 2015). This shows that the foreign financial and technical assistance will continue to play an important role in Tajikistan's development including food security in near future as well.

CHAPTER 6

CONCLUSION

Human security has gained importance in international relations after end of Cold War. It has seven elements - economic, food, health, environmental, personal, community and political. Food security comes under 'freedom from want' approach in human security. It remains central to human security as it ensures survival of an individual. Threats to food security like poverty and hunger are also threats to human security. These threats are transnational in character having the potential to endanger global security. Weak states struggle to achieve food security as they lack sufficient economic resources. Food insecurity, in turn, also helps in generating a weak state structure as a large number of people migrate to other countries in search of employment to achieve food security. This decreases manpower in agriculture sector which suffers due to neglect and food production comes down. Regional economic cooperation could be one of the ways to ensure food security as trade barriers are lowered and regional infrastructure can be improved to facilitate flow of food from surplus to deficient areas. States should try to ensure food security for their people, especially the marginalised sections, as propounded by John Rawls through his principle of 'distributive justice'. It means states should make sure that the least advantaged sections of society like women, children, elderly and poor have access to food. Concept of food justice also implies that marginalised sections should be protected against hunger despite existence of social and economic inequalities. Distributive justice has implications for food security at international, national and household level. At international level, least developed countries should be helped by developed countries through better trade and agriculture agreements to ensure their food security. At national level, it means that state governments should shield less empowered sections from hunger. At household level, distributive justice means food security of women and children should not be threatened. There are linkages between food security and political stability. Conflict and political instability lead to food insecurity, as food could be used a weapon by the warring factions. Conflict also decreases agriculture production which creates food problems. On the other hand, food insecurity could also create social unrest and political instability, as happened during the 2007-08 global food crisis. However, food problems alone rarely lead to political instability and existence of other factors like political repression, unemployment and corruption combine to cause social and political instability.

The genesis of present day food insecurity in Tajikistan lies in the policy of cotton monoculture introduced by the Tsarist regime in Central Asia and later followed vigorously by the former Soviet Union. Tsarist Russia saw Central Asia as a potential cotton growing area and this was one of the main reasons why Russia conquered this region. Most parts of present day Tajikistan were parts of emirate of Bukhara which was despotically ruled by its emirs. The agriculture remained technically backward while hunger and starvation prevailed in the republic. Bukhara had been traditionally a grain growing area but the Russians encouraged cotton cultivation in the emirate. Russian banks, firms and other credit institutions were providing credit to Central Asian farmers to grow cotton. Bukhara was integrated in to the capitalist Russian economy through construction of Trans-Caspian railway and Orenburg-Tashkent rail line which facilitated huge supplies of Central Asian cotton to European Russia. Prices of Central Asian cotton rose by 74 percent in Moscow between 1891 and 1914 which increased cotton cultivation in Bukhara by six times between 1880 and 1915. This increase in cotton came at the expense of grains and foodstuffs were supplied to Bukhara by

Moscow through Orenburg-Tashkent rail line. This rail line was cut-off during civil war which disrupted food supplies to Bukhara, creating famine in the emirate. The Basmachi movement started fighting against Russian rule in Bukhara. Both, the Soviet government and the Basmachis used food as a strategic weapon to win public support against each other. The areas of Bukhara came under Tajikistan when it was made a Soviet republic in 1929. Basmachi activity delayed economic and political consolidation of the Soviet power in Tajikistan and its development levels lagged behind other republics in Central Asia. Joseph Stalin started his collectivisation drive to replace Lenin's New Economic Policy in his bid for socialist reconstruction of Soviet agriculture. Collectivisation had social, economic and political implications for Tajikistan. Socially, it strengthened tribal, regional and clan loyalties in Tajikistan. Economically, it increased cotton cultivation replacing grain cultivation. Politically, the Communist Party of Tajikistan was purged by Stalin and Russians or the Slavs assumed powerful positions in the party. During the Second World War, Soviet Union faced food shortages and Tajikistan increased grain cultivation to supply food to soldiers fighting at the war front. Soviet Union resumed pro-cotton policies in Tajikistan after the war by offering high cotton procurement prices to farmers. In 1952, the procurement price of cotton per ton was almost 37 times higher than that of grains. Food problems started in Tajikistan during 1980s, as it was witnessing rapid population growth. Food supply could not match population growth in the republic creating food shortages. Gorbachev's reforms of glasnost and perestroika increased poverty and unemployment in Tajikistan. It had lowest consumption of food per capita in Soviet Union. Cereal production decreased by 17 percent and food production by 12 percent in Tajikistan between 1988 and 1991 and it was forced to import around 80 percent of its food requirements. Food shortages were one of the underlying causes of 'Dushanbe riots' that broke out in 1990. Tajikistan declared its independence from Soviet Union on September 9, 1991. Glasnost had unleashed hidden political forces in Tajikistan and different factions started to compete in order to fill the power vacuum created by fall of Soviet Union.

Tajikistan was embroiled in a civil war after it gained independence in 1991. Different rivals were competing for controlling power and natural resources like cotton and land. The civil war had a devastating impact on the economy and agriculture of Tajikistan. GDP declined by 60 percent between 1991 and 1997 while the total economic loss by this war was around USD 10 billion. In 1995, agriculture output declined by 40 percent compared to its 1991 level. The flow of food supplies from Moscow was stopped creating food shortages and forcing the government to start food rationing. The daily bread usage was limited between 170-249 grams. This was just 40 percent of the 600 grams limit fixed by Soviet authorities during the Second World War. Kulob and GBAO even faced economic blockades which created famine conditions in these provinces. People were forced to eat even tree bark in Kulob. Since the government lacked enough economic resources to support agriculture, it started land reforms to privatise agrarian set up and encourage farmers to increase food production. These reforms were already delayed due to civil war. The reforms have increased land under household plots which has increased food production. However, there are a number of problems in these reforms. The land remains a state property and the individuals only have land use rights. Land reforms have not been completed due to slow pace. Local officials still ask farmers to grow cotton to fulfil cotton quotas. The awareness about the reforms remains low and farmers have to pay extra money to secure land use rights. There is lack of mechanisation in agriculture while irrigation systems need repair. The state, however, does not have economic capacity to modernise the agriculture.

Food insecurity has also impacted society in Tajikistan. A large number of people, mainly males have migrated to other countries for finding employment in order to be food secure. The agriculture lacks manpower and faces neglect which reduces food production adding to food problems. Tajik diet is rich in fats and lacks antioxidants which lead to cardiovascular diseases.

Diseases related to iodine and iron deficiency are also widespread in Tajikistan. The food crisis during civil war and the severe drought in 2001 had led to fertility decline in Tajikistan. Since a large number of males have migrated from the country, females are heading the households and are also working in their farms along with their children. Tajikistan's social security schemes are small, lack funds and cover a small number of people and most of the people vulnerable to food insecurity do not get state protection. Climate change could decrease crop yields in Tajikistan while temperature is expected to rise in the country. This could further create food shortages in Tajikistan and vulnerable groups like women, children, poor and elderly would be at risk. The economy of Tajikistan is in a state of transition struggling to be self-sustaining. Around half of the GDP depends on remittances from abroad and disruption of these remittances could hinder food security of the people who depend on them. Tajikistan has lowest development levels in Central Asia along with Kyrgyzstan. In the Human Development Index 2013, Tajikistan ranked 133 out of 187 countries in 2013. It is important to note that Tajikistan's HDI value has come down from 0.610 to 0.607 between 1990 and 2013 corresponding to 0.02 percent decrease per annum. Income disparity is wide and consumption of the richest 10 percent in Tajikistan is six times that of the poorest 10 percent. Lack of income generating opportunities hinders poor peoples' access to food. Tajikistan has faced food insecurity created by political instability, as was evident during the civil war. However, it is unlikely that food insecurity could create political instability in Tajikistan, as the people still remember the hardships faced during the civil war and they prefer relative stability to uncertain future.

In view of the failure on the part of state institutions in addressing the food crisis, the international actors are trying to fill the deficit. Tajikistan's National Development Strategy (2015-2030) and its Poverty Reduction Strategy 2010-2012 are the main documents that relate to its developmental planning. These documents underline the fact that since Tajikistan is the poorest state in Central Asia, it requires foreign aid, grants and assistance for its development. These documents see an important role of foreign aid in Tajikistan. The focus of foreign aid in Tajikistan has now shifted to sustainable development assistance from humanitarian assistance. Food security assistance forms a component of sustainable development assistance. Earlier, Tajikistan received huge food aid from international community as part of humanitarian assistance, mainly during the civil war and some years after it. However, in times of crises like floods, earthquakes and compound crisis like that of 2008, Tajikistan could still need food aid for the affected people. The donor agencies get together and launch Consolidated Appeals Process (CAP) in times of severe crises. This appeal makes a rough estimate of the money required to overcome the crisis and requests humanitarian donations from the world community to gather required amount of funds (UN Office of the High Commissioner for Human Rights Website). Since the economy of Tajikistan has been recovering in the previous decade, the international agencies shifted their approach from humanitarian assistance to sustainable development assistance. Here, there is no specific focus on food security and equal priority is given to all sectors that impact food security like energy, water, transport, health and environment. This signifies the development oriented approach to ensure food security. The support of the international community to Tajikistan's development is evident from the fact that per capita foreign aid increased from USD 35.9 in 2002 to USD 57.4 in 2013. It had even increased to USD 78.3 in 2009, when Tajikistan was facing the compound crisis of water-energy-food problems (Foreign Aid Review 2013). The international donors and the government have been trying to enhance food security by aligning their activities. The land reforms launched by the Tajik authorities have received financial and technical support from the international donors. The international community complements efforts made by government of Tajikistan for ensuring food security of the masses. The UN agencies help the Tajik government in formulating its development strategy while other development partners devise their policies in Tajikistan according to this strategy. Efforts have been made to coordinate foreign aid through the Development Coordination Council. However, some donors are suspicious of Tajik government's commitment to reform and governance record. Corruption is also an issue of concern for them and they seek more openness in the Tajik economic and political system. However, this has not stopped the international community from helping Tajikistan in its development efforts. They provide technical assistance, capacity building and financial support to Tajikistan for achieving its food security. Tajikistan needs foreign assistance in its efforts to achieve its three strategic goals – energy security, food security and to solve Tajikistan's communication deadlock. The Development Coordination Council has announced its support to Tajikistan for assisting the country in achieving goals of its National Development Strategy between 2016 and 2030 (Development Coordination Council February 10, 2015). This shows that the foreign financial and technical assistance will continue to play an important role in Tajikistan's development including food security in near future as well.

REFERENCES

BOOKS

Abazov, Rafis (2005), *Cultures Of The World: Tajikistan*, New York: Cavendish, Marshall Corporation.

Abazov, Rafis (2008), *"Palgrave Concise Historical Atlas of Central Asia"*, New York: Palgrave MacMillan.

Abdel, Mohammed and Rahim Mohamed (2009), *Climate Change and Sustainable Development: New Challenges for Poverty Reduction*, Glos: Edward Elgar Publishing. Inc.

Abdullaev, Kamoludin and Shahram Akbarzadeh (2010), *"Historical Dictionary of Tajikistan"*, Maryland: The Scarecrow Press Inc.

Abdurakhimova, N A (2005), "Tsarist Russia and Central Asia", in Chahryar Adle et al. (eds.) *History of Civilizations of Central Asia: Towards the contemporary period: from the mid-nineteenth to the end of the twentieth century Vol VI*, Paris: UNESCO Publisher.

Akiner, Shirin (2001), *"Tajikistan: Disintegration or Reconciliation?"*, The Royal Institute of International Affairs, London.

Akiner, Shirin (2005), "Political Processes in Post-Soviet Central Asia", in M P Amineh and H Houweling (eds.) *Central Eurasia in Global Politics. Conflict, Security, and Development*, Leiden: Koninklijke Brill NV.

Alastair McAuley (1992), 'The Central Asian Economy', in M. Ellman and V. Kontorovich (eds), The Disintegration of the Soviet Economic System, London: Routledge quoted in Stringer, Alex (2003), "Soviet Development in Central

Asia – A Classical Colonial Syndrome?", in Tom Everett Heath (eds.) *Central Asia – Aspects of Transition*, London: RoutledgeCurzon.

Allworth, Edward (eds.) (1994), *"Central Asia: 130 Years of Russian Dominance, A Historical Overview"*, London: Duke University Press.

Ananiev, A G (1926), "Promyshlennye vozmozhnosti TASSR', in Narodnoe khoziaistvo Tadzhikistana (Dushanbe: Izdatelstvo Gosplana TASSR), p. 179, quoted in Nourzhanov, Kirill and Christian Bleuer (2013), *"Tajikistan – A Political and Social History"*, Canberra: ANU E Press.

Anderson, John (1997), *"The International Politics of Central Asia"*, Manchester: Manchester University Press.

Atkin, Michael (1992), *"The International Grain Trade"*, Cambridge: Woodhead Publishing Ltd.

Atkin, Muriel (1997), "Country Profile – Tajikistan", in Glenn E Curtis (eds.), *"Kazakstan, Kyrgyzstan, Tajikistan, Turkmenistan, and Uzbekistan: Country Studies,"* Federal Research Division, Library of Congress.

Atkin, Muriel (2011), "Tajikistan – From de facto Colony to Sovereignty in Central Asia", in Sally N Cummings and Raymond Hinnebusch (eds.) *Sovereignty After Empire: Comparing the Middle East and Central Asia,* Edinburgh: Edinburgh University Press Ltd.

Babu, Suresh Chandra and Valerie Rhoe (2006), "Food Security and Poverty in Central Asia", in S C Babu and S Djalalov (eds.) *Policy Reforms and Agriculture Development in Central Asia,* New York: Springer.

Babu et. al. (2006), "Policy Reforms and Poverty in Central Asia with Special Focus on Kyrgyzstan", in S C Babu and S Djalalov (eds.) *Policy Reforms and Agriculture Development in Central Asia,* New York: Springer.

Babu, Suresh Chandra and Debdata Sengupta (2006), "Policy Reforms and Agriculture Development in Central Asia: An

Overview of Issues and Challenges", in S C Babu and S Djalalov (eds.) *Policy Reforms and Agriculture Development in Central Asia*, New York: Springer.

Baransky, N N (1956), *"Economic Geography of the U.S.S.R."*, Moscow: Foreign Languages Publishing House.

Barnard, Phillepe J (1966), *Planning in the Soviet Union*, Oxford: Pergamon Press.

Barona, J L (2010), *"The Problem of Nutrition: Experimental Science, Public Health, and Economy in Europe 1914-1945"*, Brussels, P.I.E. Peter Land SA.

Barrett, Christopher (2013), "Food or Consequences: Food Security and its Implications for Global Socio-political Stability", in Christopher Barrett (eds.) *Food Security and Socio-political Stability*, Oxford, OUP.

Bartol'd, V V (1927), "Istoriia kul'turnoi zhizni Turkestana", Leningrad, 123, quoted in Vaidyanath, R (1967), *"The Formation of the Soviet Central Asian Republics – A Study in Soviet Nationalities Policy 1917-1936"*, New Delhi, People's Publishing House.

Bartol'd V V (1997), "Sart", quoted in Bergne, Paul (2007), *"The Birth of Tajikistan – National Identity and the Origins of the Republic"*, New York: I B Tauris & Co Ltd.

Batalden, Stephen K. and Sandra L. Batalden (1997), *The Newly Independent States of Eurasia*, Arizona: The Oryx Press.

Becker, Seymour (2004), *"Russia's Protectorates in Central Asia: Bukhara and Khiva, 1865 1924"*, London: RoutledgeCurzon.

Behnke, Roy (2008), *The Socio-economic Causes and Consequences of Dissertification in Central Asia*, Dordrecht: Springer.

Bergne, Paul (2007), *"The Birth of Tajikistan – National Identity and the Origins of the Republic"*, New York: I B Tauris & Co Ltd.

Beshimov, Baktybek et al. (2011), "A New Phase in the history of Ferghana Valley, 1992-2008", in S. Frederick Starr (eds.) *Ferghana Valley: The Heart of Central Asia*, New York: M E Sharpe Inc.

Birgerson, Susanne Michelle (2002), *After the Breakup of a Multi-ethnic Empire: Russia Successor States and Eurasian Security*, Westport: Praeger Publishing.

Bliss, Frank (2006), *"Social and Economic Change in the Pamirs (Gorno-Badakhshan, Tajikistan)"*, Oxon: Routledge.

Bobodzhanova, Khursheda (2012), "Food Safety Issues in Tajikistan", in Hami Alpas et. al. (eds.) *Strategies for Achieving Food Security in Central Asia*, Dordrecht: Springer.

Booth, K. (1995), "Dare to Know: International Relations Theory Versus the Future", in K. Booth and S. Smith (eds.) *International Relations Theory Today*, Philadelphia: Penn State University Press.

Briggs, Asa and Patricia Clavin (2003), *"Modern Europe, 1789-Present"*, Oxon: Routledge.

Bornet, Jean-Marc (1998), "The International Committee of the Red Cross and the conflict in Tajikistan", in Djalili et. al. (eds.) *Tajikistan: The Trials of Independence*, Surray: Curzon Press.

Brodovskii (1910), "Ocherk proizvodstva khlopka v Srednei Azii", Sredniaia Aziia, Almanakh..., Feb, 156, quoted in Pierce, Richard A (1960), *"Russian Central Asia 1867-1917: A Study in Colonial Rule"*, California: University of California Press.

Brown, Bess A (1998), "The Civil War in Tajikistan, 1992-1993", in Djalili et. al. (eds) *Tajikistan: The Trials of Independence*, Surrey: Cirzon Press.

Buzan, Berry (1991), *People, States and Fear: An Agenda for International Security Studies in the Post-Cold War Era*, Colo: Lynne Lienner Publishers Inc.

Buzan, Berry et al. (1997), *Security: A New Framework for Analysis*, Colo: Lynne Lienner Publishers Inc.

Capisani, Giampaolo R (2000), *"The Handbook of Central Asia – A Comprehensive Survey of the New Republics"*, New York: I B Tauris Publishers.

Caroe, Olaf (1967), *"Soviet Empire – The Turks of Central Asia and Stalinism"*, New York: St Martin's Press.

Cohen, Roberta and Francis Mading Deng (1998), *"The Forsaken People: Case Studies of the Internally Displaced"*, Virginia: R R Donnelley & Sons Co.

Cole, J P and F C German (eds.) (1961), *"A Geography of the USSR – The Background to a Planned Economy"*, London: Butterworth & Co. (Publishers) Limited.

Collier, P et. al. (2003), *Breaking the Conflict Trap: Civil War and Development Policy*, Oxford: OUP.

Collingham, Lizzie (2011), *"The Taste of War: World War Two and the Battle for Food"*, New York, Penguin Books.

Collins, Kathleen (2006), *"Clan Politics and Regime Transition in Central Asia"*, Cambridge: Cambridge University Press.

Collins, K (2003), "Tajikistan: Bad Peace Agreements and Prolonged Civil Conflict", in Chandra Lekha Sriram and Karin Wermester (eds.) *From Promise to Practice: Strengthening UN Capacities for the Prevention of Violent Conflict*, Colorado: Lynne Rienner Publishers.

Cotterell, Arthur (2011), *"Asia: A Concise History"*, Singapore: John Wiley & Sons (Asia) Pvt. Ltd.

Craumer, Peter (1995), "Rural and Agricultural Development in Uzbekistan", London: Royal Institute of International Affairs, pp 29-31, quoted in Stringer, Alex (2003), "Soviet Development in Central Asia – A Classical Colonial Syndrome?", in Tom Everett Heath (eds.) *Central Asia – Aspects of Transition*, London: RoutledgeCurzon.

Craumer, Peter R (1992), "Agricultural Change, Labor Supply and Rural Out-Migration in Soviet Central Asia", in Robert A Lewis (eds.) *Geographic Perspectives on Soviet Central Asia*, London: Routledge.

Cross, Sharyl and Marina A Oborotova (1994), *"The New Chapter in United States-Russian Relations: Opportunities and Challenges"*, Westport: Praeger Publishers.

Curzon, George (1889), *"Russia in Central Asia in 1889 and the Anglo-Russian Question"*, London: Longman Green and Co, quoted in Lloyd, Sarah J (1998), "Land-locked Central Asia: Implications for Future", in Dick Hodder et. al. (eds.) *Land-locked States of Africa and Asia*, London: Frank Cass Publishers.

d'Encausse, Hélène Carrère (1966), *"Islam and the Russian Empire: Reform and Revolution in Central Asia"*, Paris, University of California Press.

d' Encausse, Helene Carrere (1994a), "Systematic Conquest, 1865 to 1884", in Allworth, Edward (eds.) (1994), *"Central Asia: 130 Years of Russian Dominance, A Historical Overview"*, London: Duke University Press.

d' Encausse, Helene Carrere (1994b), "Organising and Colonising the Conquered Territories", in Allworth, Edward (eds.) (1994), *"Central Asia: 130 Years of Russian Dominance, A Historical Overview"*, London: Duke University Press.

d' Encausse, Helene Carrere (1994c), "The Fall of Czarist Empire", in Allworth, Edward (eds.) (1994), *"Central Asia: 130 Years of Russian Dominance, A Historical Overview"*, London: Duke University Press.

d' Encausse, Helene Carrere (1994d), "The National Republics Lose Their Independence", in Allworth, Edward (eds.) (1994), *"Central Asia: 130 Years of Russian Dominance, A Historical Overview"*, London: Duke University Press.

Dadmehr, Nasrin (2003), "Regionalism and Weakness", in Robert I Rotberg (eds) *State Failure and State Weakness in a Time of Terror*, Washington: Brookings Institution Press and the World Peace Foundation.

Davies, R W and Stephen G Wheatcroft (2004), *"The Years of Hunger: Soviet Agriculture, 1931-1933 (Industrialisation of Soviet Russia Vol 5)"*, New York: Palgrave Macmillan.

Dellenbrant J. A. (1986), *The Soviet Regional Dilemma: Planning, People and Natural Resources,* New York: M E Sharpe, Inc.

Deshpande, Ramesh (2006), "Land Reform and Farm Restructuring in Central Asia: Progress and Challenges Ahead", in S C Babu and S Djalalov (eds.) *Policy Reforms and Agriculture Development in Central Asia,* New York: Springer.

Deutsch, Robert (1986), *"The Food Revolution in the Soviet Union and Eastern Europe",* Boulder: Westview Press.

Demko, G J and Roland J Fuchs (eds.) (1974), *"Geographical Perspectives in the Soviet Union – A Selection of Readings",* Columbus: Ohio State University Press.

Dinorshoev, M (2005), "Tajikistan," in Chahryar Adle et al. (eds.) *History of Civilizations of Central Asia: Towards the contemporary period: from the mid-nineteenth to the end of the twentieth century Vol VI,* Paris: UNESCO Publisher.

Dijk et. al. (2008), *"Encyclopedia of the Cold War",* London: Routledge.

Dukhovny, Viktor A and Stulina Galina (2008), "Water and Food Security in Central Asia", in Chandra A. Madramootoo et. al. (eds.) *Water and Food Security in Central Asia,* Dordrecht: Springer.

Epkenhans, Tim (2010), "Muslims without learning, clergy without faith: Institutions of Islamic learning in the Republic of Tajikistan", in Michael Kemper et. al. (eds.) *Islamic Education in the Soviet Union and Its Successor States,* Oxon: Routledge.

Faber, M J (2008), "Human Security from Below: Freedom from Fear and Lifeline Operations", in Monica den Boer and Jaap de Wilde (eds.) *The Viability of Human Security,* Amsterdam: Amsterdam University Press.

Falkingham, Jane et. al. (1997), "Household Welfare in Central Asia: an introduction to the issues", in Jane Falkingham et. al. (eds.) *Household Welfare in Central Asia,* Basingstoke: Macmillan, pp 1-18.

Fraser, Glenda 'The Basmachi – II', Central Asian Survey Vol. 6

(2), 1987, p. 8, quoted in Marshall, Alexander (2003), "Turkfont - Frunze and the development of Soviet counter-insurgency in Central Asia", in Tom Everett Heath (eds.) *Central Asia – Aspects of Transition*, London: Routledge Curzon.

Friedman L (2005), "Living Standards and National Security of Central Asian Countries", in Irina Morozova (eds.) *Towards Social Stability and Democratic Governance in Central Eurasia*, Amsterdam, IOS Press.

Friedman, L A (1994), "Economic Crisis as a Factor of Building up Socio-Political and Ethnonational Tensions in the Countries of Central Asia and Transcaucasia", in V V Naumkin (eds.) *Central Asia and Transcaucasia: Ethnicity and Conflict*: Westport: Greenwood Press.

Feinstein, Alan Shawn (1993), *"The Hunger Report 1993"*, Switzerland: Gordon and Breach Science Publishers.

Geiss, Paul Georg (2003), *"Pre-tsarist and Tsarist Central Asia: Communal Commitment and Political Order in Change"*, London: Routledge Curzon.

Ghasimi, Reza (1994), *"Tajikistan – A World Bank Country Study"*, Washington: The World Bank.

Gibson, Mark (2012), *"The Feeding of Nations: Redefining Food Security for the 21st Century"*, Florida: CRC Press.

Gomart, Elizabeth (2003), "Between Civil War and Land Reform: Among the Poorest of the Poor in Tajikistan" in Nora Dudwick et. al. (eds.) *When Things Fall Apart: Qualitative Studies of Poverty in the Former Soviet Union*, Washington: The World Bank.

Grand, Jean-Michel et. al. (2001), "Tajikistan: What Role for Nongovernmental Organisations", in Action Against Hunger (eds.) *The Geopolitics of Hunger, 2000-2001: Hunger and Power*, London, Lynne Rienner Publishers.

Hampson, Fen Osler (2001), *Madness in Multitude: Human Security and World Order*, London: Oxford University Press.

Harris, Colette (2004), *"Control and Subversion - Gender*

Relations in Tajikistan", London, Pluto Press.

Harris, Colette (2006), *"Muslim Youth: Tensions and Transitions in Tajikistan"*, Oxford: Westview Press.

Hirlekar, K S (1945), *"Soviet Asia: The Power Behind U.S.S.R."*, Bombay: Avanti Prakashan.

Heath, Tom Everett eds. (2003), *"Central Asia – Aspects of Transition"*, London: Routledge Curzon.

Hulse, J. H. (1995), *Science Agriculture and Food Security,* Ottawa: Monograph Publishing.

Ibbotson, Sophie and Max Lovell-Hoare (2013), *"Tajikistan"*, Connecticut: The Globe Pequot Press Inc.

Istoriya Uzbekskoi SSR, book 2, vol 1, p 138, quoted in d'Encausse, Hélène Carrère (1966), *"Islam and the Russian Empire: Reform and Revolution in Central Asia"*, Paris, University of California Press.

Johnson, D Gale (1996), "Why Is It So Difficult to Replace a Failed Economic System? The Former USSR," in John M. Antle and Daniel A. Sumner (eds.) *The Economics of Agriculture*, vol. 1, Selected Papers of D. Gale Johnson, Chicago: University of Chicago Press.

Jonson, Lena (2006), *"Tajikistan in the New Central Asia: Geopolitics, Great Power Rivalry and Radical Islam"*, London: I B Tauris & Co Ltd.

Jonson, Lena (2004), *"Vladimir Putin and Central Asia: The Shaping of Russian Foreign Policy"*, London: I B Tauris & Co Ltd.

Kaldor, Mary H and Shannon D. Beebe (2010), *The Ultimate Weapon is No Weapon: Human Security and the New Rules of War and Peace*, New York: Perseus Books Group.

Karim, Farhad (1993), "Re-Imagining Tajikistan: Exclusion in the Age of Nations", in Phyllis Bennis and Michel Moushabeck (eds.) *Altered States: A Reader in the New World Order,* New York, Olive Branch Press.

Kassenova, Nargis (2011), "EU Central Asian bilateral cooperation", in Alexander Warkotsch (eds.) *The European Union and Central Asia*, Oxon: Routledge.

Kassymbekova, Botakoz (2011), "Humans as territory: forced resettlement and the making of Soviet Tajikistan, 1920–38", *Central Asian Survey*, 30:3-4, 349-370.

Kaufman, Richard F. and John P. Hardt (1993), *Former Soviet Union in Transition*, New York: M E Sharpe, Inc.

Kaushik, Devendra (1970), *"Central Asia in Modern Times: A History from the Early 19th Century"*, Moscow: Progress Publishers.

Kenez, Peter (2006), *"A History of the Soviet Union from the Beginning to the End"*, Cambridge: Cambridge University Press.

Kevlihan, Rob (2013), *"Aid, Insurgencies and Conflict Transformation: When Greed is Good"*, Oxon: Routledge.

Khalid, Adeeb (2007), *"Islam After Communism: Religion and Politics in Central Asia"*, California, University of California Press.

Khan, Azizur Rahman and Dharam Ghai (1979), *"Collective Agriculture and Rural Development in Rural Central Asia"*, London, The Macmillan Press Ltd.

Khan, Sarfraz (2003), *"Muslim Reformist Political Thought – Revivalists, modernists and free will"*, London: Routledge Curzon.

Khanam R (eds.) (2005), *"Encyclopaedic Ethnography of Middle-East and Central Asia, Volume 1"*, New Delhi: Global Vision Publishing House.

Kisliakov, N A (1959), "Sem'ia I brak u Tadzhikov", Moscov, pp 16-17, quoted in Vaidyanath, R (1967), *"The Formation of the Soviet Central Asian Republics – A Study in Soviet Nationalities Policy 1917-1936"*, New Delhi, People's Publishing House.

Kort, Michael (2004), *"Nations in Transition: Central Asian*

Republics", New York: Facts on File Inc.

Kudat, Ayse et al. (2000), Social *Assessment and Agriculture Reform in Central Asia and Turkey (World Bank Technical Papers)*, Washington: World Bank Publications.

Kugelman, Michael (2013), "Introduction" in Michael Kugelman and S L Levenstein (eds.) *The Global Farms Race: Land Grabs, Agricultural Investment and Scramble for Food Security*, Washington: Island Press.

Kuhn, Thomas (1962), *The Structure of Scientific Revolutions*, Chicago: University of Chicago Press.

Laruelle, Marlene and Sebastien Peyrouse (2013), *"Globalizing Central Asia: Geopolitics and the Challenges of Economic Development"*, New York: M E Sharpe Inc.

Lavrishchev, A (1969), *"Economic Geography of the USSR"*, Moscow: Progress Publishers.

Leninskii sbornik (A Lenin Collection), II, p 204, quoted in Lyashchenko, Peter I (1970), *"History of the National Economy of Russia to the 1917 Revolution"*, New York: Octagon Books.

Lewis, R.A. (1992), *Geographic Perspectives on Soviet Central Asia*, London: Routledge.

Lezhnev, Sasha (2005), *"Crafting Peace: Strategies to Deal with Warlords in Collapsing States"*, Lanham: Lexington Books.

Liebowitz, Ronald D (1992), "Soviet Geographical Imbalances and Soviet Central Asia", in Robert A Lewis (eds.) *Geographic Perspectives on Soviet Central Asia*, London: Routledge.

Logofet, D (1909), "Strana bezpraviya", St Petersburg, pp 32-90, quoted in d'Encausse, Hélène Carrère (1966), *"Islam and the Russian Empire: Reform and Revolution in Central Asia"*, Paris, University of California Press.

Lorch, Rajul Pandya (2000), "Prospects for Global Food Security: A Central Asian Context", in Suresh Babu and Alisher Tashmatov (eds.) *"Food Policy Reforms in Central Asia: Setting the Research Priorities"*, Washington: International

Food Policy Research Institute.

Lloyd, Sarah J (1998), "Land-locked Central Asia: Implications for Future", in Dick Hodder et. al. (eds.) *Land-locked States of Africa and Asia*, London: Frank Cass Publishers.

Luknitsky, Pavel (1954), *"Soviet Tajikistan"*, Moscow, Foreign Language Publishing House.

Luong, Pauline Jones (2004), *"Institutional Change and Political Continuity in Post-Soviet Central Asia: Power, Perceptions and Pacts"*, Cambridge: Cambridge University Press.

Lyashchenko, Peter I (1970), *"History of the National Economy of Russia to the 1917 Revolution"*, New York: Octagon Books.

Mack, Glen R and Asele Surina (2005), *"Food culture in Russia and Central Asia"*, Westport: Greenwood Press.

Makhamov, K (1981), *"Formirovanie i razvitie iuzhno-tadzhikiskogoTPK"*, Planovoe Khoziaistvo, 10, quoted in Dellenbrant, J A (1986), *"The Soviet Regional Dilemma – Planning, People and Natural Resources"*, New York: M E Sharpe, Inc.

Markowitz, Lawrence P (2013), *"State Erosion: Unlootable Resources and Unruly Elites in Central Asia"*, New York: Cornell University Press.

Mandel, William (1944), *"The Soviet Far East and Central Asia"*, New York: The Dial Press Inc, quoted in Vaidyanath, R (1967), *"The Formation of the Soviet Central Asian Republics – A Study in Soviet Nationalities Policy 1917-1936"*, New Delhi, People's Publishing House.

Markham, J W (2002), *"A Financial History of the United States – Vol. III"*, New York: M E Sharpe Inc.

Markowitz, Lawrence P (2013), *"State Erosion: Unlootable Resources and Unruly Elites in Central Asia"*, New York, Cornell University Press.

Marshall, Alexander (2003), "Turkfont - Frunze and the development of Soviet counter-insurgency in Central Asia", in

Tom Everett Heath (eds.) *Central Asia – Aspects of Transition*, London: RoutledgeCurzon.

Martin, Richard C (2003), *"Encyclopedia of Islam & the Muslim World"*, New York: McMillan Reference.

Masov, Rahim (1996), *"The History of a National Catastrophe"*, Translated and Edited by Iraj Bashiri, The University of Minnesota.

Matley, Ian Murray (1967), "Agriculture Development", in Edward Allworth (ed.), *Central Asia: One Hundred Thirty Years of Russian Dominance, A Historical Overview*, London: Duke University Press.

Matley, Ian (1981), "Central Asia and Kazakhstan", in I S Koropeckyj and Gertrude E Schroeder (eds.) *Economics of Soviet Regions* New York: Praeger Publishers.

Matley, I M (1994a), "Agricultural Development", in Allworth, Edward (eds.) (1994), *"Central Asia: 130 Years of Russian Dominance, A Historical Overview"*, London: Duke University Press.

Matley, I M (1994b), "Industrialisation (1865-1964)", in Allworth, Edward (eds.) (1994), *"Central Asia: 130 Years of Russian Dominance, A Historical Overview"*, London: Duke University Press.

Matthews, Allan (2003), *"Regional Integration and Food Security in Developing Countries"*, Rome: Food and Agriculture Organization of the United Nations.

McLean, Jennifer and Thomas Greene (1998), "Turmoil in Tajikistan: Addressing the Crisis of Internal Development", in Roberta Cohen and Francis Mading Den (eds.) *The Forsaken People: Case Studies of the Internally Displaced*, Washington: The Brookings Institution.

Medvedev, Zhores A (1987), *"Soviet Agriculture"*, New York: W W Norton & Company.

Mehta, Vinod (1978), *"Soviet Economic Development and Structure"*, New Delhi: Sterling Publishers Pvt Ltd.

Minahan, James (1998), *"Miniature Empires: A Historical Dictionary of the Newly Independent States"*, Oxon: Routledge.

Monogarova, L F (1949), "Iazgulemtsy Zapadnogo Pamira", *Sovetskaia etnografiia*, No. 3, pp. 93, 99, quoted in Nourzhanov, Kirill and Christian Bleuer (2013), *"Tajikistan – A Political and Social History"*, Canberra: ANU E Press.

Mullojanov, Parviz (2005), "General Overview Tajikistan: Politics", in Eldar Islamov (ed.) *Central Eurasia Analytical Annual*, Sweden: CA&CC Press.

Nourzhanov, Kirill and Christian Bleuer (2013), *"Tajikistan – A Political and Social History"*, Canberra: ANU E Press.

Nove, Alec (1969), *"An Economic History of the USSR"*, London, The Penguin Press.

Nove, Alec and J A Newth (1967), *"The Soviet Middle East: A Model for Development?"*, London: George Allen & Unwin Ltd.

Olcott, Martha Brill (2014), *"Tajikistan's Difficult Development Path"*, New Delhi: KW Publishers Pvt Ltd.

Olimov, M A and Saodat Olimova (2002), "Ethnic Factors and Local Self-Government in Tajikistan', in Valery Tishkov and Elena Filippova eds. *Local Governance and Minority Empowerment in the CIS*, Budapest: LGI Books/Open Society Institute, p. 248.

Pala, Ayhan (2015), "A Chronology of Central Asia", in Kemal Kantarci et. al. (eds.) *Tourism in Central Asia: Cultural Potential and Challenges*, Florida: CRC Press.

Pallot J. and Shaw Dennis J. B. (1981), *Planning in Soviet Union*, London: Biddles Ltd, Guildford and King's Lynn.

Patricia A and Melcarek H (2011), "Food Justice Movement", in D Mulvaney, & P Robbins (Eds), *Green food: An A-to-Z guide*, California: Sage Publications.

Parivalovskaya, G A et. al. (1987), "The South Tajik Territorial Production Complex", in Shah Manzoor Alam and Atiya

Habeeb Kidwai (eds.) *Regional Imperatives in Utilization and Management of Resources: India and the USSR*, New Delhi: Naurang Rai Concept Publishing Company.

Peacock, Eugenia (1993), "Eugenia Peacock" in Anna Horsbrugh-Porter (eds.) *Memories of Revolution: Russian Women Remember*, New York: Routledge.

Peimani, Hooman (2009), *"Conflict and Security in Central Asia and the Caucasus"*, California: ABC CLIO.

Perepelitsyna, L A (1976), "Rol russkoi kultury v razvitii kultur narodov Srednei Azii", Moscow: Nauka, p. 8, quoted in Nourzhanov, Kirill and Christian Bleuer (2013), *"Tajikistan – A Political and Social History"*, Canberra: ANU E Press.

Pierce, Richard A (1960), *"Russian Central Asia 1867-1917: A Study in Colonial Rule"*, California: University of California Press.

Podkolzin, A (1968), *"A Short Economic History of the USSR"*, Moscow: Progress Publishers.

Pomfret, Richard (1995), *"The Economies of Central Asia"*, New Jersey: Princeton University Press.

Pomfret, Richard (2008), "Tajikistan, Turkmenistan and Uzbekistan", in Kym Anderson and Johan F M Swinnen (eds.) *Distortions to Agricultural Incentives in Europe's Transition Economies*, Washington: The World Bank.

Pomfret, Richard (2006), "Economic Reform and Performance in Central Asia", in S C Babu and S Djalalov (eds.) *Policy Reforms and Agriculture Development in Central Asia*, New York: Springer.

Poujol, C and V Fourniau (2005), "Trade and Economy (2nd Half of 19th Century to Early 20th Century)", in Chahryar Adle et al. (eds.) *History of Civilizations of Central Asia: Towards the contemporary period: from the mid-nineteenth to the end of the twentieth century Vol VI*, Paris: UNESCO Publisher.

Peyton, William and Zelda K Coates (1951), *"Soviets in Central Asia"*, London: Lawrence & Wishart Ltd.

Radjapova, R. Y. (2005), "Establishment of Soviet Order in Central Asia (1914-1924)," in Chahryar Adle and Madhavan K. Palat (eds.) *History of Civilization of Central Asia – Vol 6*, Paris: UNESCO Publishing.

Rahimov, R R (1989), "Sovetskaya etnografia (The Soviet Ethnographic Journal)", No. 1, 1989, p 117, quoted in Masov, Rahim (1996), *"The History of a National Catastrophe"*, Translated and Edited by Iraj Bashiri, The University of Minnesota.

Rahul, Ram (1997), *"Central Asia: An Outline History"*, New Delhi: Concept Publishing Company.

Rahul, Ram (1995), *"Bukhara: The Emirate"*, New Delhi: Vikas Publications House Pvt. Ltd.

Rahul, Ram (2000), *"Central Asia: A Textbook History"*, New Delhi: Munshiram Manoharlal Publications Pvt. Ltd.

Rakowska-Harmstone, Teresa (1970), *"Russia and Nationalism in Central Asia – The Case of Tadzhikistan"*, Maryland: The Johns Hopkins Press.

Ratliff, Walter R (2010), *"Pilgrims on the Silk Road: A Muslim-Christian Encounter in Khiva"*, Eugene: Wipf & Stock Publishers.

Rawls, John (2001), *"Justice as fairness: A restatement"*, Cambridge, Harvard University Press.

Roche, Sophie (2014), *"Domesticating Youth: Youth Bulges and their Socio-political Implications in Tajikistan"*, New York: Berghahn Books.

Roudik, Peter L (2007), *"The History of the Central Asian Republics"*, Westport: Greenwood Press.

Rothschild, Emma (2007), "What is Security", in Barry Buzan and Lene Hansen (eds), *International Security: Widening Security*, Volume 3, London: Sage Publication Ltd.

Roy, Olivier (2000), *"The New Central Asia: The Creation of Nations"*, New York: I B Tauris Publishers.

Rozevitsa, Y R (1908), "Poiezdka v iuzhnuiu I sredniuiu Bukharu v 1906 g." Izviestiia Imperatorskago Russkago Geograficheskago Obshchestva, XIX, p 70-73, quoted in d' Encausse, Helene Carrere (1994b), "Organising and Colonising the Conquered Territories", in Allworth, Edward (eds.) (1994), *Central Asia: 130 Years of Russian Dominance, A Historical Overview*", London: Duke University Press.

Rumer, Boris (1989), "*Soviet Central Asia: A Tragic Experiment*", Boston: Unwin Hyman.

Runge et. al. (2003) "*Ending Hunger in Our Lifetime: Food Security and Globalization*", Maryland: John Hopkins University Press.

Rywkin, Michael (1982), *Moscow's Muslim Challenge: Soviet Central Asia*, New York: M E Sharpe Inc.

Sacks, Michael Paul (1992), "Work Force Composition, Patriarchy, and Social Change", in Robert A Lewis (eds.) *Geographic Perspectives on Soviet Central Asia*, London: Routledge.

Saidmuradov, H M (ed.) (1985), "Narodnoe khoziaistvo Tadzhikistana v period formirovaniia ekonomicheskikh predposylok razvitogo sotsializma", Dushanbe: Donish, quoted in Nourzhanov, Kirill and Christian Bleuer (2013), "*Tajikistan – A Political and Social History*", Canberra: ANU E Press.

Safarov, "Kolonial'naia revoliutsiia: opyt Turkestana, p 34, quoted in Pierce, Richard A (1960), "*Russian Central Asia 1867-1917: A Study in Colonial Rule*", California: University of California Press.

Sampath, T V (2006), "Policy Reforms and Agriculture Development Challenges", in S C Babu and S Djalalov (eds.) *Policy Reforms and Agriculture Development in Central Asia*, New York: Springer.

Sampath, T V (2006b), "Farmers Response to Land Privatization in Tajikistan", in S C Babu and S Djalalov (eds.) *Policy Reforms and Agriculture Development in Central Asia*, New York: Springer.

Sattar, Sarosh and Mohib, Shabih (2007), "Tajikistan: Cotton Farmland Privatisation", in Aline Coudouel et. al. *Poverty and Social Impact Analysis of Reforms: Lessons and Examples from Implementation*, Washington: The World Bank.

Sharma, R R (1979), *"A Marxist Model of Social Change – Soviet Central Asia: 1917-1940"*, Meerut: Macmillan Company of India Ltd.

Sharma, R R (2001), "State-building in Tajikistan: Problems and Prospects", in Mahavir Singh (eds.) (2001) *India and Tajikistan – Revitalising a Traditional Relationship*, Kolkata: Anamika Publishers & Distributors (P) Ltd.

Sedik, David (2012), "The Feed-Livestock Nexus: Livestock Development Policy in Tajikistan", in Victor R Squires (eds.) *Rangeland Stewardship in Central Asia: Balancing Improved Livelihoods, Biodiversity Conservation and Land Protection*, New York, Springer.

Sehring, Jenniver (2009), *"The Politics of Water Institutional Reform in Neo-patrimonial States - A Comparative Analysis of Kyrgyzstan and Tajikistan"*, Heidelberg: Meppel Publishers.

Sen, Amartya (1981), *Poverty and Famines: An Essay on Entitlement and Deprivation*, Oxford: Clarendon Press.

Severin, Barbara S (1993), "Differences in food production and food consumption among the Republics of former Soviet Union", in Richard F Kaufman and John P Haradt (eds.) *The Former Soviet Union in Transition*, New York: M E Sharpe.

Shaw, D J (2007), *"World Food Security - A History since 1945"*, New York: Palgrave Macmillan.

Shaw, H J (2014), *"The Consuming Geographies of Food: Diet, Food Deserts and Obesity"*, Routledge: Oxon.

Shipov, A (1857-58), "Khlopchatobumahnaya promyshlennost i vazhnost yeyo znacheniya dlya rossii", Moscow, p 42, quoted in Kaushik, Devendra (1970), *"Central Asia in Modern Times: A History from the Early 19th Century"*, Moscow: Progress Publishers.

Shoemaker, Wesley M (2014), *"Russia and The Commonwealth of Independent States 2014"*, Lanham: Stryker-Post Publications.

Spoor, Max (2000), "White gold versus Food Self-sufficiency in former Soviet Central Asia", in Aad van Tilburg et al. (eds.) *Agricultural Markets Beyond Liberalization*, New York: Kluwer Academic Publishers.

Spoor, Max (2009), "Rural poverty, cotton production and environmental degradation in Central Eurasia", in Mohamed Abdel Rahim and M. Salih (eds.) *Climate Change and Sustainable Development: New Challenges for Poverty Reduction*, Cheltenham: Edward Elgar Publishing Ltd.

Stedman, S J (2014), "Food and Security", in R L Naylor (ed) *The Evolving Sphere of Food Security*, New York: Oxforn University Press.

Stahlin, Karl, "Russisch Turkestan gestern und heute", p 16, quoted in Pierce, Richard A (1960), *"Russian Central Asia 1867-1917: A Study in Colonial Rule"*, California: University of California Press.

Stringer, Alex (2003), "Soviet Development in Central Asia – A Classical Colonial Syndrome?", in Tom Everett Heath (eds.) *Central Asia – Aspects of Transition*, London: Routledge Curzon.

Swinnen, Johan and Herck, K V (2013), "Food Security and Socio-political Stability in Eastern Europe and Central Asia", ", in Christopher Barrett (eds.) *Food Security and Socio-political Stability*, Oxford, OUP.

Tadjbakhsh, S and Anuradha .M. Chenoy (2007), *Human Security: Concepts and Implications*, Oxon: Routledge.

Terliatskas V and V Baldishis (1990), "Tak nuzhny li respublikanskie dengi?" EKO, No. 3, p 136, quoted in Nourzhanov, Kirill and Christian Bleuer (2013), *"Tajikistan – A Political and Social History"*, Canberra: ANU E Press.

Vaidyanath, R (1967), *"The Formation of the Soviet Central Asian Republics – A Study in Soviet Nationalities Policy 1917-1936"*,

New Delhi, People's Publishing House.

Voznesensky, N A (1948), *"The Economy of the USSR during World War II,"* Washington: Public Affairs Press, pp 56-57, quoted in Matley, I M (1994a), "Agricultural Development", in Allworth, Edward (eds.) (1994), *"Central Asia: 130 Years of Russian Dominance, A Historical Overview"*, London: Duke University Press.

V.I.luferev, Khlopkovodstvo v Turkestane [Leningrad, 1925], pp. 150–152. Quoted in Becker, Seymour (2004), *"Russia's Protectorates in Central Asia: Bukhara and Khiva, 1865 1924"*, London: RoutledgeCurzon.

Wheeler, Geoffrey (1964), *"The Modern History of Soviet Central Asia"*, New York: Frederick A Praeger.

Wegerich, Kai (2003), "Water - The difficult path to a sustainable future for Central Asia", in Tom Everett Heath (eds.) *Central Asia – Aspects of Transition*, London: Routledge Curzon.

Wooden, Amanda E and Christoph H Steefs (2009), "Multivaried and interacting paths of change in Central Eurasia", in Amanda E Wooden and Christoph H Steefs (eds.) *The Politics of Transition in Central Asia and the Caucasus Enduring legacies and emerging challenges,* Oxon: Routledge.

Zdravookhranenie Tadzhikistana (1990), No. 2, p. 21, quoted in Nourzhanov, Kirill and Christian Bleuer (2013), *"Tajikistan – A Political and Social History"*, Canberra: ANU E Press.

Zokirov, S and K Umarov (2011), "Economic Development in the Ferghana Valley Since 1991", in S. Frederick Starr (eds.) *Ferghana Valley: The Heart of Central Asia*, New York: M E Sharpe Inc.

ARTICLES

Akbarzadeh, Shahram (1996), "Why did Nationalism fail in Tajikistan", *Europe-Asia Studies*, Vol 48, No 7, 1105-1129.

Azzarri, Carlo and Alberto Zezza (2010), "International migration and nutritional outcomes in Tajikistan", *Food Policy,* 36, 54-

70.

Babu, Suresh and Alisher Tashmatov (eds.) (2000), *"Food Policy Reforms in Central Asia: Setting the Research Priorities"*, Washington: International Food Policy Research Institute.

Beatrice, Penati (2007), 'The Reconquest of East Bukhara: The Struggle against the Basmachi as a Prelude to Sovietization', *Central Asian Survey*, Vol. 26, No. 4, pp. 522, 533.

Benjamin, Shepherd (2012), "Thinking critically about food security", *Security Dialogue*, 43 (3), 195-212.

Bone, Robert M (1967), "Regional Planning and Economic Regionalization in the Soviet Union", *Land Economics*, Vol. 43, No. 3 (Aug., 1967), pp. 347-354.

Bleuer, Christian (2012), "State-building, migration and economic development on the frontiers of northern Afghanistan and southern Tajikistan", *Journal of Eurasian Studies,* Volume 3, Issue 1, January 2012, Pages 69–79.

Bush, Ray (2010), "Food Riots: Poverty, Power and Protest", *Journal of Agrarian Change*, Vol. 10 No. 1, January 2010, pp. 119–129.

CIA World Factbook Website, (Online Web), Accessed 6 April 2014 URL: https://www.cia.gov/library/publications/the-world-factbook/geos/ti.html.

Chen et. al. (1992), "Health Crisis in Central Asian Republics", *Economic and Political Weekly,* June 6.

Cohen, MJ and Andersen, Per Pinsterup (1999), "Food Security and Conflict", *Social Research: An International Quarterly,* Volume 66, No. 1 (Spring 1999): 375-416.

Ferrando, Olivier (2011), "Soviet population transfers and interethnic relations in Tajikistan: assessing the concept of ethnicity", *Central Asian Survey*, 30:1, 39-52.

Foroughi, Payam (2002), "Tajikistan: Nationalism, Ethnicity, Conflict, and Socio-economic Disparities--Sources and Solutions", *Journal of Muslim Minority Affairs*, 22:1, 39-61.

Fuchs, Roland J and G J Demko (1979), "Geographic Inequality Under Socialism", *Annals of the Association of American Geographers,* Vol. 69, No. 2, June 1979.

Gures, Gulash (2011), "State-building in Tajikistan in the post-independence period civil war, regime consolidation and September 11", *Contemporary Central Asia,* Vol. XV, No. 1, pp 38-62.

Haberli, C and Smith, F (2014), "Food Security and Agri-Foreign Direct Investment in Weak States: Finding the Governance Gap to Avoid Land Grab", *The Modern Law Review,* 77(2) MLR 189–222.

Haqnazar, Imomnazar (2004), "Migrants from Badakhshan", Khorog, Mountain Societies Development Support Programme (Aga Khan Fund Project), quoted in Olimova, Saodat (2005), "Impact of external migration on development of mountainous regions", Strategies for Development and Food Security in Mountainous Areas of Central Asia, *International Workshop*: Dushanbe.

Heinzig, Dieter (1983), "Russia and the Soviet Union in Asia: Aspects of Colonialism and Expansionism", *Contemporary Southeast Asia,* Vol. 4, No. 4 (March 1983), pp. 417-450.

Hierman, Brent and Navruz Nekbakhtshoev (2014), "Whose land is it? Land reform, minorities, and the titular "nation" in Kazakhstan, Kyrgyzstan, and Tajikistan," *Nationalities Papers: The Journal of Nationalism and Ethnicity,* 42:2, 336-354.

Holdsworth, M (1952), "Soviet Central Asia, 1917-1940", *Soviet Studies,* Vol. 3, No. 3 (Jan., 1952), pp. 258-277.

Hopkins, R F and Puchala, D J (1978), "Perspectives on the international relations of food", *International Organisation,* Vol. 32, No. 3.

I. Lenin, Polnoe sobranie sochinenii [Complete collection of works], vol. 4 (Moscow 1960), p. 86, quoted in Heinzig, Dieter (1983), "Russia and the Soviet Union in Asia: Aspects of Colonialism and Expansionism", *Contemporary Southeast*

Asia, Vol. 4, No. 4 (March 1983), pp. 417-450.

Kassymbekova, Botakoz (2011), "Humans as territory: forced resettlement and the making of Soviet Tajikistan, 1920–38", *Central Asian Survey*, 30:3-4, 349-370.

Kasymov, Shavkat (2013), "Regional fragmentation in Tajikistan: The shift of powers between different identity groups", *Asian Geographer*, 30:1, 1-20.

Kaw, A. Mushtaq (2006), "Changing Land Tenures, Agrarian Reforms and Peasantry in Post-Soviet Central Asian Republics: A Historico-Legal Framework", *International Journal of Central Asian Studies*, Vol 11, 42-58.

Khodjamurodov, Ghafur and Bernd Rechel (2010), "Tajikistan – Health System Review", *Health Systems in Transition*, 12(2):1–154.

Kokaisl, P (2013), "Soviet Collectivisation and Its Specific Focus on Central Asia", *Agris on-line Papers in Economics and Informatics*, Vol 5, No 4, pp 121-133.

Koropeckyj, I S (1967), "The Development of Soviet Location Theory before the Second World War: I", *Soviet Studies*, Vol. 19, No. 1 (Jul 1967), pp 1-28.

Lerman, Zvi et al. (2003), "Agricultural Output and Productivity in the Former Soviet Republics", *Economic Development and Cultural Change,* Vol. 51, No. 4 (July 2003), pp. 999-1018.

Mandel, William M (1942), "Soviet Central Asia", *Pacific Affairs*, Vol. 15, No. 4 (Dec., 1942), pp. 389-409.

Mason, Frances (2001), "AAH in Tajikistan: a flexible response based on analysing the causes of malnutrition", (Online Web), Accessed 25 Mar 2014 URL: http://www.ennonline.net/fex/14/aah.

Mearsheimer, John (1995), "A Realist Reply", *International Security* 20: 82-93.

Mohapatra, N K (2013), "Migration and Its Impact on Security of Central Asia", *India Quarterly,* 69(2) 133–157.

Mohapatra, N K (2013), "Political and Security Challenges in Central Asia: The Drug Trafficking Dimension" *International Studies*, 44, 2 (2007): 157–74.

Nakaya, Sumie (2009), "Aid and transition from a war economy to an oligarchy in post-war Tajikistan", *Central Asia Survey*, 28:3, 259-273.

Nello, Susan Senior (1992), "The Food Situation in the ex-Soviet Republics", *Soviet Studies*, Vol. 44, No. 5 (1992), pp. 857-880.

Newton, Francis (1976), "Soviet Central Asia: Economic Progress and Problems", *Middle Eastern Studies,* Vol. 12, No. 3, Special Issue on the Middle Eastern Economy(Oct., 1976), pp. 87-104.

Nissen, Soren W. (2004), "Tajiks' promised land: A farm of one's own", *OSCE Magazine*, Vol. 1 No 3, 4-7.

Niyazi, Aziz (2002), "Migration, Demography and Socio-Ecological Processes in Tajikistan", JCAS Symposium Series, Vol. 9, pp. 169–71, quoted in Nourzhanov, Kirill and Christian Bleuer (2013), *"Tajikistan – A Political and Social History"*, Canberra: ANU E Press.

Nove, Alec (1970), "Soviet Agriculture under Brezhnev", *Slavic Review*, Vol. 29, No. 3 (Sep., 1970), pp. 379-410.

Nygaard, D et. al. (2005), "Seizing Opportunities to Promote Development and Improve Food Security in the Mountainous Regions of Central Asia", International Workshop Dushanbe, Tajikistan, June 6-10.

Olimova, Saodat (2005), "Impact of external migration on development of mountainous regions", Strategies for Development and Food Security in Mountainous Areas of Central Asia, *International Workshop*: Dushanbe.

Oudenhoven, Frederik J W van and L Jamila Haider (2010), "Imagining alternative futures through the lens of food in the Afghan and Tajik Pamir mountains", *Revue d'ethnoécologie*, Vol. 2, Contribution de la biodiversité à l'alimentation.

Patel, Raj and Philip McMichael (2009), "A Political Economy of the Food Riot," *Review*, XXXII, 9-35.

Patrick, Stewart (2006), "Weak States and Global Threats: Fact or Fiction?", *The Washington Quarterly* 29:2, 27-83.

Rowe, William C (2009), "Kitchen Gardens in Tajikistan: The Economic and Cultural Importance of Small-Scale Private Property in a Post-Soviet Society", *Human Ecology*, Vol. 37, No. 6, pp. 691-703.

Rowe, William C (2010), "Agrarian adaptations in Tajikistan: land reform, water and law", *Central Asian Survey*, 29:2, 189-204.

Reenock, C et. al. (2007), "Regressive Socioeconomic Distribution and Democratic Survival," International Studies Quarterly, 51 (3), 677-699.

Schroeder, G E (1973), "Regional Differences in Incomes and Levels of Living in the USSR", in V N Bandera and Z L Melnyk (eds.) *The Soviet Economy in Regional Perspective,* New York: Praeger Publishers, pp 167-95, quoted in Fuchs, Roland J and G J Demko (1979), "Geographic Inequality Under Socialism", *Annals of the Association of American Geographers,* Vol. 69, No. 2, June 1979.

Slim, Randa M and Faredun Hodizoda (2002), "Tajikistan: From Civil War to Peace- building", quoted in Gures, Gulash (2011), "State-building in Tajikistan in the post-independence period civil war, regime consolidation and September 11", *Contemporary Central Asia*, Vol. XV, No. 1, pp 38-62.

Tarry, Sarah (1999), "'Deepening' and 'Widening': An Analysis of Security Definitions in the 1990s", *Journal of Military and Strategic Studies*, Vol 2, No 1.

Taaffe, R N (1962), "Transportation and Regional Specialization: The Example of Soviet Central Asia", *Annals of the Association of American Geographers*, Volume 52, Issue 1, pp 88-89.

TsGART, f. 12, op. 1, d. 35, l. 55. Vystuplenie Karamova. III Chrezvychainyi Vsetadzhikskii S'ezd Sovetov. Stenogramma. 1929, quoted in Kassymbekova, Botakoz (2011), "Humans as territory: forced resettlement and the making of Soviet Tajikistan, 1920–38", *Central Asian Survey*, 30:3-4, 349-370.

Von Atta, Don (2009), "White Gold" or Fool's Gold? The Political Economy of Cotton in Tajikistan", *Problems of Post-Communism*, vol. 56, no. 2, March/April, pp. 17–35.

Vyas, V S (2000), "Ensuring Food Security: The State, Market and Civil Society," *Economic and Political Weekly*, Vol 35, No 50, 4402-4407.

Wadekin, K E (1990), "Fattori di crisi dell'economia agro-alimentare sovietica", Rivista de Politica Agraria, pp. 13-22, quoted in Nello, Susan Senior (1992), "The Food Situation in the ex-Soviet Republics", *Soviet Studies*, Vol. 44, No. 5 (1992), pp. 857-880.

Walt, Stephen (1991), "The Renaissance of Security Studies", *International Studies Quarterly* 35 (2): 211-39.

Wegerich, Kai (2001), "Not a simple path - A sustainable future for Central Asia", Occasional Paper No 28, *Water Issues Study Group*, School of Oriental and African Studies (SOAS): University of London.

Wheeler, G E (1955), "Soviet Policy in Central Asia", *International Affairs*, Vol. 31, No. 3 (Jul., 1955), pp. 317-326.

NEWS SOURCES

Addleton, Jonathan (2014), "Tajikistan Transformed: Feeding the Future", May 20, (Online Web), Accessed 10 Nov 2014 URL: http://blog.usaid.gov/2014/05/tajikistan-transformed-feeding-the-future/.

Agence France-Presse (2001), "UN warns of need for food aid to drought-stricken Tajikistan", April 26, (Online Web), Accessed Jan 18, 2013 URL: http://reliefweb.int/report/tajikistan/un-warns-need-food-aid-drought-stricken-tajikistan.

Agence France-Presse (2001), "Tajikistan facing famine unless aid sent: WFP", October 13, (Online Web), Accessed Jan 18, 2013 URL: http://reliefweb.int/report/tajikistan/tajikistan-facing-famine-unless-aid-sent-wfp.

Aioubov, Salimjon (2008), "Tajikistan: Tensions Rising Over

Food Prices In Remote East", June 18, (Online Web), Accessed May 1, 2015 URL: http://www.rferl.mobi/a/1144643.html.

Andrianova, Anna (2015), "Russia's 2014 Economic Growth Rate Declines to Lowest Since 2009", (Online Web), Accessed April 10, 2015 URL: http://www.bloomberg.com/news/articles/2015-01-30/russia-s-2014-economic-growth-rate-declines-to-lowest-since-2009.

Arsenault, Chris (2012), "Risk of water wars rises with scarcity", Al Jazeera, August 26, (Online Web), Accessed Jan 15, 2013 URL: http://www.aljazeera.com/indepth/features/2011/06/2011622193147231653.html.

Asia Plus (2006), "Drought causes serious damage to grain farms in mountain areas of Kulob", (Online Web), Accessed Jan 18, 2013 URL: http://news.tj/en/news/drought-causes-serious-damage-grain-farms-mountain-areas-kulob.

Asia Plus (2006), "Severe electricity shortages lead to increase in prices of bread in northern Tajikistan", (Online Web), Accessed Jan 18, 2013 URL: http://www.news.tj/en/news/severe-electricity-shortages-lead-increase-prices-bread-northern-tajikistan.

Asia Plus (2008), "Pests pose serious threat to Tajikistan's food security, says expert", (Online Web), Accessed Jan 18, 2013 URL: http://news.tj/en/news/pests-pose-serious-threat-tajikistan-s-food-security-says-expert.

Asia Plus (2009), "EAEC countries develop food security concept", May 20, (Online Web), Accessed Dec 18, 2014 URL: http://news.tj/en/news/eaec-countries-develop-food-security-concept.

Asia Plus (2011), "Wheat and flour prices continue to rise in Tajikistan", (Online Web), Accessed Jan 18, 2013 URL: http://news.tj/en/news/wheat-and-flour-prices-continuing-rise-tajikistan.

Asia Plus (2011), "Expensive food imports may become 'major burden' in Tajikistan, says FAO expert", February 16, (Online Web), Accessed Dec 18, 2014 URL: http://www.news.tj/en/

news/expensive-food-imports-may-become-major-burden-tajikistan-says-fao-expert.

Asia Plus (2013), "TI's Corruption Perception Index of 2013 lists Tajikistan 154th among 177 countries", (Online Web), Accessed Jan 18, 2013 URL: http://news.tj/en/news/ti-s-corruption-perception-index-2013-lists-tajikistan-154th-among-177-countries.

Asia Plus (2013), "IsDB provides additional $2.1 million loan for the Dushanbe water supply rehabilitation project", (Online Web), Accessed Jan 18, 2013 URL: http://www.asiaplus.tj/en/news/isdb-provides-additional-21-million-loan-dushanbe-water-supply-rehabilitation-project.

Asia Plus (2013), "GDP per capita in Tajikistan reportedly recorded at 1,000 USD", July 26, (Online Web), Accessed Jan 18, 2013 URL: http://news.tj/en/news/gdp-capita-tajikistan-reportedly-recorded-1000-usd.

Asia Plus (2013), "Tajikistan pursues open-door policy, says Tajik leader", (Online Web), Accessed Jan 18, 2015 URL: http://news.tj/en/news/tajikistan-pursues-open-door-policy-says-tajik-leader.

Asia Plus (2015), "FAO launches new project in Tajikistan", February 9, (Online Web), Accessed Jan 18, 2013 URL: http://news.tj/en/news/fao-launches-new-project-tajikistan.

Asia Plus (2015), "WFP: Impact of the Russian economic slowdown will be felt more severely in spring", (Online Web), Accessed Jan 18, 2015 URL: http://www.news.tj/en/news/wfp-impact-russian-economic-slowdown-will-be-felt-more-severely-spring.

Asia Plus (2015), "Chinese investors reportedly lease more than 6,300 ha of arable lands in Tajikistan", January 15, (Online Web), Accessed Dec 18, 2014 URL: http://news.tj/en/news/chinese-investors-reportedly-lease-more-6300-ha-arable-lands-tajikistan.

BBC Monitoring Global Newsline - Central Asia Political, August 4, 2012, "Food prices rises after military actions in troubled

Tajik region" through Author's BBC subscription of the service.

Bhutta, Zafar (2014), "Power project: IDB agrees to fill financing gap in CASA-1000 project", October 29, (Online Web), Accessed Jan 18, 2013 URL: http://tribune.com.pk/story/782601/power-project-idb-agrees-to-fill-financing-gap-in-casa-1000-project/.

Broening, Stephens (1972), "Soviet Union Reports Crop Failure; 30 Million Tons Shy in Grain Harvest", *The Telegraph*, June 6, (Online Web), Accessed Jan 15, 2013 URL: https://news.google.com/newspapers?nid=2209&dat=19721106&id=TZw rAAAAIBAJ&sjid=DvwFAAAAIBAJ&pg=7093,840759&hl =en.

"Bread Shortage in Tajikistan", May 2, 1995, Russian News, (Online Web), Accessed Jan 15, 2013 URL: http://www.russianmentor.net/RussianLibrary/section_17/efrn_03_25.htm.

CBS News (2011), "Egyptians Riot in the Streets in 1977", (Online Web), Accessed 17 Sept 2014 URL: http://www.cbsnews.com/news/egyptians-riot-in-the-streets-in-1977/.

Central Asia Online (2009), "Uzbekistan cuts gas supply to Tajikistan", (Online Web), Accessed Jan 18, 2013 URL: http://centralasiaonline.com/en_GB/articles/caii/features/2009/01/06/feature-02.

Charles, Dan (2014), "Can Quinoa Take Root On The 'Roof Of The World'?", (Online Web), Accessed 10 July 2014 URL: http://www.npr.org/blogs/thesalt/2014/08/21/342183903/can-quinoa-take-root-on-the-roof-of-the-world.

Chorshanbiyev, Payrav (2014), "14 percent of Tajik households last year lived below poverty line", Asia Plus, 25 July, (Online Web), Accessed 19 Jan 2014 URL: http://news.tj/en/news/14-percent-tajik-households-last-year-lived-below-poverty-line.

"Contaminated Wheat Kills 24 in Tajikistan", New York Times, Jan 19, 1993, (Online Web), Accessed Jan 15, 2013 URL: http://www.nytimes.com/1993/01/19/world/contaminated-wheat-kills-24-in-tajikistan.html.

Crossette, Barbara (1995), "Iraq Sanctions Kill Children, U.N. Reports", New York Times, December 1, (Online Web), Accessed Jan 15, 2013 URL: http://www.nytimes.com/1995/12/01/world/iraq-sanctions-kill-children-un-reports.html.

Euractive (2014), "Corruption hampers EU aid in Central Asia: Court of Auditors", (Online Web), Accessed 1 August 2014 URL: http://www.euractiv.com/development-policy/court-auditors-corruption-hamper-news-532880.

Eurasianet (2007), "Central Asia: Governments, Banks Gradually Open Up To Islamic Banking", (Online Web), Accessed 10 Feb 2014 URL: http://www.eurasianet.org/departments/insight/articles/pp071307.shtml.

Eurasianet Website (2015), "Tajikistan Ponders Future Without Opposition", (Online Web) Accessed 18 April 2015 URL: http://www.eurasianet.org/node/72381.

Farchy, Jack (2014), "Tajikistan looks to China as Russian remittances dry up", (Online Web), Accessed Jan 18, 2015 URL: http://www.ft.com/cms/s/0/2c87ee20-58f9-11e4-9546-00144feab7de.html#slide4.

IRIN News (2004), "TAJIKISTAN: World Bank installs early warning system at Lake Sarez", August 5, (Online Web), Accessed Jan 18, 2013 URL: http://www.irinnews.org/report/24473/tajikistan-world-bank-installs-early-warning-system-at-lake-sarez.

IRIN News (2007), "TAJIKISTAN: Lake Sarez disaster preparedness proceeding well", May 23, (Online Web), Accessed Jan 18, 2013 URL: http://www.irinnews.org/report/72328/tajikistan-lake-sarez-disaster-preparedness-proceeding-well.

Khovar (2012), "Uzbekistan completely cut off the supplying of natural gas to Tajikistan", (Online Web), Accessed Jan 18, 2013 URL: http://khovar.tj/eng/foreign-policy/2549-uzbekistan-completely-cut-off-the-supplying-of-natural-gas-to-tajikistan.

html.

Kucera, Joshua (2013), "The Aga Khan's tightrope walk in Tajikistan", (Online Web), Accessed Jan 18, 2013 URL: http://www.aljazeera.com/indepth/opinion/2013/08/2013828121815583542.html.

Mennen, Tiernan (2014), "Tajikistan: Legal aid boosts food security and agriculture investment", November 5, (Online Web), Accessed 10 Nov 2014 URL: http://usaidlandtenure.net/commentary/2014/11/tajikistan-legal-aid-boosts-food-security-agricultural-investment.

Najibullah, Farangis (2008), "Tajikistan: UN Urges Food Aid, As Anger Mounts Over Energy Crisis", (Online Web), Accessed Jan 18, 2013 URL: http://www.rferl.org/content/article/1079499.html.

Pannier, Bruce (2008), "Central Asia: Locust Invasion Worsens Region's Food Woes", (Online Web), Accessed Jan 18, 2013 URL: http://www.rferl.org/content/article/1144537.html.

Pannier, Bruce (2011), "Tajikistan Agrees To Allow Chinese Farmers To Till Land", Radio Free Europe Radio Library, January 28, (Online Web), Accessed Jan 15, 2013 URL: http://www.rferl.org/content/tajikistan_china/2289623.html.

Pyrkalo, Svitlana (2014), "Tajikistan to get Auchan: first hypermarket financed by EBRD", (Online Web), Accessed 10 Feb 2015 URL: http://www.ebrd.com/news/2014/tajikistan-to-get-auchan-first-hypermarket-financed-by-ebrd.html.

New Europe Online (2015), "EBRD lends a helping hand to Tajikistan's water rehabilitation network", (Online Web), Accessed 10 Feb 2015 URL: http://www.neurope.eu/article/ebrd-lends-helping-hand-tajikistan%E2%80%99s-water-rehabilitation-network.

Radio Free Europe Radio Liberty (2011), "UN Official: Trains Stuck In Uzbekistan Could Cause Tajik Food Shortage", (Online Web), Accessed Jan 18, 2013 URL: http://www.rferl.org/content/un_official_says_trains_stuck_in_uzbekistan_could_cause_tajik_food_shortage/24421481.html.

Russia Today (2014), "UN warns world must produce 60% more food by 2050 to avoid mass unrest", March 10, (Online Web), Accessed May 15, 2015 URL: http://rt.com/news/world-food-security-2050-846/.

Schmemann, Serge (1993), "War Bleeds Ex-Soviet Land at Central Asia's Heart", *New York Times*, Feb 21, (Online Web), Accessed Jan 15, 2013 URL: http://www.nytimes.com/1993/02/21/world/war-bleeds-ex-soviet-land-at-central-asia-s-heart.html.

Symonds, Peter (1998), "Social unrest undermines Suharto regime", (Online Web), Accessed 17 Sept 2014 URL: http://www.wsws.org/en/articles/1998/02/suha-f10.html.

The Times of Central Asia (2012), "Tashkent blocks Dushanbe from importing Turkmen gas", (Online Web), Accessed Jan 18, 2013 URL: http://www.timesca.com/news/10281-tashkent-blocks-dushanbe-from-importing-turkmen-gas.

The Times of Central Asia (2015), "World Bank to continue supporting Tajikistan", (Online Web), Accessed Jan 22, 2014 URL: http://www.timesca.com/news/14954-world-bank-to-continue-supporting-tajikistan.

"Tajikistan: Cotton Harvest Relies Heavily on Child Labor", (Online Web), Accessed 02 May 2014 URL: http://www.eurasianet.org/departments/insightb/articles/eav110309.shtml.

"Tajik Cotton Heists", The Moscow Times, July 26, 1995, (Online Web), Accessed Jan 15, 2013 URL: http://www.themoscowtimes.com/sitemap/paid/1995/7/article/tajik-cotton-heists/336740.html.

Tahir, Muhammad (2011), "Governments Move To Thwart 'Arab Spring' In Central Asia", April 28, (Online Web) Accessed 18 April 2015 URL: http://www.rferl.org/content/governments_move_to_thwart_arab_spring_in_central_asia/16796618.html.

Trilling, David (2014), "Tajikistan: Migrant Remittances Now Exceed Half of GDP", (Online Web), Accessed Jan 18, 2013 URL: http://www.eurasianet.org/node/68272.

Vinson, Mark (2015), "Marginalization of Tajikistan's Political Opposition Could Threaten Security", (Online Web) Accessed 18 April 2015 URL: http://www.jamestown.org/single/?tx_ttnews%5Btt_news%5D=43696&tx_ttnews%5Bb ackPid%5D=7&cHash=fff358f6f283baffd6c5259c667ca36e#. VTEzQyGqqkp.

Wall, Tim (2014), "Food Wars Could Rage by 2050", April 18, (Online Web), Accessed May 15, 2015 URL: http://news.discovery.com/earth/weather-extreme-events/food-wars-could-rage-by-2050-140418.htm.

Williams, Marcia (2014), "Top 10 facts you didn't know about the First World War", (Online Web), Accessed Dec 18, 2014 URL: http://www.theguardian.com/childrens-books-site/2014/jul/01/top-10-first-world-war-facts-marcia-williams.

Yanovska, Maria (2012), "Dododzhon Atovulloev : " I left the Sklifa - there was not safe ", January 31, (Online Web), Accessed May 15, 2015 URL: http://www.fergananews.com/article.php?id=7260?print=1.

THESES

Bautista, Castillo R C (2006), *"Tajikistan: informal politics in the consolidation of a new hegemony"* Ph. D Thesis, Universidad de las Américas Puebla.

Clifford, David M (2009), *"Marriage and fertility change in post-Soviet Tajikistan"*, Ph. D Thesis, Southampton, University of Southampton.

Larsen, Laura (2012), *"Repurposing the Great Grain Robbery in Canada"*, Ph. D Thesis, University of Saskatchewan.

Lata, Prem (1989), *"Parameters of Agrarian Reconstruction and Modernization in Soviet Central Asia: A Case Study of Tajikistan 1930 – 1980"*, Ph. D Thesis, New Delhi, Jawaharlal Nehru University.

Mandler, Andreas (2011), *"Coping with Post-Soviet Agriculture Knowledge and Local Governance in Horticultural Production in Tajikistan"*, Ph. D Thesis, Bonn: University of Bonn.

ONLINE SOURCES

Akiner, Shirin and Barnes, Catherine (2001), "The Tajik civil war: Causes and dynamics", (Online Web) Accessed 18 April 2014 URL: http://www.c-r.org/accord-article/tajik-civil-war-causes-and-dynamics.

Akramov, K T and Ganga Shreedhar (2012), "Economic Development, External Shocks, and Food Security in Tajikistan", (Online Web), Accessed 07 Mar 2014 URL: www.ifpri.org/sites/default/files/publications/ifpridp01163.pdf.

AKDN Website, (Online Web), Accessed 10 Nov 2014 URL: http://www.akdn.org/faq.asp.

Al-Eyd, Ali et. al. (2012), "Global Food Price Inflation and Policy Responses in Central Asia", (Online Web) Accessed 18 April 2014 URL: https://www.imf.org/external/pubs/ft/wp/2012/wp1286.pdf.

Alkire, Sabina (2003), "A Conceptual Framework of Human Security", [Online: Web] Accessed 11 Mar. 2013 URL: www.crise.ox.ac.uk/pubs/workingpaper2.pdf.

Amir, Omair and Albert Berry (2013), "Challenges of Transition Economies – Economic Reforms, Emigration and Employment in Tajikistan", in *Social Protection, Growth and Employment: Evidence from India, Kenya, Malawi, Mexico, Peru and Tajikistan*, UNDP, (Online Web) Accessed 18 Mar 2013 URL: http://www.undp.org/content/undp/en/home/librarypage/poverty-reduction/inclusive_development/social-protection--growth-and-employment--evidence-from-india--k/.

Aminjanov et. al (2009), "Case Study of Aid Effectiveness in Tajikistan", (Online Web), Accessed 1 August 2014 URL: http://www.brookings.edu/~/media/research/files/papers/2009/10/aid-tajikistan-aminjanov/10_aid_tajikistan_aminjanov.pdf.

Amirov, B. (2000), "Agricultural Policy Reforms in Tajikistan", [Online: Web] Accessed on 21 Mar. 2013 URL: www.ifpri.org/sites/default/files/pubs/pubs/books/fprca.pdf.

Asadov, Shokhboz (2013), "Food Security and the Agricultural

Cooperation Agenda in Central Asia with a Focus on Tajikistan", (Online Web) Accessed 20 Mar 2013 URL: www. ucentralasia.org/.../UCA-IPPA-WP16-FoodSecurity-Eng.pdf.

ADB (2011), "Tajikistan Government and Development Coordination Council Review Progress of the Development Agenda", (Online Web), Accessed 1 August 2014 URL: http:// www.adb.org/news/tajikistan-government-and-development-coordination-council-review-progress-development-agenda.

ADB Development Effectiveness Brief (2013), (Online Web), Accessed 10 Feb 2014 URL: adb.org/sites/default/files/pub/.../ tajikistan-adb-15-years-partnership.pdf.

Asian Development Bank (2013), "Assessment of Agriculture and Rural Development", (Online Web), Accessed 28 Mar 2014 URL: www.adb.org/sites/default/files/linked.../8-Agriculture-Rural-Dev.pdf.

ADB Country Assistance Program Evaluation (2014), "Tajikistan Responding to the Changing Development Conditions", (Online Web), Accessed 10 June 2014 URL: www.adb.org/ sites/default/files/evaluation.../files/cape-tajikistan_0.pdf.

ADB Country Operations Business Plan 2014-2016, (Online Web), Accessed 10 June 2014 URL: www.adb.org/.../tajikistan-country-operations-business-plan-2014-2016.

Bajpai, Kanti (2000), "Human Security: Concepts and Measurements", [Online: Web] Accessed 14 Feb. 2013 URL: www.hegoa.ehu.es/.../Human_security_concept_and_ measurement.pdf.

Bashiri, Iraj (1996), "Islam and Communism: Tajikistan in Transition", (Online Web) Accessed Dec 26, 2013 URL: http:// www.angelfire.com/rnb/bashiri/Tajtransition/Transition.html.

Bashiri, Iraj (1997), "From the Manghits to a Democratic State", (Online Web), Accessed 25 Feb 2014 URL: www.angelfire. com/rnb/bashiri/Manghit/Manghits.html.

Bashiri, Iraj (1999), "Tajikistan: An Overview", (Online Web), Accessed 19 Jan 2014 URL: http://www.angelfire.com/rnb/

bashiri/Tajikistan/TajikistanOverview.pdf.

Bertelsmann Stiftung's Transformation Index (BTI) (2014), "Tajikistan Country Report", (Online Web), Accessed 27 April 2014 URL: www.bti-project.de/uploads/tx_itao.../BTI_2014_ Tajikistan.pdf.

Beuter, Thomas (2007), "Tajikistan Market Profile (Draft)", (Online Web) Accessed 23 Feb, 2013 URL: www.untj.net/ index.php?...tajikistan-market-profile-june-2007...2007.

Bora, Saswati et. al. (2010), "Food Security and Conflict", (Online Web), Accessed 17 Sept 2014 URL: http://www-wds. worldbank.org/external/default/WDSContentServer/WDSP/ IB/2011/06/01/000333037_20110601012349/Rendered/PDF/ 620340WP0Food00BOX0361475B00PUBLIC0.pdf.

Bliss, Frank (2012), "Agrarian Reform of the Republic of Tajikistan – A Roadmap for Local Governance and Agriculture Management Institutions Reform (DRAFT)", (Online Web) Accessed 13 Oct 2013 URL: www.researchgate.net/... Institutional...Tajikistan/.../0a85e532f58aaa4f18.

Brinkman, H J and C S Hendrix (2010), "Food Insecurity and Conflict: Applying the WDR Framework" (Online Web), Accessed 1 August 2014 URL: https://openknowledge. worldbank.org/bitstream/.../WDR2011_0025.pdf.

Brinkman, HJ and Hendrix, SJ (2011), "Food Insecurity and Violent Conflict: Causes, Consequences, and Addressing the Challenges" (Online Web), Accessed 17 Sept 2014 URL: https://www.wfp.org/content/occasional-paper-24-food-insecurity-and-violent-conflict-causes-consequences-and-addressing-.

Breu, T and H Hurni (2003), "The Tajik Pamirs : Challenges of Sustainable Development in an Isolated Mountain Region", (Online Web) Accessed Dec 26, 2013 URL: https://www.cde. unibe.ch/CDE/pdf/The_Tajik_Pamirs.pdf.

Burchi, Francesco and De Muro, Pasquale (2012), "A Human Development and Capability Approach to Food Security: Conceptual Framework and Informational Basis", (Online

Web), Accessed 10 Sept 2014 URL: www.undp.org/.../
Capability%20Approach%20Food%20Security.pdf.

Caccavale, Oscar Maria (2005), "Land Reform in Tajikistan:
Economic Effects on Private Frams", [Online: Web] Accessed
8 Mar. 2011 URL: papers.ssrn.com/sol3/papers.cfm?abstract_
id=999944.

CAREC Website, (Online Web), Accessed 10 July 2014 URL:
http://www.carecprogram.org/.

Carles, Jacques and Montfort, Paul-Florent (2010), "Food Security
and National Defense, A Geopolitical Perspective", April 19,
(Online Web) Accessed 18 October 2013 URL: http://www.
momagri.org/UK/points-of-view/Food-Security-and-National-
Defense-A-Geopolitical-Perspective_661.html#ANCRTOP.

Christmann et. al. (eds.) (2009), "Food Security and Climate
Change in Central Asia and the Caucasus", (Online Web)
Accessed Feb 27, 2013 URL: https://apps.icarda.org/
wsInternet/wsInternet.asmx/DownloadFileToLocal?filePath
=Regional_program_reports_archive/CAC/Food_security_
Caucasus.pdf&fileName=Food_security_Caucasus.pdf.

Commission on Human Security (2003), (Online Web) Accessed
18 April 2015 URL: http://reliefweb.int/sites/reliefweb.int/
files/resources/91BAEEDBA50C6907C1256D19006A9353-
chs-security-may03.pdf.

Cornish, Paul (2014), "Rationing And Food Shortages During
The First World War", (Online Web), Accessed 1 August 2014
URL: http://www.iwm.org.uk/history/rationing-and-food-
shortages-during-the-first-world-war.

Development Coordination Council Website (2015),
"Development Partners will Continue to Support Tajikistan in
Improving Country's Economic Competitiveness", February
10, (Online Web) Accessed 18 April 2015 URL: http://www.
untj.org/dcc/index.php/news/141-development-partners-
will-continue-to-support-tajikistan-in-improving-country-s-
economic-competitiveness.

Duncan, Jennifer (2000), "Agricultural Land Reform and Farm

Reorganization in Tajikistan", (Online Web) Accessed 23 Oct 2013 URL: www.landesa.org/wp-content/uploads/2011/01/RDI_106.pdf.

EBRD Strategy for Tajikistan (2012), (Online Web), Accessed 10 June 2014 URL: www.ebrd.com/downloads/country/strategy/tajikistan.pdf.

EBRD Tajikistan Website, (Online Web), Accessed 10 July 2014 URL: http://www.ebrd.com/tajikistan.html.

Economic Commission for Europe (2004), "Environmental Performance Reviews – Tajikistan", (Online Web), Accessed 25 April 2014 URL: http://www.unece.org/fileadmin/DAM/env/epr/epr_studies/tajikistan.pdf.

Encyclopedia Iranica Online, "Economy in Tajikistan", (Online Web) Accessed 21 Mar 2014 URL: http://www.iranicaonline.org/articles/economy-xii-in-tajikistan.

Encyclopedia of the Nations Website, (Online Web), Accessed 15 April 2014 URL: http://www.nationsencyclopedia.com/geography/Slovenia-to-Zimbabwe-Cumulative-Index/Tajikistan.html.

Encyclopaedia Britannica Website, "Entitlement Failure", (Online Web), Accessed 10 Sept 2014 URL: http://www.britannica.com/EBchecked/topic/201392/famine/277563/Entitlement-failure#ref1007457.

Encyclopaedia Britannica Website, "World Food Council", (Online Web), Accessed 10 Sept 2014 URL: http://www.britannica.com/EBchecked/topic/648301/World-Food-Council-WFC.

Eurasian Center for Food Security Country Report Tajikistan (2012), (Online Web), Accessed 05 May 2014 URL: ecfs.msu.ru/docs/wb_conf/Country%20report-Tajikistan_ENG.doc.

Evans, Richard J (2012), "Food Fights: The use of food as a weapon during World War II", (Online: Web) Accessed June 14 2014 URL: http://www.thenation.com/article/167059/food-fights#.

Eurasian Development Bank Website (2014), "Kazakhstan says

SCO should have food security programme", (Online Web) Accessed 18 April 2015 URL: http://eabr.org/e/press_center/ news-region/?id_4=45356&from_4=11.

Falkingham, Jane (2000), "A Profile of Poverty in Tajikistan", (Online Web) Accessed Dec 26, 2013 URL: eprints.lse. ac.uk/6453/1/A_Profile_of_Poverty_in_Tajikistan.pdf.

Falkingham J (2000a), "Country Briefing Paper—Women and Gender Relations in Tajikistan", (Online Web), Accessed 02 May 2014 URL: http://reliefweb.int/sites/reliefweb.int/ files/resources/F59C64EEDBBEFE77C1256934004651B0-tajikwomen.pdf.

FAO Website, (Online Web), Accessed 10 July 2014 URL: http:// www.fao.org/about/en/.

FAO Technical Cooperation Department Website, (Online Web), Accessed 10 July 2014 URL: https://extranet.fao.org/fpmis/ FPMISReportServlet.jsp?div=&type=countryprofileopen&lan guage=EN&countryId=TJ.

FAO (1996), "Rome Declaration on World Food Security", (Online Web), Accessed 10 Sept 2014 URL: http://www.fao. org/docrep/003/w3613e/w3613e00.HTM.

FAO (1996), "Persistent Bread Shortages and Hardship in Tajikistan", Special Alert No 264, (Online Web), Accessed 28 Mar 2014 URL: http://www.fao.org/docrep/004/w0339e/ w0339e00.htm.

FAO/WFP (2000), "FAO/WFP Crop and Food Supply Assessment Mission to Tajikistan", (Online Web), Accessed 25 Mar 2014 URL: http://www.fao.org/docrep/004/x7844e/x7844e00.htm.

FAO (2001), "Tajikistan faces serious food deficit", August 14, (Online Web), Accessed 4 April 2014 URL: http://www.fao. org/english/newsroom/global/gw0107-e.htm.

FAO (2001), "FAO/WFP Crop and Food Supply Assessment Mission to Tajikistan", (Online Web), Accessed 25 Mar 2014 URL: http://www.fao.org/docrep/004/y1534e/y1534e00. htm#P58_8144.

FAO (2002), "FAO/WFP Crop and Food Supply Assessment Mission to Tajikistan", (Online Web) Accessed 22 April 2014 URL: http://www.fao.org/docrep/005/y7285e/y7285e00.htm.

FAO (2003), "Trade Reforms and Food Security", (Online Web), Accessed 17 Sept 2014 URL: http://www.fao.org/docrep/005/y4671e/y4671e06.htm.

FAO (2006), "Food Security Policy Brief", (Online Web), Accessed 10 Sept 2014 URL: http://www.fao.org/forestry/13128-0e6f36 f27e0091055bec28ebe830f46b3.pdf.

Food & Agriculture Organisation (2009), "Evaluation of FAO Activities in Tajikistan", (Online Web) Accessed 13 Oct 2013 URL: www.fao.org/.../user.../1_Tajikistan_FAO_Cooperation_2009_MR.pdf.

FAO (2011), "Agro-industry National Policy Framework – Tajikistan", (Online Web), Accessed 1 August 2014 URL: http://www.fao.org/fileadmin/user_upload/Europe/documents/Publications/AI_briefs/Tajikistan_ai_en.pdf.

FAO (2013), "State of Food Insecurity in the World", (Online Web), Accessed 1 August 2014 URL: http://www.fao.org/docrep/018/i3434e/i3434e00.htm.

FAO (2014), "Crop and Food Security Assessment in Tajikistan", (Online Web), Accessed 05 May 2014 URL: http://reliefweb.int/sites/reliefweb.int/files/resources/1_CFSAM_REPORT_2013_Eng_Final.pdf.

FAO (2014a), "Main Official Reference Documents on Food Security – Tajikistan", (Online Web), Accessed 21 Mar 2014 URL: http://95.142.83.122/downloads/MAIN%20OFFICIAL%20REFERENCE%20DOCUMENTS%20ON%20FOOD%20SECURITY.pdf.

Fay, Marianne and Hrishi Patel (2008), "A simple index of vulnerability to climate change," Background paper prepared for World Bank report. Washington, DC, quoted in World Bank (2009), "Adapting to Climate Change in Europe and Central Asia", (Online Web), Accessed 02 May 2014 URL: http://www.worldbank.org/eca/climate/ECA_CCA_Full_Report.

pdf.

Food Security and Poverty Bulletin No 1 (2014), (Online Web), Accessed 18 April 2014 URL: http://www.stat.tj/en/img/38f3e f5251e7e073f22380beb403deee_1403332876.pdf.

Food for Peace (2008), "Franklin Delano Roosevelt Addresses the Delegates to The United Nations Conference on Food and Agriculture", (Online Web), Accessed 10 Sept 2014 URL: http://www.schiller-institut.de/seiten/wirtschaft/foodwatch/ english/fdr.htm.

Foroughi, Payam (2012), "Nations in Transit: Tajikistan", (Online Web) Accessed 12 Jan 2013 URL: https://www.freedomhouse. org/report/nations-transit/2012/tajikistan#.VKVfZSuUeYA.

Fumagalli, Matteo (2008), "The 'Food-Energy-Water' Nexus in Central Asia: Regional Implications of and the International Response to the Crises in Tajikistan", (Online Web), Accessed 27 April 2014 URL: aei.pitt.edu/11082/1/1731[1].pdf.

GAA Tajikistan Program Factsheet, (Online Web), Accessed 1 August 2014 URL: www.duschanbe.diplo.de/contentblob/.../ DWHH_factsheet_10_2011.pdf.

Golay, Christophe (2010), "The Food Crisis and Food Security: Towards a New World Food Order?", (Online Web) Accessed 18 January 2014 URL: http://poldev.revues.org/145.

Government of Tajikistan (2002), "Poverty Reduction Strategy", (Online Web), Accessed 28 Mar 2014 URL: http://planipolis. iiep.unesco.org/upload/Tajikistan/PRSP/Tajikistan%20 PRSP%202002.pdf.

Google Translation of Dododzhon Atovulloev's interview with Maria Yanovska for Ferghana News, January 31, 2012, (Online Web), Accessed 02 May 2014 URL: http://www.fergananews. com/article.php?id=7260?print=1.

Granit et. al. (2010), "Regional Water Intelligence Report Central Asia", (Online Web) Accessed Dec 26, 2013 URL: www. watergovernance.org/.../Reports/Paper-15_RWIR_Aral_Sea. pdf.

Grebmer, K V et. al. (2011), "The Challenge of Hunger: Taming Price Spikes and Excessive Food Price Volatility", (Online Web) Accessed 18 April 2014 URL: www.ifpri.org/sites/default/files/publications/ghi11.pdf.

Harsch, Ernest (2008), "Price Protests Expose State Faults," (Online: Web) Accessed 15 Apr. 2013 URL: http://www.un.org/africarenewal/magazine/july-2008/price-protests-expose-state-faults.

Hendrix, CS and Haggard, Stephen (2009), "International Food Prices, Regime Type, and Protest in the Developing World", (Online Web), Accessed 17 Sept 2014 URL: https://cshendrix.files.wordpress.com/2007/03/hh_foodpricesprotest_forweb.pdf.

Hendrix, Cullen et. al. (2009), "Grievance and Opportunity: Food Prices, Political Regime, and Protest", (Online: Web) Accessed October 14 2014 URL: http://www.researchgate.net/profile/Beatriz_Magaloni/publication/228433892_Grievance_and_opportunity_food_prices_political_regime_and_protest/links/0046352c18c7e95f2c000000.pdf.

Historic Documents (1944), "The Economic Bill of Rights", (Online Web), Accessed 1 Nov 2014 URL: http://www.ushistory.org/documents/economic_bill_of_rights.htm.

Hofman, Irna (2017), "Tajikistan: Searching for Food Security", (Online Web), Accessed 1 April, 2018

URL: https://eurasianet.org/s/tajikistan-searching-for-food-security.

Huasheng, Zhao, quoted in Zikibayeva, Aigerim (2011), "What Does the Arab Spring Mean for Russia, Central Asia and the Caucasus", (Online Web) Accessed 18 November 2014 URL: csis.org/files/publication/110912_Zikibayeva_ArabSpring_Web.pdf.

Human Development Report (2014), "Explanatory note on the 2014 Human Development Report composite indices – Tajikistan", (Online Web), Accessed 10 July 2014 URL: http://hdr.undp.org/sites/all/themes/hdr_theme/country-notes/TJK.

pdf.

IsDB Website, (Online Web), Accessed 10 July 2014 URL: www. isdb.org.

IFRC (2001), "Silent humanitarian crisis unfolding in Tajikistan, says Red Cross Red Crescent", (Online Web), Accessed 30 Mar 2014 URL: http://www.ifrc.org/en/news-and-media/ press-releases/europe/tajikistan/silent-humanitarian-crisis-unfolding-in-tajikistan-says-red-cross-red-crescent/.

IPCC (2007), "Climate Change 2007: Mitigation of Climate Change" Cambridge: Cambridge University Press, quoted in Christmann et. al. (eds.) (2009), "Food Security and Climate Change in Central Asia and the Caucasus", (Online Web) Accessed Feb 27, 2013 URL: https://apps.icarda.org/ wsInternet/wsInternet.asmx/DownloadFileToLocal?filePath =Regional_program_reports_archive/CAC/Food_security_ Caucasus.pdf&fileName=Food_security_Caucasus.pdf.

Integrated Regional Information Networks (IRIN) (2008), "Tajikistan: People begin to flee northern town due to water shortages", (Online Web), Accessed 27 Mar 2014 URL: http:// reliefweb.int/report/tajikistan/tajikistan-people-begin-flee-northern-town-due-water-shortages.

International Crisis Group (ICG) (2005), "The Curse of Cotton: Central Asia's Destructive Monoculture", (Online Web) Accessed 9 Oct 2013 URL: http://www.crisisgroup.org/en/ regions/asia/central-asia/093-the-curse-of-cotton-central-asias-destructive-monoculture.aspx.

ICG (2009), "Tajikistan: On the Road to Failure", (Online Web), Accessed 29 April 2014 URL: http://www.crisisgroup.org/~/ media/Files/asia/central-asia/tajikistan/162_tajikistan___on_ the_road_to_failure.pdf.

IFAD Tajikistan Website, (Online Web), Accessed 10 July 2014 URL: http://operations.ifad.org/web/ifad/operations/country/ home/tags/tajikistan.

IFAD Website, (Online Web) Accessed 18 April 2015 URL: http:// www.ifad.org/governance/index.htm.

International Federation of Red Cross (2001), "Tajikistan and Uzbekistan: Drought", (Online Web), Accessed 30 Mar 2014 URL: https://ifrc.org/docs/appeals/rpts01/tjuzdr01b1.pdf.

International Food Policy Research Institute (2012), "Sustainable Food Security Under Land, Water, and Energy Stresses", (Online: Web) Accessed October 14 2014 URL: http://www.ifpri.org/ghi/2012/sustainable-food-security-under-land-water-energy-stresses.

International Monetary Fund (2003), "Republic of Tajikistan: Selected Issues and Statistical Appendix", (Online Web), Accessed 06 Mar 2014 URL: www.imf.org/external/pubs/ft/scr/2005/cr05131.pdf.

International Monetary Fund (2004), "Republic of Tajikistan: Second Review Under the Three-Year Arrangement Under the Poverty Reduction and Growth Facility, and Request for a Waiver of Performance Criterion", (Online Web), Accessed 1 August 2014 URL: https://www.imf.org/external/pubs/cat/longres.cfm?sk=17139.0.

Joint Country Partnership Strategy 2010–2012, (Online Web), Accessed 1 August 2014 URL: http://www.adb.org/sites/default/files/institutional-document/32376/files/cps-taj-2010-2012.pdf.

Kaldor, Mary (2007), "Human Security: A New Strategic Narrative for Europe", *[Online: Web] Accessed 20 Jan. 2010 URL: papers.ssrn.com/sol3/papers.cfm?abstract_id=1062033.*

KOC, Ali A (2012), "Agriculture Sector Diversification Concept for the Republic of Tajikistan (DRAFT)", (Online Web) Accessed 13 Sept 2013 URL: www.researchgate.net/...Tajikistan/.../0a85e532f58aaa4f18000000.

Kelly, Charles (2009), "Field note from Tajikistan Compound disaster - A new humanitarian challenge?", (Online Web) Accessed 18 April 2015 URL: www.jamba.org.za/index.php/jamba/article/viewFile/32/32.

Knuth, Lidija (2008), "Tajikistan: Institutional, Policy and Legislative Framework of Food Security of Tajikistan", (Online

Web) Accessed 23 Jul 2013 URL: www.fao.org/docrep/016/ ap600e/ap600e.pdf.

Kuryliw, Valentina (2002), "The Holodomor, 1932-1933 A Ukrainian Genocide", (Online: Web) Accessed October 14 2014 URL: http://www.faminegenocide.com/resources/hessay. htm.

League of Nations (1935), "The Problem of Nutrition Vol – 2: Report on the Physiological Bases of Nutrition", (Online Web), Accessed 1 August 2014 URL: http://archive.org/stream/ problemofnutriti02leaguoft/problemofnutriti02leaguoft_djvu. txt.

Lerman, Zvi and David Sedik (2008), "The Economic Effects of Land Reform in Tajikistan", (Online Web) Accessed 23 Oct 2013 URL: ftp://ftp.fao.org/docrep/fao/011/aj285e/aj285e00. pdf.

Lerman, Zvi (2012), "Agrarian Reform of the Republic of Tajikistan – Farm Reform and Restructuring Cooperative Development Report", (Online Web) Accessed 23 Jul 2013 URL: http://www.agriculture-reform.tj/images/DOCs/Reports/ FAO%20reports/Final%20Draft_Dehkan%20Farm%20 and%20Cooperative_Zvi%20Lerman_July%2017-2012_eng. pdf.

Long, Andie (2013), "Stories of Impact: Improving Water Quality in Tajikistan During Flood Emergencies", (Online Web), Accessed 1 August 2014 URL: http://xylemwatermark. com/2013/03/07/mercy-corps-tajikistan/.

"Living Standards Improvement Strategy of Tajikistan for 2013-2015", (Online Web) Accessed 13 Oct 2013 URL: http://www. tj.undp.org/content/dam/tajikistan/docs/legal_framework/ UNDP_TJK_MidTermReview_eng.pdf.

Magauin, Yedige (2008), "A Tragedy Kazakhstan Must Never Forget", December 8, (Online Web), Accessed 11 Jan 2014 URL: http://www.rferl.org/content/A_Tragedy_Kazakhstan_ Must_Never_Forget/1357455.html.

Malthus, T R (1798), "An Essay on the Principle of Population",

(Online Web), Accessed 10 Sept 2014 URL: http://www.esp. org/books/malthus/population/malthus.pdf.

Malashenko, Alexey (2012). "Tajikistan: Civil War's Long Echo", (Online Web) Accessed 18 November 2014 URL: carnegieendowment.org/files/MalashenkoBrifing_14-3-12_ eng_web.pdf.

Maletta, Hector (2014), "From Hunger to Food Security: A Conceptual History", (Online Web), Accessed 10 Sept 2014 URL: papers.ssrn.com/sol3/Delivery.cfm?abstractid=2484166.

Mandler, Andreas (2010), "Social and Political Context of Agriculture Advisory Aervice in Tajikistan," [Online: Web] Accessed 21 Feb. 2013 URL: www.mace-events.org/ greenweek2010/6382-MACE/.../Mandler_feb.pdf.

Matveeva, Anna (2008), "External Democracy Promotion in Post-Conflict Zones: Evidence from Case Studies", (Online Web) Accessed 23 Mar 2013 URL: http://aix1.uottawa.ca/~czurcher/ czurcher/Transitions_files/Final%20Report%20Tajikistan.pdf.

Maxwell, Daniel (2012), "Food Security and its Implication for Political Stability: A Humanitarian Perspective," (Online: Web) Accessed Apr. 14 2013 URL: http://www.fao.org/fileadmin/ templates/cfs_high_level_forum/documents/FS-Implications-Political_Stability-Maxwell.pdf.

McGovern, Jim (2011), "Food Security Is National Security", (Online Web) Accessed 12 Jan 2013 URL: http://wfpusa.org/ blog/food-security-national-security.

Middleton, Robert (2013), "Sustainable Livelihoods in a Fragile Environment - Case Studies from the Tajik Pamirs", (Online Web) Accessed Jan 21, 2013 URL: www.pamirs.org/ Sustainable-Livelihoods.pdf.

Ministry of Agriculture of Republic of Tajikistan (2011), "Crop and Food Security Assessment Mission Report – Tajikistan", (Online Web) Accessed 13 Oct 2013 URL: www.fao.org/ docrep/015/an110e/an110e00.pdf.

Ministry of Agriculture, Tajikistan (2012), "The Agriculture

Reform Program of Republic of Tajikistan", (Online Web), Accessed 27 April 2014 URL: http://moa.tj/wp-content/ Program_Taj_Rus_Eng_ready.pdf.

Ministry of Foreign Affairs of Tajikistan Website, (Online Web), Accessed 05 May 2014 URL: http://mfa.tj/en/three-strategic-goals/three-strategic-goals.html.

Ministry of Agriculture, China Website (2013), "SCO Seminar on Food Security opens", (Online Web) Accessed 18 April 2015 URL: http://english.agri.gov.cn/news/dqnf/201309/ t20130905_20196.htm.

Mirzoeva, Viloyat (2009), "Gender Issues in Land Reform in Tajikistan", (Online Web), Accessed 05 May 2014 URL: www. asu.lt/erd/lt/33224.

Mogelgaard, Kathleen (2013), "Faster-Than-Expected Population Growth in Many "Feed the Future" Countries", (Online Web), Accessed 29 April 2014 URL: http://www.newsecuritybeat. org/2013/08/faster-than-expected-population-growth-feed-future-countries/.

Muckenhuber, David (2013), "Why Has the Arab Spring Skipped Central Asia (So Far)?", February 8, (Online Web) Accessed 18 April 2015 URL: http://theglobalobservatory.org/2013/02/ why-the-arab-spring-has-skipped-central-asia-so-far/.

Mukhamedova, Nozilakhon and Kai Wegerich (2014), "Land Reforms and Feminization of Agricultural Labor in Sughd Province, Tajikistan", (Online Web), Accessed 28 Mar 2014 URL: www.iwmi.cgiar.org/Publications/IWMI_Research_ Reports/.../rr157.pdf.

Mullojanov, Parviz (2014), "Tajikistan 2014: Challenges and Risks", (Online Web) Accessed 18 November 2014 URL: http://www.ipp.kg/en/news/2853/.

NATO Website, (Online Web), Accessed 1 August 2014 URL: http://www.nato.int/cps/en/natolive/topics_50312.htm.

National Development Strategy 2015, (Online Web), Accessed 21 Mar 2014 URL: amcu.gki.tj/eng/images/stories/nds_en.pdf.

Niyozov, Sarfaroz (2004), "The Realities of Being a Woman-Teacher in the Mountains of Tajikistan", (Online Web) Accessed 18 April 2014 URL: http://asiecentrale.revues.org/695#ftn30.

OECD (2014), "Society at a Glance: Asia/Pacific 2014", (Online Web) Accessed 18 April 2014 URL: http://www.oecd-ilibrary. org/deliver/8114171ec018.pdf?itemId=/content/chapter/soc_ aag-2014-18-en&mimeType=application/pdf.

Overseas Development Institute Briefing Paper (1997), "Global Hunger and Food Security after the World Food Summit", (Online Web), Accessed 10 Sept 2014 URL: http://www.odi. org/sites/odi.org.uk/files/odi-assets/publications-opinion-files/2630.pdf.

Oxfam (2008), "Reaching Tipping Point? Climate Change and Poverty in Tajikistan", (Online Web) Accessed 23 Oct 2013 URL: http://www.oxfam.org.hk/content/98/content_3493en. pdf.

Oxfam (2010), "Climate Change and water shortages closing in on Tajikistan and Central Asia", (Online Web), Accessed 05 May 2014 URL: http://www.oxfam.org/en/pressroom/ pressreleases/2010-02-17/climate-change-and-water-shortages-closing-tajikistan-and-central.

Oxfam (2014), "Oxfam Highlights Critical Lessons Learned in IPCC Report", (Online: Web) Accessed December 14, 2014 URL: http://peoplefoodandnature.org/blog/oxfam-highlights-critical-lessons-learned-in-ipcc-report/.

Perry, J R (1996), "From Persian to Tajik to Persian: Culture, politics and law reshape a Central Asian language", quoted in Encyclopedia Iranica Online, (Online Web), Accessed 19 Jan 2014 URL: https://www.google.co.in/url?sa=t&rct=j& q=&esrc=s&source=web&cd=4&cad=rja&uact=8&ved= 0CC4QFjAD&url=http%3A%2F%2Fwww.iranicaonline. org%2Farticles%2Ftajik-i-the-ethnonym-origins-and-applicati on&ei=fq23VPLrGNfCsATOu4GQBQ&usg=AFQjCNGyKgI lVqRh3PBziXyVnCH8fPizcw&bvm=bv.83640239,d.cWc.

Peyrouse, Sebastien (2009), "The multiple paradoxes of the

agriculture issue in Central Asia", (Online Web) Accessed Jan 27, 2013 URL: aei.pitt.edu/13583/1/WP6-EN.pdf

Peyrouse, Sebastien (2013), "Policy Memo: Food Security in Central Asia: A Public Policy Challenge", (Online Web) Accessed Feb 27, 2013 URL: http://www.ponarseurasia.org/sites/default/files/policy-memos-pdf/Pepm_300_Peyrouse_Sept2013.pdf.

Porteous, O (2003), "Land Reform in Tajikistan: From the Capital to the Cotton Fields", (Online Web) Accessed 13 Oct 2013 URL: eastagri.org/files/tajikistanlandreform.pdf.

Poverty Reduction Strategy 2010-2012, (Online Web), Accessed 21 Mar 2014 URL: http://www.imf.org/external/pubs/ft/scr/2012/cr1233.pdf.

President Rahmon's Speech at the FAO Summit (1996), (Online Web), Accessed 10 July 2014 URL: http://www.fao.org/docrep/003/x0736m/rep2/tajik.htm.

President Rahmon Speech at WTO, Switzerland (2012)", (Online Web) Accessed 22 April 2014 URL: http://www.tajikembassy.be/content/statement-president-tajikistan-general-council-meeting-accession-tajikistan-wto.

Robic et. al. (2010), "Understanding Energy Poverty: Case Study – Tajikistan", (Online Web), Accessed 27 April 2014 URL: www.indiaenergycongress.in/montreal/library/pdf/339.pdf.

Romm, Cari (2014), "The World War II Campaign to Bring Organ Meats to the Dinner Table", (Online Web), Accessed 1 Nov 2014 URL: http://www.theatlantic.com/health/archive/2014/09/the-world-war-ii-campaign-to-bring-organ-meats-to-the-dinner-table/380737/.

Roston, Tom (2012), "A Brief History of Food & War", (Online: Web) Accessed June 14 2014 URL: http://www.foodrepublic.com/2012/01/11/brief-history-food-war.

Rupert, James (1991), "The Strange State of Soviet Central Asia", (Online: Web) Accessed 15 Dec, 2013, URL: http://aliciapatterson.org/stories/strange-state-soviet-central-asia.

Russiapedia Online "Collectivisation" (Online Web), Accessed 19 Jan 2014 URL: http://russiapedia.rt.com/of-russian-origin/collectivization/.

Save the Children (2009), "Modernising Foreign Assistance Insights from the field: Tajikistan", (Online Web), Accessed 1 August 2014 URL: http://www.savethechildren.org.uk/sites/default/files/docs/Modernizing_Foreign_Assistance_-Tajikistan_1.pdf.

Schmitz, Andrea and Alexander Wolters (2012), "Political Protest in Central Asia. Potentials and Dynamics", (Online Web) Accessed 18 Mar 2013 URL: www.swp-berlin.org/fileadmin/contents/.../2012_RP07_smz_wolters.pdf.

Scott, Adam et. al. (2008), "Climate Change and Food Security in Tajikistan: A Backgrounder", (Online Web) Accessed 9 Oct 2013 URL: www.untj.net/index.php?...climate-change-and-food-security-in-tajikistan.

Sen, Amartya (1981b), "Ingredients of Famine Analysis: Availability and Entitlements", The Quarterly Journal of Economics, Vol. 96, No. 3. (Aug., 1981), pp. 433-464, (Online: Web) Accessed June 14 2014 URL: http://www.hss.caltech.edu/~camerer/SS280/SenQJE81.pdf.

Sihag, Balbir Singh (2014), "Kautilya's Proactive and Pragmatic Approach to National Security", (Online: Web) Accessed June 14 2014 URL: www.du.ac.in/du/uploads/events/20102014_Abstract.pdf.

Simon, George-Andre (2012), "Food Security: Definition, Four dimensions, History", (Online Web), Accessed 10 Sept 2014 URL: www.fao.org/fileadmin/templates/ERP/uni/F4D.pdf.

Smith, Barbara Clark (2012), "Food rioters and the American Revolution", (Online Web), Accessed 17 Sept 2014 URL: https://libcom.org/history/food-rioters-american-revolution-barbara-clark-smith.

Son, Hyun H (2011), "Evaluating Social Protection Programs in Tajikistan", (Online Web) Accessed Jan 21, 2013 URL: www.adb.org/.../evaluating-social-protection-programs-tajikistan.

Speckard, Daniel (2014), "From Food Security to National Security", (Online Web) Accessed 12 Jan 2013 URL: http://www.worldfooddayusa.org/daniel_speckhard.

Speech of Emamoli Rahmon at WTO (2012), (Online Web), Accessed 07 Mar 2014 URL: http://www.tajikembassy.be/content/statement-president-tajikistan-general-council-meeting-accession-tajikistan-wto.

Spoor, Max (1993), "Transition to Market Economies in Former Soviet Central Asia: Dependency, Cotton and Water", (Online: Web) Accessed 10 Dec, 2013, URL: maxspoor.files.wordpress.com/2011/07/cottoncentralasia_ejdr1993.pdf.

State Agency for Hydrometeorology of the Committee for Environmental Protection (2008), "The Second National Communication of the Republic of Tajikistan under the United Nations Framework Convention on Climate Change" (Online Web), Accessed 02 May 2014 URL: http://unfccc.int/resource/docs/natc/tainc2.pdf.

State of the Union Address (1941), "Annual Message to Congress on the State of the Union", (Online Web), Accessed 1 Nov 2014 URL: http://www.fdrlibrary.marist.edu/pdfs/fftext.pdf.

Suleri, A Q (2012), "Hunger: A National Security Threat", (Online Web) Accessed 12 Jan 2013 URL: http://unchronicle.un.org/article/hunger-national-security-threat/.

Tadjbakhsh, Shahrbanou (1996), "Economic Regionalism in Tajikistan", (Online Web) Accessed Jan 15, 2013 URL: www.ucis.pitt.edu/nceeer/1996-809-08-2-Tadjbakhsh.pdf.

TAJSTAT Website (2014), "Statistical Agency under President of the Republic of Tajikistan", (Online Web), Accessed 19 Jan 2014 URL: http://www.stat.tj/en/.

Tajikistan Committee of Emergency Situations and Civil Defence (2010), "Disaster Risk Management Programme Document", (Online Web), Accessed 28 Mar 2014 URL: http://reliefweb.int/sites/reliefweb.int/files/resources/Disaster%20Risk%20Management%20Programme%20Document%20Phase%20III.pdf.

Tajikistan Profile on World Bank Website, (Online Web), Accessed 19 Jan 2014 URL: http://data.worldbank.org/country/tajikistan.

Tajikistan Development Partner Profiles (2014), (Online Web), Accessed 10 Feb 2015 URL: untj.org/dcc/files/2014-2015/Strategic-Framework/dpp_2014_en.pdf.

Tajikistan Demographic and Health Survey (2012), (Online Web), Accessed 05 May 2014 URL: https://dhsprogram.com/pubs/pdf/FR279/FR279.pdf.

Tajikistan Agriculture Rehabilitation Project (2014), (Online Web), Accessed 10 June 2014 URL: http://www.adb.org/sites/default/files/in407-14.pdf.

Tajikistan Foreign Aid Review (2013), (Online Web), Accessed 02 May 2014 URL: http://amcu.gki.tj/eng/index.php?option=com_content&task=view&id=22&Itemid=56.

Temel, Tugrul (2012), "An Institutional Assessment of the Food Security Information System in Tajikistan", (Online Web), Accessed 21 Mar 2014 URL: http://www.researchgate.net/publication/260990901_An_Institutional_Assessment_of_the_Food_Security_Information_System_in_Tajikistan.

Teodosijevic, Slobodanka B. (2003), "Armed Conflicts and Food Security", (Online: Web) Accessed 15 Jan. 2013 URL: www.fao.org/righttofood/kc/.../vl/.../armed%20conflicts%20and%20FS.pdf.

Tetley, Khaleel and Marhabo Jonbekova (2005), "Development of Social Organisation in Tajikistan: MSDSP's Approach in the Mountainous Areas", (Online Web), Accessed 1 August 2014 URL: http://www.akdn.org/publications/2005_akf_mountains_paper10_english.pdf.

The Economist (2012), "Water wars in Central Asia Dammed if they do", (Online Web), Accessed 02 May 2014 URL: http://www.economist.com/node/21563764.

The Great Soviet Encyclopedia Online, 3rd Edition (1970-1979), (Online Web), Accessed 25 Feb 2014 URL: http://

encyclopedia2.thefreedictionary.com/Bukhara+Khanate.

Timmer, C P (2010), "Behavioural dimensions of food security", (Online: Web) Accessed June 14 2014 URL: http://www.pnas. org/content/109/31/12315.full.pdf.

Trenholm, Sandra (2012), "Food Conservation during WWI: "Food Will Win the War", (Online Web), Accessed 1 August 2014 URL: http://www.gilderlehrman.org/collections/ treasures-from-the-collection/food-conservation-during-wwi-%E2%80%9Cfood-will-win-war%E2%80%9D.

UN Website, (Online Web), Accessed 10 Sept 2014 URL: http:// www.un.org/en/documents/udhr/.

UN Office of the High Commissioner for Human Rights Website, (Online Web), Accessed 1 August 2014 URL: http://www. ohchr.org/EN/AboutUs/Pages/AppealsProcess.aspx.

UNDP (2010), "Tajikistan Monthly Risk Monitoring & Warning Report", (Online Web), Accessed 29 April 2014 URL: http:// untj.org/files/Publications/DRMP/Compound%20crisis%20 in%20Tajikistan-Early%20warning%20indicators/TJK%20 Riskmonitoring%20August%202010%20eng.pdf.

UNDP (2011), "Capacity Building for Disaster Risk Management in Tajikistan", (Online Web), Accessed 30 Mar 2014 URL: http://www.undp.org/content/tajikistan/en/home/ourwork/ crisispreventionandrecovery/successstories/capacity-building-for-disaster-risk-management-in-tajikistan.html.

UNICEF Albania Website, (Online Web), Accessed 17 Sept 2014 URL: www.unicef.org/albania/Food_Security_ANG.pdf.

UNICEF (2010), "Strategic Repositioning of the UNICEF-supported WASH in Schools Programme in Tajikistan", (Online Web), Accessed 05 May 2014 URL: http://www. washinschoolsmapping.com/projects/pdf/TajikistanStrategic. pdf.

UNICEF (2012), "Tajikistan nutrition Report" (Online Web), Accessed 05 May 2014 URL: http://www.unicef.org/tajikistan/ Tajikistan_Nutrition_Report_Eng.pdf.

UNOCHA (2008), "Consolidated Appeals Process (CAP): Tajikistan Humanitarian Food Security Appeal 2008-2009", (Online Web), Accessed 27 Mar 2014 URL: http://reliefweb. int/report/tajikistan/consolidated-appeals-process-cap-tajikistan-humanitarian-food-security-appeal-2008.

UNOCHA (2008a), "Revision of the Tajikistan Compound Crises Flash Appeal 2008", (Online Web), Accessed 25 Mar 2014 URL: http://www.unocha.org/cap/appeals/revision-tajikistan-compound-crises-flash-appeal-2008.

UNOCHA (2012), "Tajikistan: 2012 humanitarian overview", (Online Web), Accessed 30 Mar 2014 URL: http://reliefweb. int/map/tajikistan/tajikistan-2012-humanitarian-overview-31-dec-2012.

United Nations Development Program (1994), "Human Development Report," (Online Web), Accessed 1 August 2014 URL: http://hdr.undp.org/sites/default/files/reports/255/ hdr_1994_en_complete_nostats.pdf.

United Nations Development Program (2008), "The Case of Tajikistan: Some Issues for Discussion", (Online Web) Accessed 17 Sept 2013 URL: http://www.unicef.org/about/ execboard/files/B-8729E-Tajikistan_case_studyFINAL_ formatted-21Jan.pdf.

United Nations Development Program (2011), "Capacity Building for Disaster Risk Management in Tajikistan", (Online Web), Accessed 30 Mar 2014 URL: http://www.undp.org/content/ tajikistan/en/home/ourwork/crisispreventionandrecovery/ successstories/capacity-building-for-disaster-risk-management-in-tajikistan.html.

United Nations in Tajikistan Website, (Online Web), Accessed 10 July 2014 URL: http://www.untj.org/index.php?option=com_ content&view=article&id=106&Itemid=760.

UNDP Tajikistan Website, (Online Web), Accessed 10 Feb 2015 URL: http://www.tj.undp.org/content/tajikistan/en/home/ ourwork/environmentandenergy/successstories/community-approach-to-food-security-and-natural-resources.html.

US State Government Consultant Document (2009), Accessed 10 Feb 2015 URL: www.state.gov/s/globalfoodsecurity/129952. htm.

US Dept. of Agriculture (2004), "Commonwealth of Independent States", (Online Web), Accessed 1 August 2014 URL: www. ers.usda.gov/media/880583/gfa15g_002.pdf.

USAID Website, (Online Web), Accessed 10 July 2014 URL: http://www.usaid.gov/tajikistan/our-work.

USAID (2004), "Land Reform and Farm Reorganization in Tajikistan", (Online: Web) Accessed 15 Jun. 2011 URL: pdf. usaid.gov/pdf_docs/PNADD469.pdf.

USAID (2011), "Livelihood and Food Security Conceptual Framework", (Online Web), Accessed 17 Sept 2014 URL: http://theliftproject.org/wp-content/uploads/2013/03/ Livelihood-and-Food-Security-Conceptual-Framework.pdf.

USAID (2014), "USAID Seeks Solutions to Malnutrition in Tajikistan", (Online Web), Accessed 21 Mar 2014 URL: http:// www.usaid.gov/tajikistan/press-releases/may-28-2014-usaid-seeks-solutions-malnutrition-tajikistan.

US Food Aid and Security Website, (Online Web), Accessed 10 Sept 2014 URL: http://foodaid.org/resources/the-history-of-food-aid/.

US Deptartment of Justice (1993), "Tajikistan Political Conditions In The Post-Soviet Era", (Online Web) Accessed 12 Jan 2013 URL: www1.umn.edu/humanrts/ins/tajiks94.pdf.

UN Economic Commission for Europe (2012), "Tajikistan Environmental Performance Review" (Online Web), Accessed 28 Mar 2014 URL: http://www.unece.org/fileadmin/DAM/ env/epr/epr_studies/TajikistanII.pdf.

Warcholak, Natasha and Parviz Boboev (2012), "Drivers of Contraception in Tajikistan: Poverty, Religion and Mothers-in-law", (Online Web), Accessed 29 April 2014 URL: http://www. unfpa.org/news/drivers-contraception-tajikistan-poverty-religion-and-mothers-law.

Website of Embassy of Uzbekistan to United Kingdom and Northern Ireland, (Online Web), Accessed 25 Feb 2014 URL: http://www.uzbekembassy.org/e/events_at_the_ embassy/28483/.

Website of Embassy of Tajikistan to Geneva, (Online Web), Accessed 02 May 2014 URL: http://www.tajikistanmission.ch/ business-and-investment/infrastructure.html.

Welthungerhilfe (2012), "What about small farmers? – The example of Tajikistan", (Online Web), Accessed 05 May 2014 URL: http://www.rural21.com/english/news/detail/article/ what-about-small-farmers-the-example-of-tajikistan-000016/.

Welthungerhilfe Website, (Online Web), Accessed 1 August 2014 URL: http://www.welthungerhilfe.de/en/about-us/who-we-are/our-vision.html.

Whitehouse, Douglas (1972), "Soviet Regional Development in 1960-69: Trends and Implications", CIA Historical Review Program Release in Full 1999 (Online Web) Accessed Jan 10, 2013 URL: www.foia.cia.gov/sites/default/files/document.../ DOC_0000292298.pdf.

Wolf, Holger C (1999), "Transition Strategies: Choices and Outcomes", (Online Web), Accessed 05 May 2014 URL: https://www.princeton.edu/~ies/IES_Studies/S85.pdf.

World Bank Website, (Online Web), Accessed 1 August 2014 URL: http://web.worldbank.org/WBSITE/EXTERNAL/NEW S/0,,contentMDK:23143909~menuPK:141310~pagePK:3437 0~piPK:34424~theSitePK:4607,00.html.

World Bank (1986), "Poverty and Hunger: Issues and Options for Food Security in Developing Countries", (Online Web), Accessed 10 Sept 2014 URL: http://www-wds.worldbank.org/ external/default/WDSContentServer/WDSP/IB/1999/09/17/0 00178830_98101901455676/Rendered/PDF/multi_page.pdf.

World Bank Country Partnership Strategy 2010-2013, (Online Web), Accessed 15 April 2014 URL: siteresources.worldbank. org/TAJIKISTANEXTN/.../Country_CPS.pdf.

World Bank (2003), "Irrigation in Central Asia Social, Economic and Environmental Consideration", (Online Web), Accessed 29 April 2014 URL: http://siteresources.worldbank.org/ECAEXT/Resources/publications/Irrigation-in-Central-Asia/Irrigation_in_Central_Asia-Full_Document-English.pdf.

World Bank (2005), "Tajikistan Trade Diagnostic Study", (Online Web) Accessed 23 Feb, 2013 URL: siteresources.worldbank.org/INTRANETTRADE/.../TajikTradeStudy.pdf.

World Bank (2007), "Integrating Environment into Agriculture and Forestry Progress and Prospects in Eastern Europe and Central Asia, Country Review Tajikistan", (Online Web), Accessed 29 April 2014 URL: http://www.worldbank.org/eca/pubs/envint/Volume%20II/English/Review%20TAJ-final.pdf.

World Bank (2008), "Tajikistan - Farm Privatization Support Project" (Online Web) Accessed 23 Jul 2013 URL: http://documents.worldbank.org/curated/en/2008/06/9722664/tajikistan-farm-privatization-support-project.

World Bank (2008a), "Tajikistan - Country environmental analysis", (Online Web) Accessed 18 Mar 2013 URL: http://documents.worldbank.org/curated/en/2008/05/9559623/tajikistan-country-environmental-analysis.

World Bank (2009), "Adapting to Climate Change in Europe and Central Asia", " (Online Web), Accessed 02 May 2014 URL: http://www.worldbank.org/eca/climate/ECA_CCA_Full_Report.pdf.

World Bank (2011), "World Bank-Tajikistan Partnership Snapshot", (Online Web) Accessed 18 Mar 2013 URL: http://siteresources.worldbank.org/INTTAJIKISTAN/Resources/Tajikistan_snapshot.pdf.

World Bank (2011b)," World Development Report", (Online Web), Accessed 17 Sept 2014 URL: https://openknowledge.worldbank.org/bitstream/handle/10986/4389/9780821384398_overview.pdf.

World Bank (2012), "World Bank Financing Promotes Key Policy Reforms in Tajikistan", (Online Web), Accessed 1

August 2014 URL: http://www.worldbank.org/en/news/press-release/2012/11/01/world-bank-financing-promotes-key-policy-reforms-tajikistan.

World Bank (2014), "Food Price Watch", (Online: Web) Accessed June 14 2014 URL: http://www.worldbank.org/content/dam/Worldbank/document/Poverty%20documents/FPW_May%20 2014_final.pdf

World Bank (2014a), "Turn Down Heat the Confronting the New Climate Normal", (Online Web), Accessed 01 Jan 2015 URL: http://www.worldbank.org/en/events/2014/11/26/turn-down-the-heat-confronting-the-new-climate-normal.

World Bank (2015), "Food Security Overview", (Online Web) Accessed 18 January 2015 URL: http://www.worldbank.org/en/topic/foodsecurity/overview.

World Bank Farm Privatisation Support Project (1999), (Online Web), Accessed 10 May 2014 URL: http://www-wds. worldbank.org/external/default/WDSContentServer/WDSP/IB/1999/09/17/000094946_99060411143160/Rendered/INDEX/multi_page.txt.

World Bank Country Partnership Strategy 2015-2018, (Online Web), Accessed 10 May 2014 URL: http://www-wds. worldbank.org/external/default/WDSContentServer/WDSP/IB/2014/05/20/000442464_20140520101548/Rendered/PDF/863720CAS0P146010Box385211B00OUO090.pdf.

World Bank Indicators – Tajikistan (2013), (Online Web) Accessed 22 April 2014 URL: https://www.google.co.in/publicdata/explore?ds=d5bncppjof8f9_&met_y=sp_pop_grow&idim=country:TJK:KGZ:UZB&hl=en&dl=en.

World Hunger and Poverty Facts and Statistics (2015), (Online Web)Accessed 18 January 2015 URL: http://www.worldhunger. org/articles/Learn/world%20hunger%20facts%202002.htm.

WFP Website, (Online Web), Accessed 10 July 2014 URL: https:// www.wfp.org/content/restoring-sustainable-livelihoods-food-insecure-people.

WFP (1996), "WFP Appeals for Urgent Food for 400,000 Desperate People in Tajikistan", (Online Web), Accessed 28 Mar 2014 URL: http://www.un.org/press/en/1996/19960327. wfp1032.html.

WFP (2005), "Tajikistan: Market Profile for Emergency Food Security Assessments", (Online Web), Accessed 02 May 2014 URL: http://documents.wfp.org/stellent/groups/public/documents/ena/wfp085164.pdf.

WFP and GoT (2008), "A Food Security, Livelihoods and Nutrition Assessment June/July 2008", (Online Web), Accessed 27 Mar 2014 URL: http://documents.wfp.org/stellent/groups/public/documents/ena/wfp188192.pdf.

World Food Program (2008), "The Silent Tsunami - the Globalization of the Hunger Challenge; Keynote address to the Peter G. Peterson Institute for International Economics", (Online Web) Accessed 18 January 2014 URL: http://www. wfp.org/eds-centre/speeches/silent-tsunami-globalization-hunger-challenge-keynote-address-peter-g-peterson-i.

World Food Program (2011), "A Regional View of Wheat Markets and Food Security in Central Asia: With a Focus on Afghanistan and Tajikistan", (Online Web) Accessed 20 Mar 2013 URL: documents.wfp.org/stellent/groups/public/documents/.../ wfp238576.pdf.

WFP (2012a), "Tajikistan Market Price Report August 2012", (Online Web), Accessed 10 July 2014 URL: documents.wfp. org/stellent/groups/public/documents/.../wfp250018.pdf.

WFP (2012), "Tajikistan Food Security Monitoring System", (Online Web), Accessed 05 May 2014 URL: https://www.wfp. org/.../tajikistan-food-security-monitoring-system-2012.

WFP (2013), "Food Security Brief – Tajikistan", (Online Web), Accessed 02 May 2014 URL: http://documents.wfp.org/stellent/groups/public/documents/ena/wfp258721.pdf.

World Health Organization (2009), "Protecting health from climate change Connecting science, policy and people", (Online Web), Accessed 02 May 2014 URL: http://www.who.

int/globalchange/publications/reports/9789241598880/en/.

World Health Organisation (2011), "High food prices contributing to malnutrition in Tajikistan", (Online Web), Accessed 05 May 2014 URL: http://www.euro.who.int/en/countries/tajikistan/news/news/2011/11/high-food-prices-contributing-to-malnutrition-in-tajikistan.

Yao, Adam Vinaman and Hubertus Ruffer (2005), "Food Security in Tajikistan: German Agro Action Strategy", (Online Web), Accessed 6 April 2014 URL: http://www.akdn.org/publications/2005_akf_mountains_paper6_english.pdf.

INTERVIEWS

Bleuer, Dr. Christian (2014), Email Interview, December 19, 2014.

Imomberdieva, Davlatbibi (2015), National Program Coordinator of Welthungerhilfe, Tajikistan, Email Interview, January 19.

Umarov, Dr. K (2015), Personal Interview at the Jawaharlal Nehru Institute of Advanced Studies, April 7.

Index